Conducting School-Based Functional Behavioral Assessments

The Guilford Practical Intervention in the Schools Series

Kenneth W. Merrell, Series Editor

Books in this series address the complex academic, behavioral, and social–emotional needs of children and youth at risk. School-based practitioners are provided with practical, research-based, and readily applicable tools to support students and team successfully with teachers, families, and administrators. Each volume is designed to be used directly and frequently in planning and delivering educational and mental health services. Features include lay-flat binding to facilitate photocopying, step-by-step instructions for assessment and intervention, and helpful, timesaving reproducibles.

Recent Volumes

Conducting School-Based Functional Behavioral Assessments

A Practitioner's Guide

SECOND EDITION

MARK W. STEEGE
T. STEUART WATSON

Foreword by Frank M. Gresham

THE GUILFORD PRESS
New York   London

© 2009 The Guilford Press
A Division of Guilford Publications, Inc.
72 Spring Street, New York, NY 10012
www.guilford.com

Printed in Canada

This book is printed on acid-free paper.

Last digit is print number: 9   8   7   6   5   4   3

Library of Congress Cataloging-in-Publication Data

Steege, Mark W.
    Conducting school-based functional behavioral assessments : a practitioner's guide / Mark W.
Steege, T. Steuart Watson. — 2nd ed.
        p. cm. — (The Guilford practical intervention in the schools series)
    Earlier ed. entered under: Watson, T. Steuart.
    Includes bibliographical references and index.
    ISBN 978-1-60623-027-5 (pbk. : alk. paper)
    1. Behavioral assessment of children—Handbooks, manuals, etc.   2. Problem children—
Behavior modification—Handbooks, manuals, etc.   3. School psychology—Handbooks, manuals,
etc.   I. Watson, T. Steuart.   II. Watson, T. Steuart. Conducting school-based functional
behavioral assessments.   III. Title.
    LB1124.W38 2009
    370.15′28—dc22
                                                                                                2008048497

MIX
Paper from
responsible sources
FSC® C004071

To my colleagues and friends at the Margaret Murphy Center for Children. Your dedicated service to students with disabilities and your commitment to applied behavior analysis has been an inspiration. Thanks for all of your support.

—M. W. S.

To those who make life worthwhile and give me immense joy: Tonya, Mackenzie, Tucker, Addison, Preston (the newest Watson), and Mom and Dad.

To Thomas: You will never know the depth of my gratitude for the early life experiences you gave me.

Finally, to those who are gone but not forgotten: Velma Watson and Marie Salley. May God bless each of you.

—T. S. W.

About the Authors

Mark W. Steege, PhD, is Professor of School Psychology at the University of Southern Maine. Dr. Steege completed his graduate training in school psychology at the University of Iowa in 1986. He is a licensed psychologist, nationally certified school psychologist, and board-certified behavior analyst. He has written numerous original research articles, book chapters, and two books on functional behavioral assessment. Dr. Steege has served several terms as a member of the editorial boards of the *Journal of Applied Behavior Analysis* and *School Psychology Review* and is presently associate editor of the *Journal of Evidence-Based Practices for Schools*. His primary research interests are the application of applied behavior analysis in the assessment and treatment of interfering behaviors with persons with developmental disabilities.

T. Steuart Watson, PhD, is Professor and Chair of the Department of Educational Psychology at Miami University in Oxford, Ohio. Dr. Watson graduated from the University of Nebraska–Lincoln in 1991, with a doctorate in school psychology and a minor in applied behavior analysis. He was awarded the 1998 Lightner Witmer Award from Division 16 of the American Psychological Association for outstanding research contributions by a young scholar. Dr. Watson is coeditor of the *Journal of Evidence-Based Practices for Schools*. He has written numerous articles, books, and book chapters on behavioral interventions, functional assessment, and the application of behavioral principles in school settings. His primary research interests are in the areas of evaluating the effects of external reinforcers on motivation, direct behavioral consultation, improving the effectiveness and efficiency of behavioral interventions, promoting treatment integrity, functional assessment methodologies, and investigating the effects of olfactory stimuli on learning.

Foreword

The overarching rationale of this book is based on a fundamental premise of assessment: the only good assessment is one that results in an effective intervention. Each chapter of this second edition makes this point repeatedly. There is an extensive literature on the use of one such assessment, functional behavioral assessment (FBA), which is largely inaccessible to school-based practitioners either because it is found in technical journals or because it has not been translated into feasible recommendations for practice. This book does an excellent job of translating what can be a technically daunting literature into practical and usable strategies for conducting FBAs in schools. It is replete with tables, forms, charts, and other aids that practitioners will find useful in their daily practice of FBA.

Apart from the plethora of useful devices, Steege and Watson include topics that should be of interest to school-based practitioners. One example is the box titled "Desperately Seeking a Diagnosis" in Chapter 1. Although many readers will certainly see the validity of Steege and Watson's argument in this box, there will be others who may take issue with their position. At the very least, this and similar discussions will cause readers to take pause and reflect on the vital elements of their daily practice.

For those readers who may be unfamiliar with the literature on FBA, Chapters 1 and 2 provide overviews on both the history and current status of functional procedures. Of special note are the errors that are typically made by school-based teams when evaluating challenging behaviors. In my own career, I have seen these errors repeated numerous times by well-meaning teams.

Although there are numerous conceptual models upon which to base practice, I found that Steege and Watson's S-M-I-R-C model encompasses the most vital elements of human behavior. This model is first presented in Chapter 2 and is then further described in Chapter 4. The complexities of everyday interactions are captured by this model and will serve school-based practitioners well if they adhere to analyzing behavior when using it. The relationship between the S-M-I-R-C model and other important concepts (e.g., response classes, matching law) is presented as well, providing readers with a more complete understanding of challenging behavior in students.

As a researcher with keen interests in applied practice, I have always been concerned about not only evaluating outcome but also evaluating the integrity of the processes used in reaching the outcome. After all, if a desirable outcome is not achieved, is it because the intervention "just didn't work" or was it because there were problems with the dynamic processes used to select the intervention? To address this issue, Steege and Watson present the Functional Behavioral Assessment Rating Scale (FuBARS), which is a "must-have" tool for any school-based team that seeks to evaluate the accuracy and completeness of its FBA procedures.

Like the first edition, perhaps the strongest feature of this book is its inclusion of instruments, forms, and procedures that have been tested in schools and found to be both efficient and effective. Two examples are the Task Analysis Recording Procedure (TARP) and the behavior-analytic problem-solving (BAPS) model. These tools, and numerous others, not only provide ample structure to practitioners who may feel uneasy about conducting FBAs but also provide seasoned practitioners with sufficient flexibility to modify the tools so that they fit the practitioners' particular needs at the moment. This is especially true of the FBA reports found in Chapter 12. These reports, which are based on the authors' real-life cases with varying degrees of length and complexity, tie together results from the procedures described in preceding chapters and illustrate the FBA process.

The final chapter, on direct behavioral consultation (DBC), for me generates the most excitement. The DBC procedures as described by Steege and Watson reflect my own philosophy and pragmatism about how consultation in the schools should be conducted. In a nutshell, DBC can be explained as "Let's do it instead of talking about doing it." If more practitioners adhered to this mantra, school-based consultation would result in more meaningful outcomes for students and would simultaneously be more reinforcing for teachers and practitioners.

I strongly recommend this second edition and believe it should be required reading in coursework in applied behavior analysis, school psychology, and special education, as the information crosses all three professions. Practitioners who adhere to and use the models and procedures outlined in this book will undoubtedly discover that they are more effective in their service delivery, which will translate into more positive outcomes for the students they serve—which is ultimately what this book is all about.

FRANK M. GRESHAM, PhD
Department of Psychology
Louisiana State University

Preface

When the second edition of a book is published, probably the most pressing question a reader can pose is, "Is it worth buying this new edition?" This question is invariably quickly followed by, "Have the authors really changed a lot here, or is it just an updated version of the first edition?" Here are our answers to these questions: If you liked the first edition, you are going to love the second edition! We have not only updated the information but have also added new chapters and revised our forms and reports to make them even more useful for school-based practitioners.

So, you ask, what exactly is different about this edition that would actually make it more useful for me? To respond, let us describe how the chapters have been altered, expanded, and added to make this edition an exciting and rewarding practical resource—whether or not you were familiar with the original book.

Chapter 1 is still titled "Introduction to Functional Behavioral Assessment," as in the first edition. We have retained much of the information from the first edition but added a box called "Desperately Seeking a Diagnosis," in which we discuss, among other issues, the futility of attempting to base intervention decisions on a diagnostic label. Many schools and practitioners still spend a great deal of time engaging in behavior that is desperately seeking the "correct" diagnosis for a student. We point out the folly of doing so and provide a meaningful alternative that makes time well spent. Readers of the first edition are undoubtedly familiar with the five errors that can occur during the functional behavioral assessment (FBA) process. Based on our ever-accumulating observations, we have modified this list by adding additional errors and revising others.

Chapter 2, Genesis of Functional Behavioral Assessment, is another of the foundation chapters. Much of its information is timeless and did not require revision. We did, however, insert new information on functional assessment procedures and their application to the school environment so that you can see how the field has progressed in a few short years. At the end of this chapter, we give you a "teaser" about our updated conceptual model for understanding behavior. In the first edition, we adhered to the A-I-B-C model: Antecedent variables–Individual variables–Behavior–Consequences. We now follow the S-M-I-R-C model: Stimulus/discriminative stimulus–Motivating operations–Individual (organism) variables–Response–C (Consequence), which is a more comprehensive model for understanding the complexity of human behavior.

Chapter 3, Legal Aspects of Functional Behavioral Assessment, required extensive updating given the recent passage of the Individuals with Disabilities Education Improvement Act (IDEIA). We have gone to considerable lengths to provide you with recent administrative rulings, court decisions, Office of Special Education Programs policy statements, and other legal guidance regarding both FBAs and behavioral intervention plans. We have done our best to combine legal and best-practice considerations into realistic applications for school-based practitioners. We have used a "Q and A" format for addressing many of the legal and best-practice parameters. We used this format based on reader feedback over the last 3 years indicating the "user-friendliness" of this format.

Our collective thoughts when looking at the completed version of Chapter 4, Everything You Always Wanted to Know about the Conceptual Foundations of Functional Behavioral Assessments . . . but Were Afraid to Ask, were that not only does it have a really long title, but the chapter is long as well. It now includes material from the first edition as well as a number of new sections, addressing topics such as motivating operations, how altered physical states directly affect behavior, a description of the S-M-I-R-C model, why response classes may be important in the FBA and intervention process, and how the matching law influences behavior in the school setting. Admittedly, some of the concepts are fairly complex and will require additional study, but we determined it was important to include these topics in the second edition.

Three significant additions were made to Chapter 5, Key Elements of Functional Behavioral Assessment. First, we expanded the FBA decision tree into two trees by separating the reinforcing and motivating consequences of behavior, in keeping with the S-M-I-R-C model. Second, we revised the key elements to correspond with the S-M-I-R-C model and with what we have learned over the past 5 years. Third, we provided an updated Functional Behavioral Assessment Rating Scale (FuBARS) that allows you to formatively and summatively assess FBAs.

Chapter 6, Observing and Recording Behavior, contains a new section on real-time recording. Much of the information from the first edition remains because the basic principles of behavioral observation and recording have not changed and the procedures we previously recommended continue to be effective. Similarly Chapter 7, Indirect Functional Behavioral Assessment, closely follows the text in the first edition. We did, however, update the forms to make them consistent with the S-M-I-R-C model.

Chapter 8, Direct Descriptive Functional Behavioral Assessment, includes the significant addition of the Task Analysis Recording Procedure (TARP), which is a means for teaching skills and recording a student's behavior within the context of instructional programming. It is an excellent tool for documenting increases in appropriate behavior while simultaneously documenting decreases in inappropriate behavior. We describe step by step how to develop individualized TARPs and how to analyze the data, and provide an example of a completed TARP and subsequent analysis as well.

Chapter 9, Brief Functional Analysis of Behavior, is all *new*! Based on feedback we received from readers of the first edition, we added this chapter. Functional *analysis* is more rigorous than functional *assessment* and is particularly useful in those cases where the FBA does not yield a clear function. Realizing that most practitioners are pressed for time, we describe a model that is both rigorous *and* time efficient. We provide examples of structural analyses (analysis of antecedents) and analyses of consequences to give practitioners a broad view of functional analysis. We then provide an extended case example of our brief functional analysis model that incorporates assessment data, a brief standard functional analysis, a confirmatory functional analysis, and a contingency reversal.

Chapter 10, Behavior-Analytic Problem-Solving Model, is likewise all new. We acknowledge that the FBA process can at times be overwhelming and data rich. And since it is sometimes difficult to see the relationships among the variables identified in the FBA, we created the behavior-analytic problem-solving (BAPS) model, which is a means for practitioners to organize and summarize their findings for the entire assessment process. In this chapter, we provide in-depth, detailed examples of how the BAPS is used with contextual variables, discriminative stimuli, motivating operations, individual mediating variables, individual behavior variables, and reinforcing consequences. We also include a BAPS Recording Form that should be useful in organizing your assessment data and arriving at meaningful and socially significant conclusions about intervention.

Chapter 11, Function-Based Interventions, discusses the essentials of positive behavioral supports and linking the results of the FBA to socially meaningful interventions. There are sections on antecedent modifications, teaching coping skills, remediating academic skills deficits, and positive and negative reinforcement, among others. There are also a multitude of examples in each section, as well as a comprehensive example with charts and graphs demonstrating the step-by-step process of linking an FBA to a function-based intervention.

Chapter 12, Sample Functional Behavioral Assessment Reports, is an updated and expanded version of Chapter 8 in the first edition. We have retained the brief FBA report and functional behavioral assessment reports and added a comprehensive psychological evaluation report sample, as well as an additional FBA report example. You will find that our reports match not only the FBA procedures we recommend, but also the S-M-I-R-C conceptual model. The interventions we offer are based on positive procedures for improving socially meaningful behaviors.

Finally, Chapter 13, Direct Behavioral Consultation, is based on our 40 years of collective experience of what constitutes effective consultation in various educational arenas. Some years ago, the concepts of direct behavioral consultation (DBC) were articulated and were differentiated from traditional behavioral consultation. In this chapter, you will learn not only the basic concepts of DBC but also the "flow" of DBC from the time of referral to resolution of the case. To assist with writing a summary of the consultation process, we included an example of a consultation summary report. Finally, be sure to make note of the chapter's concluding sections, "The Quiet Crisis" and "American Idle."

We hope that this second edition will be as rewarding in your practice as it has been for us to collect, synthesize, and write. In closing, please remember the wise words from one of our school psychology colleagues, Kevin Jones, who observed, "If you wanted to predict the flight of a bumble bee, you could examine still frames of 30+ busy bees. Or you could examine the motion picture of a single bee."

MARK W. STEEGE
T. STEUART WATSON

Contents

List of Figures and Tables

FIGURES

TABLES

1

Introduction to Functional Behavioral Assessment

Once in possession of a set of terms we may proceed to a kind of description of behavior by giving a running account of a sample of behaviors as it unfolds itself in some frame of reference. This is a typical method in natural history. . . . It may be classified as a narration. . . . From data obtained in this way it is possible to classify different kinds of behavior and to determine relative frequencies of occurrence. But although this is, properly speaking, a description of behavior, it is not a science in the accepted sense. We need to go beyond mere observation to a study of functional relationships. We need to establish laws by virtue of which we may predict behavior, and we may do this only by finding variables of which behavior is a function.
—B. F. SKINNER (1938, p. 8)

This quote from Skinner 70 years ago captures the very essence of this entire book that merely describing and classifying behavior is insufficient for anything beyond those two tasks. To change the lives of students in a positive and meaningful way, we need to understand the functional relationship between variables present in the environment and a student's behavior. It is folly, however, to think that we can identify and isolate the relative effects of *every* variable in a student's environment and its impact on his or her behavior. What we can do is identify the *most likely* variables and then evaluate the relationship between a variable or set of variables and its or their subsequent effect on behavior.

Students who display interfering behavior in the classroom challenge the resources of schools, social service agencies, and their families. An inordinate amount of time, energy, and resources are expended attempting to develop strategies to address the behaviors exhibited by these students and to make them more successful in the classroom. When students are referred to school-based teams because of problematic behavior in the classroom, the multidisciplinary team[1] often discusses what action to take regarding the behavior of the

---

[1]School-based assistance teams are often referred to as "multidisciplinary teams," "transdisciplinary teams," "student support teams," and "functional behavioral assessment teams." Regardless of the name, their purpose is roughly the same, and we use these terms interchangeably throughout the book.

individual in crisis. Invariably, in an urgent attempt to resolve the immediate crisis, the team discusses the inappropriateness and severity of the problem behavior and develops a set of procedures for responding to the individual when the problem behavior recurs instead of arranging environmental conditions to prevent it from occurring. Too often, what has been lost in this process is a comprehensive analysis of the conditions that contribute to the occurrence of problem behavior. In addition to this lack of analysis, there is a historic reliance on making a "correct diagnosis" that has significantly interfered with the provision of meaningful services to children (see the box Desperately Seeking a Diagnosis below).

DESPERATELY SEEKING A DIAGNOSIS

During the 1970s, there was considerable discussion about the negative impact of labeling children. A commonly held position was that the stigma associated with the label of "special ed" would haunt a student for life and have long-term detrimental effects on a student's social–emotional functioning. During that era, parents/guardians were often very resistant to the identification of their child as having a disability. Labels such as "mental retardation," "autism," "learning disability," and "emotionally disturbed" were viewed as stigmatizing and damaging. During that era, team members often deliberated at length about whether or not a student was truly disabled and in need of special education services or rather mildly delayed and in need of general education modifications. The team recognized the student needed help, but saw special education identification as the *last resort*. Fast forward to 2008.

In today's world of education, diagnoses are not a "scarlet letter" and special education is often viewed as the *only hope*. Indeed, in our experience, team members are often so focused on identifying the disability that little time or attention is given to solving the student's problems. Within these systems, when a student has been referred for academic, social–emotional, developmental, or behavioral "issues," team members typically conduct norm-referenced assessments to determine if the child meets the criteria for eligibility for special education services. If so, the child is diagnosed (i.e., labeled with a special education classification). So what's wrong with that, you ask? Nothing so far. It's when the team stops there—at the diagnosis—that a major disservice to the child begins. Without going into a huge discussion about the advantages and disadvantages of norm-referenced assessment, let's just say that from our reading of the empirical literature relative to designing individually tailored interventions to address the educational needs of students, norm-referenced assessments and the resulting diagnoses have serious limitations:

- *The diagnosis does not inform intervention.* Consider the case of a 4-year-old who has recently been diagnosed with autistic disorder. How does this diagnosis inform a parent, teacher, or therapist about the most effective instructional methodologies to teach academic, social, or functional life skills? How does the diagnosis lead to the design of behavioral supports to address severe interfering behaviors? In short, at best a diagnosis might point you in the right general direction, but it will not provide you with the information you need to design effective interventions for that individual student.

- *The blame game.* Now, consider the case of the 15-year-old student who has been recently diagnosed with anxiety disorder. In this case, the diagnosis was provided by an outpatient mental health clinic. After reviewing the reports from the clinic, individualized education program (IEP) team members breathed a sigh of relief and said: "Well, there's not much we can do about that. Anxiety is a medical condition. That explains why she has been struggling in school. Until the anxiety is addressed, there is nothing we can do."

(continued)

(box continues)

In our experience, we have seen school teams fall victim to the allure of diagnosis to drive their professional practices.

Why, Then, Do Practitioners Use a Diagnostic Model?

Many practitioners have defined their practice of school psychologists with the quest for the most precise diagnosis as their "holy grail." I (Steege) recently provided consultation with a school psychology practitioner who presented me with a case in which he had spent hours interviewing and reinterviewing teachers and family members about the child's developmental history, had administered numerous norm-referenced behavior rating scales, and had spent hours reviewing the DSM-IV. When I asked him what was the purpose of the assessment, his answer was "To give an accurate diagnosis." Can you can imagine my shock at this statement!?!

With other practitioners, the notion of a diagnosis is more instrumental. In short, it lets you off the hook. Within this perspective, now that the team has identified the diagnosis, the blame for interfering behavior or academic failure is placed squarvwely on the shoulders of the student. This often leads to a mutually beneficial, albeit somewhat twisted, symbiotic relationship between the practitioner and the school system. Within this model, the student's problems are his or hers and his or hers alone. The problems are not related to school-based variables. From this perspective, there is no need to examine the adequacy of instruction, the rate of reinforcement delivered by teaching staff, the level of organization within the school system, the schoolwide behavioral support system (or lack thereof), and so on. This often boils down to a "You scratch my back and I'll scratch yours" professional relationship.

It also depends on how we define our jobs. Many practitioners define their role as assisting the team in determining the diagnosis and subsequent special education placement. Under this model, "It's my job to do the testing and help determine eligibility. . . . It's the job of the special education staff to figure out what to do." Within this model, special education services are often viewed as the only way that additional supports are available. In extreme cases, but not infrequently, special education services are viewed as an entitlement.

In contrast to the diagnostic model of practice, we endorse a comprehensive assessment model that takes into consideration a wide range of variables that influence human behavior. Despite the limitation of the diagnostic model, we believe that it is important to consider diagnostic information as part of our collaborative problem-solving model. In subsequent chapters, you will see how we consider diagnostic information as an "individual mediating variable," one of several variables that interact in complex ways to maintain interfering behaviors. What we do not endorse is a model that looks at any one variable as the *sole cause* of human behavior. Human behavior is a complex enterprise, so it is critical that we understand all of the contributing variables when we set forth to develop person-centered and individually tailored interventions.

THE "GOOD OLD DAYS"

Prior to the introduction of functional behavioral assessment (FBA) methodologies, interventions to treat severe behavior problems typically involved a process wherein team members conducted informal interviews and observations of the referred individual and, based on these findings, identified specific interventions. The selection of interventions was often a personal decision, with practitioners implementing preferred interventions or procedures with which they were very familiar. Practitioners typically used one or more of the follow-ing processes in selecting interventions:

- *Topography-based interventions.* A member of the team reviewed the research lit-erature and chose an intervention that had been demonstrated to be effective with indi-viduals who displayed topographically similar problem behaviors. For example: " I con-ducted a comprehensive review of the literature regarding interventions used to address oppositional–defiant behavior. I recommend that we consider implementing a treatment package addressing Sally's oppositional–defiant behaviors that includes the following com-ponents: (1) guided compliance training, (2) behavioral contracting, (3) cognitive-behavioral counseling twice weekly, (4) family therapy once weekly, (5) differential reinforcement of other behavior (DRO), and (6) differential reinforcement of incompatible behaviors (DRI)." Or "I just heard about a study conducted in Portland where they found pickles were effec-tive in reducing aggression. Apparently gherkins were more effective than dill pickles. Let's try pickle therapy using gherkins to reduce the aggressive behaviors exhibited by Steve." This method is akin to selecting interventions from a manual where topography of behavior is the primary feature (see the discussion below).
- *Case-based interventions.* The team chose an intervention that had been imple-mented and was thought to have been effective with another individual who displayed simi-lar problem behaviors. For example: "Remember Billy. Billy displayed very similar behav-iors. We used time-out with Billy and it seems to help. Let's try time-out with Sue."
- *Individual/team preference-based interventions.* Individuals and teams sometimes develop a tendency whereby they default to "preferred" interventions. These interventions may become preferences because (1) they have actually worked in the past, (2) they require very little effort, (3) they fit neatly into the established classroom/school routine, (4) they involve strategies and skills already in the teacher's repertoire, and/or (5) they are consis-tent with the school's philosophy or policy regarding intervention. This list is certainly not exhaustive: most readers will probably be able to add at least one or two additional reasons as to why teams develop intervention preferences. The important things are to recognize when this is happening and interrupt this process before it is too late and inappropriate or ineffective interventions are selected.

INTERFERING BEHAVIOR

Throughout this guide, we will be using the term "interfering behavior" to refer to those behaviors that have historically been referred to as "maladaptive," "inappropriate," "dysfunc-tional," "disruptive," "challenging," and "problematic." We prefer this term for several reasons: (1) it is consistent with the language of the Individuals with Disabilities Education Act (IDEA); (2) it conveys the idea that the behavior is interfering in some way with the individual's social, emotional, behavioral, and/or academic development or that of his or her peers; (3) it makes no prior assumptions about the appropriateness/inappropriateness or other qualities of the behavior; (4) it does not convey the message that some behaviors result in a "bad" adaptation because any behavior that is functional is by definition adaptive (that is why we dislike the term "maladaptive"); and (5) it does not convey the idea that some behaviors have the "wrong" function as does the term "dysfunctional."

THE SHIFTING SANDS OF TREATMENT APPROACHES

In the early 1980s, a dramatic shift in the conceptualization of problem behaviors and the development of FBA methodologies emerged. The "new thinking" of that era gave consideration to the environmental etiology of problem behaviors as a basis for the rational selection of treatment procedures (Mace & Roberts, 1993). Interventions were to be based on the *function* rather than merely the *form* of the behavior. This meant, for example, that interventions addressing behaviors maintained by negative reinforcement (e.g., escape from tasks) would be different than interventions focusing on behaviors maintained by positive reinforcement (e.g., social attention). The following examples illustrate the difference between addressing the form versus the function of behavior:

- Chris, a 7-year-old student diagnosed with an emotional disability, engages in shouting, swearing, and throwing of materials when asked to complete science lab worksheets.
- Arlene, a 12-year-old student with a diagnosis of mild mental retardation, displays high-pitched vocalization, as well as throwing work materials, when teachers work directly with her peers within the classroom.
- Felix, a 14-year-old with a diagnosis of autistic disorder, exhibits inappropriate verbalizations and throwing of objects in a variety of settings, at different times of day, and with various peers and staff members.

A review of these examples indicates that the *form* of interfering behaviors exhibited by Chris, Arlene, and Felix are very similar—although not identical (i.e., all three individuals engage in inappropriate vocal behaviors and throw objects/materials). Despite the similarity in *form* or appearance, the *function* of the interfering behaviors may be very different in each of the cases. For example, the results of comprehensive functional behavioral assessments indicated that, for Chris, interfering behaviors were motivated by negative reinforcement (i.e., escape from and/or avoidance of difficult tasks), whereas Arlene's behaviors were motivated by positive reinforcement (i.e., access to staff attention). Felix's behaviors were motivated by automatic positive reinforcement (i.e., the sensory consequences produced by the occurrence of these behaviors). Again, in each of these examples, the target behaviors were similar in form but the motivation (i.e., function) for each person was strikingly individualized.

Given that interventions matched to the function of behavior typically result in more effective and efficient outcomes compared to interventions based on the form of behavior, the intervention developed for each individual should be distinctly different from the interventions developed for the others. For instance:

- An intervention package for Chris might involve manipulating task difficulty, escape extinction, and teaching a more appropriate response to signal that assistance or a brief break is needed.
- For Arlene, treatment might involve providing attention contingent upon the absence of the behaviors for increasingly longer periods of time (DRO), attention extinction, and teaching a more appropriate means of obtaining adult attention.
- For Felix, intervention might consist of providing the opportunity for increased sen-

sory stimulation through more appropriate behaviors and teaching new behaviors that result in sensory activation.

It is important to note that although completing an FBA may lead to the identification of a *single function* of a specific behavior (e.g., negative reinforcement only as opposed to positive reinforcement and automatic reinforcement), in many cases a specific behavior may be reinforced by *multiple functions* (e.g., avoidance of academic tasks *and* social attention from peers).

The team has a number of resources available to assist them in choosing interventions, among them some type of intervention manual (e.g., *The Pre-Referral Intervention Manual* [PRIM-3rd ed.])[2] in which behavior is categorized according to topography (e.g., hitting, out-of-seat behavior, swearing, refusing to do work). Once a target behavior is selected, the team simply locates that behavior in the manual and chooses from among 50 listed interventions—that's right, 50 possible interventions for each target behavior! There are no guidelines on which intervention is likely to be most effective, nor are there guidelines on how to select interventions for a particular student. Quite obviously, function is not considered in these types of publications. Thus, their helpfulness is limited by their lack of attention to the function of behavior as well as their lack of creativity in intervention design (e.g., reinforce an opposite behavior). Too often the processes described above lead to the selection of ineffective interventions that at best result in no changes in problem behaviors but oftentimes lead to an increase in the frequency, intensity, and/or duration of problem behaviors. The results of these hastily developed and premature interventions are often ineffective programming, an escalation in the intensity of the original problem behavior, and/or the display of related but more severe forms of the problem behavior.

A more thoughtful and systematic approach for addressing these challenging behaviors is *functional behavioral assessment* (FBA). Although the basic principles of FBA have been in existence for several decades in related professions (e.g., applied behavior analysis, behavior modification, and developmental disabilities; see Chapter 2 for a more in-depth discussion), it was not until the passage of Public Law 105-17 that the term become meaningful for most school psychologists and other school-based practitioners. Because of its relative "newness" within the educational domain, we will attempt to accomplish several goals in this brief introductory chapter:

- Provide a definition and description of FBA.
- Describe some of the most common errors associated with FBA.
- Provide an overview of types of FBA methodologies.

WHAT IS FUNCTIONAL BEHAVIORAL ASSESSMENT?

Behaviors do not occur "out of the blue." Behavior does not occur in a vacuum. Rather, behavior occurs in reaction to a complex array of interacting variables (environmental, indi-

---

[2]First published in 1988. Available from Hawthorne Educational Services, Inc., 800 Gray Oak Drive, Columbia, MO 65201.

vidual, biological, motivational, and instructional, to name a few). Only by identifying the relationships between the unique characteristics of the individual and the contextual variables that trigger and reinforce behavior can we begin to truly understand human behavior and work in concert with the person and those in his or her environment to develop interventions that lead to socially significant and meaningful behavior change. *Identifying these relationships is the core of FBA.*

> **FBA defined: Simply put, FBA is an investigative process that results in an understanding of why behaviors occur. More formally, FBA is a set of assessment procedures that results in the identification and description of the relationships between the unique characteristics of the individual and the contextual variables that trigger, motivate, and reinforce behavior. The FBA is used as the basis for designing individually tailored interventions.**

This book is intended to be a resource that provides school-based practitioners with conceptual models and applied procedures for assessing problem behaviors that interfere with a student's personal, academic, and social development and functioning. All of the procedures and models presented in this book are designed to assist the practitioner in understanding *why* an individual displays a behavior in a particular setting at a particular time. Our models of FBA follow a problem-solving process demonstrating how an array of assessment methodologies can be used to understand the whys of behavior and design and evaluate positive behavioral support interventions. Thus, FBA is not one specific methodology. Rather, it is an amalgamation of techniques that have the same purpose: *identifying the variables that control a behavior and using that knowledge to design individualized interventions.*

THE NEED FOR OBJECTIVE AND INDIVIDUALIZED BEHAVIORAL ASSESSMENTS (OR, THE COMMON ERRORS COMMITTED DURING FUNCTIONAL BEHAVIORAL ASSESSMENTS)

Decisions regarding the development and evaluation of interventions with students who exhibit problem behaviors should be based on objective and accurate information. Failing to do so often results in ineffective programming. Consider the following scenario:

> As a member of the student assistance team (SAT), the school psychologist was asked to provide comprehensive assessment to develop a positive behavioral support plan with Jerry, an adolescent with autism who exhibited aggressive behaviors (e.g., hair pulling, hitting, biting others). When the school psychologist asked school staff to offer an example of an occurrence of aggressive behavior, an educational technician reported an incident in which she had asked the student to fold a laundry basket of towels, saying, "Jerry, it is time to fold towels. These are the towels you have already washed and dried. I'm sure that you can fold these towels. You have folded towels before. Do you want help, or can you do these all by yourself?" She reported that Jerry immediately jumped out of his chair, lunged toward her, grabbed her by the hair, and wrestled her to the floor. This resulted in a three-person physical restraint that lasted 44 minutes. The educational technician stated that the reason Jerry engaged in aggressive behavior was his clear and obvious dislike of folding towels. Some practitioners may stop at

this level of information gathering because (1) they have a firsthand description of the sequence of events that led to the physical restraint, (2) it is a reasonable hypothesis that Jerry reacted in such an aggressive manner because he obviously dislikes folding towels, and/or (3) they are being pressured by the team or other school personnel to quickly design an intervention plan because of the potentially dangerous nature of the aggressive behavior. While on the surface this may appear to be an accurate conclusion, the results of a subsequent *comprehensive* FBA indicated otherwise. The educational technician's error in this case was an *error of association* (see the accompanying box).

In the case of Jerry, the educational technician made an *error of association*. In this example, folding towels was *associated* with the occurrence of aggressive behavior but was not functionally related. That is, folding towels was not the antecedent that acted as a trigger for Jerry's aggressive behavior. The association of two variables (e.g., folding towels and aggressive behavior) does not necessarily mean that there is a functional relationship between those variables. This is similar to the research adage "Correlation does not mean causation."

To conduct an FBA, one must gather more than just one report of a single incident using more than one method. The educational technician had prematurely concluded, based on this one incident, that the trigger for Jerry's aggressive behavior was indeed folding towels. Having some knowledge of the various functions of behavior, she further stated that it appeared that his aggressive behavior was motivated by "escape from and/or avoidance of towel folding." Quite reasonably, she also stated that she did not want to introduce towel folding in the future out of fear of an aggressive response. After interviewing the educational technician, the school psychologist conducted a comprehensive FBA that included interviews with other staff, direct observations, ongoing data collection of aggressive behavior and related variables (i.e., antecedents and consequences), and a brief functional analysis. Data from the various sources demonstrated that aggressive behavior was unrelated to towel folding. Instead, aggression was found to be triggered by excessive verbal instructions and reinforced by the cessation of verbal instructions. Had an intervention been implemented based on the premature (and incorrect) hypothesis that the towel-folding task triggered aggressive behavior, it is highly unlikely that such an intervention would have been effective. Manipulating the towel-folding task in some way without altering the length of verbal instructions would have been ineffective and may have resulted in any combination of the following consequences:

- Ineffective treatment for Jerry.
- Increased risk of potential physical danger to Jerry, the educational technician, and other staff because the aggressive behavior would likely have continued, perhaps worsened, and resulted in additional physical restraints.
- A more restrictive placement for Jerry.
- Decreased confidence in FBA from the SAT.

The *error of association* committed by the educational technician was only one type of error that can occur within the FBA process. Other types of errors include

- Recency error of perception.
- Primacy error of perception.
- Error of misplaced precision.
- Error of inaccurate FBA.
- Error of exaggeration.
- Error of generalization.

With the *recency error of perception*, interviewees report the most recent occurrence of a behavior and attribute its occurrence to variables that were present during the incident. This error is illustrated by the following example:

Jaime was a student in a fourth-grade regular education class. He was referred to the SAT because of frequent disruptive outbursts in class that sometimes included swearing and minor property damage. During the initial stages of the FBA process, the school psychologist interviewed the classroom teacher. She indicated that she thought his outbursts were the result of an abrupt transition from a relatively unstructured, highly physical activity (e.g., recess or gym class) because the most recent episode had occurred within the first 20 minutes after gym class. In fact, she reported that she believed most of his outbursts had occurred after gym or recess. Again, based on what is known about some children's difficulty in making transitions from one activity to another, particularly from an unstructured situation to a more structured classroom environment, the teacher's initial hypothesis seemed quite reasonable. Just to be certain, however, the school psychologist decided that a more comprehensive FBA was necessary in order to validate the teacher's hypothesis and to accurately identify some of the temporally proximate (see the accompanying box) triggers of Jaime's outbursts. The school psychologist conducted several direct observations of Jaime in his classroom, including those times immediately after lunch recess and gym and at other randomly selected times. In addition, the teacher agreed to keep track of Jaime's outbursts using a time-based scatterplot (e.g., see Interval Recording Procedure in Chapter 8) and an antecedent checklist (e.g., see Task Difficulty Antecedent Analysis Form in Chapter 8). When combined, these data revealed two findings that were significant for understanding Jaime's outbursts and for planning intervention: (1) on occasion, his outbursts occurred after recess or gym, but only infrequently; (2) more than 65% of Jaime's outbursts occurred immediately after his teacher issued a negative comment regarding either the quality or the quantity of his academic work output.

The *primacy error of perception* is similar to the recency error of perception except, in this case, interviewees report the initial occurrence of interfering behavior and attribute its cause to variables that were present at that time. Both types of errors can result in very misleading information about the topography and function(s) of interfering behaviors. For example:

Sheryl was an eighth-grade junior high student receiving special services for children diagnosed with specific learning disabilities. In addition to her diagnosed learning disabilities in math and reading, her social skills were quite poor. More specifically, she often threatened her classmates with physical harm although she had not yet reached the point of physical aggression. When a member of the SAT interviewed one of her teachers about the verbal aggression, the teacher was quite certain that she knew the reason behind Sheryl's verbal aggression: teasing from classmates regarding her sometimes poor academic performance. To support her hypothesis, the teacher recalled the first time she directly witnessed Sheryl threatening a classmate, which was about 10 weeks prior to the interview. The student had teased Sheryl about her inability to read a selected paragraph, and Sheryl responded by threatening to beat her up if she didn't stop teasing her. The teacher concluded by saying that although she didn't always hear what was going on, she was convinced that the teasing was the reason behind Sheryl's verbally aggressive behavior. Although the initial incident as described by the teacher may indeed have been accurate, it may or may not have reflected what was *currently* happening to prompt and maintain Sheryl's verbal threats. Hence, more FBA was indicated to determine the extant cues that trigger (antecedents) and the consequences that maintain Sheryl's verbal threats.

The *error of misplaced precision* is illustrated in the following case example:

A preschooler with autism was receiving intensive in-home applied behavior analysis service. A comprehensive data collection system was used to record the frequency of each of several problem behaviors (e.g., self-injury, aggression, tantrums, stereotypy). For example, staff used a tally mark system (i.e., //// //) to record each occurrence of the specified problem behaviors. This data-recording procedure yielded the rate of occurrences of problem behavior per day. During a program evaluation, a consulting psychologist noted that the recording of the frequency of all problem behaviors resulted in imprecise measures of several of the behaviors. For example, the length of the tantrum behaviors varied considerably, from a few seconds to several minutes. Thus, a frequency count of one tantrum that lasted 5 seconds is not equivalent to one tantrum that lasted 28 minutes. Moreover, the tally system offered no information about the contextual variables associated with each of the problem behaviors. In this example, the data-recording procedures were not matched to the dimensions of each behavior. Comprehensive individualized FBA procedures that included frequency, duration, and performance-based behavioral recording procedures were developed. Additionally, an individualized scatterplot data-recoding form (see Interval Recording Procedure in Chapter 8) was developed that resulted in the identification of controlling variables. This is an example of the *error of misplaced precision* because, although there was great concern and care for recording the frequency of several behaviors, the effort put forth on collecting frequency data would have been more beneficial if it had been placed on gathering more relevant data.

The *error of inaccurate functional behavioral assessment* is demonstrated in the following case example:

A student with a history of social emotional and learning difficulties was referred for psychological evaluation regarding oppositional and defiant behaviors (e.g., refusing to comply with teacher requests and refusing to complete assignments). Based on informal interviews and anecdotal observations, the school psychologist concluded that the problem behaviors were motivated by social attention (specifically, the attention the student received from the one-on-one teacher assistant whenever problem behavior occurred). Based on that conclusion, a "time-out procedure" to address problem behavior was implemented for several weeks. During that time, the frequency and duration of oppositional and defiant behaviors increased markedly. A second referral to the school psychologist led to a more comprehensive FBA. This time, the school psychologist conducted an assessment that included a structured interview, direct observations, and brief functional analysis procedures. The combined assessment results indicated that problem behavior was motivated by avoidance or termination of academic tasks, not the student's desire for social attention. The time-out intervention, while designed to reduce problem behavior, was actually serving to reinforce and strengthen oppositional and defiant behaviors because academic tasks were terminated contingent upon oppositional or defiant behavior so that the student could be placed in time-out. Based on the results of the more comprehensive FBA, a positive behavioral support plan incorporating antecedent modification and functional communication training was developed. The revised procedure, which was based on the results from an accurate FBA, resulted in a significant decrease in problem behaviors and a marked increase in task participation, task completion, and task accuracy.

The *error of exaggeration* is illustrated in the following example:

Floyd is a student who receives special education services under the handicapping condition of serious emotional disability (SED). Floyd was referred for psychological evaluation because he displayed oppositional–defiant behaviors (e.g., verbally refusing to complete academic assignments, throwing books, ripping up assignments) within both general education and resource room special education settings. During an interview regarding these behaviors, one of Floyd's teachers stated that "He *always* misbehaves when I ask him to do his work." When asked to elaborate she said, "Every time I ask him to complete an assignment he throws one of his tantrums." The school psychologist conducted three observations within each of the classroom settings and found that while Floyd exhibited oppositional–defiant behaviors, there was not a perfect correspondence between direction to complete assignments and interfering behaviors. The school psychologist kept track of the number of times Floyd was given a directive, the number of times he complied, and the number of times he displayed interfering behaviors. The results showed that given task demands, the conditional probability of task completion was 32%, the probability of oppositional–defiant behavior was 36%, and the probability of neither was 32%. Further observations and analysis showed that the vast majority of occurrences of interfering behavior followed teacher direction for Floyd to participate in reading-based activities. While there are times when a behavior "always" follows an antecedent, in our experience, words and phrases such as "always" and "every time" are flags that further investigation and direct observations are needed.

The *error of generalization* may occur both across and within students.

The error of generalization *across students* occurs when team members assume that the variables contributing to the interfering behaviors exhibited by Student A are the same set of variables contributing to the identical behavior exhibited by Student B. For example, the error of generalization across students is evidenced when team members assume that because Jimmy is exhibiting swearing behavior to gain attention from classmates, Carter is also swearing to gain social attention from peers. Further analysis revealed that the function of swearing behaviors exhibited by Jimmy was social attention, but that the function of swearing displayed by Carter was escape-avoidance of difficult assignments.

The error of generalization across behaviors occurs when the evaluator assumes that because one behavior is motivated by a specific function that *all* interfering behaviors are related to that function. For example, consider the case of Erin, a student with mild developmental disabilities, who displays multiple interfering behaviors (e.g., aggression, property destruction, swearing, and hand biting). During the initial phases of the FBA, the behavior analyst conducting the FBA hypothesized that aggression and property destruction were both reinforced by escape from difficult tasks. The behavior analyst next assumed that the other behaviors were also reinforced by negative reinforcement. Subsequent function-based interventions were only successful in treating aggression and property destruction behaviors, while swearing and hand-biting behaviors increased over time. Additional FBA procedures determined that swearing and hand biting were not reinforced by negative reinforcement (i.e., escape from demanding tasks); rather, these behaviors were maintained by positive reinforcement in the form of social attention from teachers). Swearing and hand biting were eliminated when an intervention package based on the results of the accurate FBA was introduced.

A central theme to identifying and correcting the errors depicted in each of these scenarios is the need to closely examine objective behavioral assessments. In each case, behavioral assessment procedures were used to record behaviors and to systematically identify controlling variables. A conclusion drawn from these examples is that an anecdotal report (i.e., interview data) alone is often an inadequate method for understanding complex behavioral interactions. Moreover, not all behavioral assessment methods are suitable for recording and evaluating all forms of behavior. When FBAs of interfering behavior are conducted, an individualized assessment process that takes into account the characteristics of the individual, the behaviors exhibited, and the environments in which these behaviors occur must be implemented. Thus, we do not recommend a "cookie-cutter" approach to FBAs. Although we acknowledge several critical components that must be included in every FBA (e.g., direct observations of behavior), the timing and extent of these and other components will likely be different for each student.

THE "NOT SO GOOD OLD DAYS": INTERVENTION MOMENTUM AND PREMATURE IMPLEMENTATION

Despite almost three decades of research demonstrating the utility of using a functional approach for determining the most effective treatment, school-based teams do not always engage in productive discussions during meetings, as the following example illustrates. Unfortunately, this meeting did not occur 20 or 15 years ago or even 10 years ago. In sad truth, this meeting occurred within the last 5 years.

I (Steege) was invited to the meeting by the parent of Chris, a student whom the team would be discussing. The purpose of the meeting was to discuss interfering behaviors that Chris had been exhibiting for several weeks. Participants at the meeting included the parent, the special education case manager, Chris's mainstream teachers, the school psychologist, a behavior specialist, an educational technician, an occupational therapist, and the principal. The meeting began with introductions of all team members. Next, the special education case manager began to describe several "behavioral incidents" over the past few weeks in which Chris displayed "silly disruptive behaviors." The team spent approximately 2 minutes discussing the target behavior(s) and less than 1 minute addressing possible antecedent, individual, or consequence variables. Several minutes were devoted to a discussion of possible diagnoses (e.g., Asperger's disorder, oppositional–defiant disorder, nonverbal learning disability, obsessive–compulsive disorder, and attention-deficit/hyperactivity disorder). The team members spent approximately 40 out of the 60 minutes of the meeting discussing the advantages and disadvantages of various intervention strategies that could be used to address these behaviors. The discussion about interventions focused on strategies that would change Chris's behaviors. Toward the end of the meeting, the team agreed to implement four or five of the strategies and "see how Chris responds to these changes." Because of my role as "invited guest" and not having worked with this team before, I spent the majority of my time observing the collaborative problem-solving process as it unfolded. On a positive note, the team members were respectful of each other's opinions and suggestions and appeared to be working very hard to develop fair and equitable strategies to reduce occurrences of "silly disruptive behaviors."

Throughout the meeting, I kept track (yes, I love to collect data) of the number of specific strategies that were suggested. This team identified 22 specific intervention strategies (time-out, response cost, a token economy program, social skills training, individual counseling, group counseling, self-esteem-building activities, peer tutoring, peer mentoring, one-on-one educational technician support, life space interviewing, brief walks around the school to reduce anxiety, brief walks to stimulate attending, and several sensory integration techniques, among others). This is a classic case of a team developing *intervention momentum*. Intervention momentum occurs when members of the team begin to suggest (oftentimes in rapid-fire motion) strategy after strategy after strategy. It's the snowball effect—or, for folks from warmer climates, it's the tidal wave effect. A team member's idea sparks an idea in another team member, whose suggestion triggers the offering of a strategy by another team member, and so on. This type of brainstorming can often be quite valuable in identifying creative and effective interventions. However, it is a much more effective and efficient process when it occurs *after* a comprehensive FBA has been conducted and the team members have a full understanding of all the variables associated with the behavior(s) of concern. This case example also illustrates another classic situation that often occurs within school and agency settings, namely, *premature implementation*. Premature implementation occurs when team members, usually out of a sense of urgency to act or to be "helpful," frantically identify and implement intervention strategies that are preceded by little if any forethought. Premature implementation, although meeting an immediate need to "do something," may in fact do nothing, or—in a worst-case scenario—may actually complicate the situation and result in an increase in the problem behavior.

The Solution:
- Conduct a comprehensive FBA.
- Use the results of the FBA to design individually tailored interventions.
- Objectively evaluate the effectiveness of the intervention.

THE EVIDENCE BASE
FOR FUNCTIONAL BEHAVIORAL ASSESSMENT

Since the early 1980s, there has been an extraordinary and steady increase of research supporting, demonstrating, and validating a wide range of FBA procedures. A central theme of this research is that the understanding of behavior needs to be conducted on an individualized basis. Numerous school-based FBA studies have shown that individual topographies of problem behavior may be maintained by various forms of reinforcement across populations of students (Radford, Aldrich, & Ervin, 2000). A recent study by Kennedy, Meyer, Knowles, and Shukla (2000) clearly illustrates this point. We have summarized the Kennedy et al. study in the accompanying box.

The findings of Kennedy et al. (2000) are consistent with previous research that has demonstrated that interventions based on the *function* of behavior rather than the *form* of behavior result in meaningful behavior change (e.g., Iwata, Dorsey, Slifer, Bauman, & Richman, 1982/1994; Carr & Durand, 1985; Steege, Wacker, Berg, Cigrand, & Cooper, 1989; Steege et al., 1990; Wacker et al., 1990). Basically, the body of research from 1982 to the present in the area of FBA clearly demonstrates that the identification of the function(s) of problem behavior is critical to the design and successful implementation of positive behavioral support interventions.

Kennedy et al. (2000) investigated the behavioral functions associated with stereotypy (body rocking, object manipulation, tapping objects, head weaving, and hand waving, among others) of five students with autism who attended age-appropriate public school placements that ranged from a full-time general education class to a self-contained special education class. Stereotypic behavior has historically been referred to as "self-stimulatory behavior," implying that sensory consequences are reinforcing and maintaining the behavior. For example, hand flapping is often considered to be a form of self-stimulatory behavior, with the explanation that the movement of the hand in front of the face produces visual stimulation that is reinforcing to the individual. The above authors conducted FBAs of a range of stereotypic behaviors, most of which might be classified as self-stimulatory. FBAs showed that stereotypy served multiple operant functions, including positive reinforcement (i.e., access to social attention) and negative reinforcement (i.e., termination of demanding tasks), and occurred in the absence of environmental reinforcement (presumably from perceptual or sensory reinforcement). Kennedy et al. demonstrated that just because a behavior looks like it serves self-stimulatory purposes does not necessarily mean that that is the function of the behavior. They found that one cannot presume the function of behavior based on the form of the behavior. They next developed tailored interventions with each student, interventions that were based on the results of the FBA. For example, for a student whose stereotypic behavior was motivated by both negative reinforcement (i.e., the occurrence of behavior revisited in the termination of a difficult

(continued)

(box continues)

task) and positive reinforcement (i.e., social attention), he or she was taught to raise his or her right hand to request attention and to sign "break" to indicate a request to terminate difficult tasks. The intervention resulted in a marked increase in functional communication skills and a decrease in stereotypic behaviors.

While there is an abundant and historically robust literature on FBA within the fields of developmental disabilities and applied behavior analysis, the widespread application of FBA in school settings is a growing phenomenon. As noted by Ervin, Ehrhardt, and Poling (2001), the number of published studies on school-based applications of FBA has grown dramatically since the early 1980s. Hanley, Iwata, and McCord (2003) identified 87 published studies in which functional analysis procedures were conducted in school settings, with the vast majority of those studies published after 1990. A recent PsychINFO search using the terms "school" and "functional assessment" or "functional analysis" yielded 324 records. When the search was limited by year of publication (2003–2008), type of publication (only peer-reviewed journal articles), and language (English only) and the titles and abstracts were examined for relevant content, 83 records were identified. Thus, in a relatively short period of 6 years, the number of articles on school-based functional assessment doubled from the number cited by Hanley et al. in about one-third the amount of time. In addition, the fields of both school psychology and special education have seen a multitude of book chapters and books devoted to the subject of FBA (Crone & Horner, 2003; Monastra, 2008; O'Neil et al., 1997; Shapiro & Kratochwill, 2000; Steege, Mace, & Brown-Chidsey, 2007; Watson & Steege, 2003). This accumulating body of knowledge is testament to the robustness of FBA and its applicability to a broad spectrum of children in a wide variety of educational settings.

BRIEF OVERVIEW
OF FUNCTIONAL BEHAVIORAL ASSESSMENT PROCEDURES

FBA goes beyond merely identifying and describing problem behavior. The FBA process is an investigative endeavor that also focuses on identifying and evaluating the variables that trigger and maintain behavior. The results of an FBA are then used as the basis for designing individually tailored intervention plans. There are three methods for conducting an FBA:

1. Indirect FBA.
2. Direct descriptive FBA.
3. Functional analysis.

Indirect functional behavioral assessment involves a variety of methods, including review of records, behavior rating scales, social skills ratings, adaptive behavior assessments, informal interviews, and semistructured interviews. The primary purposes of indirect FBA procedures are to (1) identify and describe behavior and (2) to generate *hypothesized* functional relationships (i.e., the identification of antecedent, individual, and consequent variables that are *associated with* the targeted interfering behavior). In the vast majority of cases, this should not be the only step of an FBA. As discussed earlier, interviewees often unintentionally report biased and erroneous information. Teams that base an FBA solely on interviews risk conducting inaccurate and invalid (and perhaps illegal) assessments that result in ineffective interventions.

Note: We have seen several examples of *one-page* FBA forms designed by practitioners and/or school district personnel. These forms are completed using interviews often conducted during a team meeting. This does not represent a best practices approach to conducting an FBA. The one-page "quick" and oftentimes "dirty" approach should be viewed as only the start of the hypothesis-testing approach.

Direct descriptive functional behavioral assessment involves the collection of observational data on the occurrence of behavior and contextual variables within the context of natural environments. These assessments involve observing and recording the specified target behavior and relevant environmental events. Direct observation of target behaviors and causal conditions within the natural environment is a procedure school-based practitioners can use that allows educational teams to construct applied interventions that are clearly indicated by the assessment data (Skinner et al., 2000). There are a variety of direct descriptive FBA methods. Selection of the method typically depends on several factors including the topography of the behavior (i.e., what it looks like) and the skills/resources of those who are conducting the assessment. At the most basic level, direct descriptive FBA involves identifying and describing the behavior, designing an appropriate behavior-recording procedure, and observing and recording the behavior and associated antecedent and consequence variables. Although valuable for identifying these potential relationships, information gathered from both indirect FBA and direct descriptive FBA are only *suggestive* of functional relationships because they do not systematically isolate and manipulate environmental variables (McComas & Mace, 2000). We will more fully discuss direct descriptive procedures in Chapter 8.

In order to *confirm* hypothesized functional relationships, it is necessary to conduct a more precise assessment in which an experimental or functional analysis is conducted. There are two types of functional analysis: (1) brief functional analysis and (2) extended functional analysis (brief functional analysis will be covered in Chapter 9). In a functional analysis, antecedents and consequences found in the student's natural environment are arranged in such a way so that their relative effects on interfering behavior can be directly observed and measured (Cooper et al., 2007). Both brief and extended functional analysis procedures involve the observation of behavior and the direct manipulation of antecedent and/or consequence variables for the purpose of empirically determining the functions of behavior. Extended functional analysis procedures (i.e., Iwata et al., 1982) involve multiple assessment trials of several minutes (e.g., up to 30 minutes) for each assessment condition (e.g., five trials of academic demand, five trials of social attention, five trials of alone), typically within an alternating treatments design. The brief functional analysis model incorporates the same general assessment methodologies as the extended functional analysis, except the number and duration of assessments of sessions is limited (e.g., 8 to 10 sessions from 10 to 15 minutes each).

Steege and Northup (1998) described a brief functional analysis procedure in which the assessment is conducted within two to three phases: (1) standard assessment, where potential maintaining variables are evaluated; (2) confirmatory assessment, where the results of the initial assessment are replicated; and (3) contingency reversal, where the identified function of problem behavior is provided contingent on appropriate behavior. More recently, Asmus et al. (2004) reported 138 case examples in which they conducted brief functional analyses of a wide range of interfering behaviors (e.g., self-injury, aggression, disruption, property destruction, noncompliance, tantrum, etc.). They reported that brief functional analysis procedures were successful in identifying reinforcing consequences with 96% of the participants. In addition, the results of function-based interventions resulted in an 80% or greater reduction of interfering behaviors in an average of 10 days with 76% of the participants.

Over the past 25 years, extensive research has validated the experimental rigor and clinical utility of functional analysis procedures. Suffice it to say, these procedures are clearly evidence-based and have emerged as the "gold standard" for conducting FBAs. When conducting an indirect or direct descriptive FBA, one is attempting to identify the same types of functional relationships that are determined via a functional analysis. Essentially, indirect and direct descriptive FBA procedures are approximations of functional analyses.

The need for comprehensive, rigorous, and objective assessment of behaviors is obvious. There are a wide range of FBA methodologies available to practitioners. A common question at workshops is "Is one method absolutely better than the others?" We can answer that with an emphatic "No!" There is no one best FBA procedure or set of procedures. In our application of FBAs across a wide range of individuals, referral issues, and settings, our methodologies have taken many forms. The particular form depends on the individual being assessed, the target behaviors, the setting, and the amount of training and experience in behavior analysis of teachers, support staff, parents, and others. To address the full range of presenting issues, practitioners need to be well trained and experienced in a wide range of assessment methodologies. In short, it is naive to expect that we can assess all behavioral issues with a single or "cookie-cutter" method (i.e., the standard battery approach) or a "shotgun" approach (use of every FBA procedure every time in hopes that we get the requisite information). Either of these approaches, which are probably often utilized in practice, are at the very least *inefficient* and likely *ineffective*. Instead, practitioners need a well-stocked arsenal of assessment methods from which they can choose. With these tools in hand, practitioners will be able to:

- Match the assessment process to the referral issues.
- Conduct assessments that result in accurate, reliable, and valid data.
- Design effective and realistic *function-based* interventions that result in meaningful improvements in the student's academic, behavioral, and social functioning.

To reiterate, this book will not tell a practitioner *which* particular FBA method to use in a given situation. Nor will it give a formulaic approach that can be applied to all FBAs conducted in a school district. Rather, it will equip the practitioner with information and skills that will facilitate improved decision making as she or he completes the FBA process, with the end results being more effective interventions and improved student outcomes.

2

Genesis of Functional Behavioral Assessment

Twenty years from now you will be more disappointed by the things that you
didn't do than by the ones you did do. So throw off the bowlines. Sail away from
the safe harbor. Catch the trade winds in your sails. Explore. Dream. Discover.
—MARK TWAIN

Since publication of the first edition of this book, a number of advances have been made,
both procedurally and in the widespread dissemination of information about functional
behavioral assessment (FBA). It is unlikely that most special educators or school psychologists would be completely unfamiliar with this topic. Familiarity, however, does not imply
knowledge of the extensive history associated with FBA and the work from which it developed. In this short chapter, we provide a very general overview of that history because we
believe that school practitioners need to be able to relate to others the relative "un-newness"
of FBA and that it is not merely another bandwagon onto which educational reform/legisla-
tion has hopped and continues to ride. We also think it is important to know why the focus
on function is so very crucial for understanding the reasons children behave the way they
do and for remedying problematic academic and social behaviors. We will also give an overview of more recent innovations in the application of the various FBA methodologies.

When Public Law 105-17, the Individuals with Disabilities Act (IDEA) was passed in
1997, terms related to FBA and intervention (such as positive behavioral supports) were
introduced into the everyday vocabulary of professionals providing psychological services
to children in educational settings:

> The team must address through a behavioral intervention plan any need for positive behav-
> ioral strategies and supports (614(d)3(B)(i)). In response to disciplinary actions by school
> personnel, the IEP team must, within 10 days, meet to develop a *functional behavioral
> assessment* plan to collect information. This information should be used for developing or
> reviewing and revising an existing behavioral intervention plan to address such behaviors
> (615(k)(1)(B)). In addition, states are required to address the in-service needs of person-

18

nel (including professionals and paraprofessionals who provide special education, general education, related services, or early intervention services) as they relate to developing and implementing positive intervention strategies (653(c)(3)(D)(vi)). (emphasis added)

The reauthorization of IDEA, the Individuals with Disabilities Education Improvement Act (IDEIA; Public Law 108-446 in 2004) reaffirmed that FBA would be part and parcel of the special education intervention process. Although these two federal laws were largely responsible for bringing FBA methodologies into the educational realm, the notion that all behaviors serve some purpose (function) actually has a lengthy history, dating back to the work of E. L. Thorndike (1898) and B. F. Skinner (1938), among others.

To get at the roots of function, let's begin with the work of Edward L. Thorndike, who coined the term *law of effect* (1898; see the accompanying box). Although the work of Thorndike did not directly influence the development of research specifically related to function, it is a predecessor to some of the concepts that Skinner used to understand human behavior. Without going into undue detail in the present context, we note that Thorndike observed over a series of trials that the behavior of cats was influenced by the consequences (escape from a box and access to food) of their behavior. That is, behaviors that resulted in escape from the box (i.e., pulling a wire or pressing a lever), and hence access to food, increased over time, whereas other behaviors that did not result in escape from the box (i.e., clawing and biting at the box) decreased. In addition, each cat spent less time in the box with each succeeding trial before it exhibited the behavior that allowed it to escape. Thus, not only were the cats learning behaviors that resulted in positive consequences, but they were exhibiting the behaviors in a more efficient fashion. Thorndike's experiments were a simple yet elegant illustration of the powerful effects that consequences can have on responding.

LAW OF EFFECT

Briefly, the law of effect states that behaviors that result in satisfying consequences are "stamped in" or tend to recur and those that result in "annoying" consequences are "stamped out" and tend not to recur.

John B. Watson, who is known as the father of behaviorism, asserted that all behaviors were the result of environmental events. He argued that psychologists should study overt behaviors and their environmental determinants and not the internal urges/drives that dominated the field of psychology at the time. Almost everyone is familiar with Watson's most famous experiment in which he conditioned a fear response in an 11-month-old infant to demonstrate the effects that environmental events can have on the development of "emotions" (J. B. Watson & Rayner, 1920). Watson's psychology was appropriately called "stimulus–response" because of the focus on the relationship between the presentation of a stimulus and the resulting response. Watson, like Ivan P. Pavlov earlier, illustrated the behavior-eliciting effects of certain stimuli. When behavior is a function of (or caused by) a stimulus that *preceded* it, the behavior is called a *respondent behavior*. The accompanying example (see box on p. 20) illustrates the principle of respondent behavior.

A REAL-LIFE EXAMPLE OF RESPONDENT BEHAVIOR

On a cool spring day, little Mackenzie, age 4, was playing on the swingset in her backyard, swinging, laughing, and singing, and pumping her legs so that she would go ever higher in the air. Unbeknownst to her, a nasty wasp had entered the area and had pinpointed her as a target for its mildly poisonous but painful stinger. Mackenzie visually detected the wasp just as it landed on her leg and inserted its stinger into her calf muscle. The wasp had inflicted a painful stimulus on Mackenzie and, like most children her age when they are hurt, she began crying and screaming and running away from the aversive stimulus (the wasp).

Several days later, Mackenzie was once again playing on the swingset in her backyard. And once again, a wasp was flying around the swingset, perhaps looking for potential targets. Mackenzie saw the wasp and immediately jumped from the swing and ran away screaming and crying, essentially exhibiting the same behavior as during her first encounter with a wasp. This encounter was different in at least one important aspect, however. This time, Mackenzie exhibited the same behavior without being stung. This is an extremely critical point because Mackenzie had not received a consequence for this encounter with the wasp yet she exhibited behavior as if she had indeed been stung. In this case, we say that her crying, screaming, and running behaviors were respondent behaviors because they resulted from, or were caused by, the presentation of a stimulus (i.e., the wasp).*

---
*This story was told here with the permission of Mackenzie Watson

---

In the early 1930s, Burrhus Frederic Skinner, who was heavily influenced by Charles Darwin in addition to Pavlov, Thorndike, and Watson, began studying the effects that consequences have on behavior as well as the stimuli that evoke behavior. Skinner primarily used rats in his laboratory and analyzed the effects that different schedules of reinforcement have on behavior. One of Skinner's most important findings was that behavior was a function of (i.e., was caused by) the consequences that followed it. For instance, Skinner's data indicated that if lever pressing was positively reinforced with food (i.e., lever presses were immediately followed by a food pellet), lever pressing increased. In this example, lever pressing is *operant behavior* because it is controlled by the consequences that followed it. If food is no longer presented after lever pressing, then lever pressing will decrease in frequency until it is no longer exhibited. The accompanying example (see box below) illustrates how the principle of operant conditioning works in the classroom to produce interfering behavior.

A REAL-LIFE EXAMPLE OF OPERANT BEHAVIOR

Barry is a third-grade student who is well liked by his peers and his teachers. He gets along well with everyone in his class, has a wonderful personality, and does well academically . . . except in math. For some reason, he has always had difficulty with even basic math concepts like addition and one digit by one digit multiplication computations. Despite his difficulty, his grades and standardized achievement scores have never been sufficiently low to warrant consideration for special education testing. Until the current school year, Barry was a model

(continued)

(box continues)

student in terms of classroom behavior. His teacher noted that recently his behavior has been getting progressively worse, especially during math instruction and while doing worksheets. What typically happens is that the teacher will either begin a lesson on math or assign a worksheet to be completed at his desk which results in Barry either complaining loudly that he can't do the work, running around the classroom, or being openly defiant of her. Quite obviously, the teacher is concerned about why he is engaging in this behavior and why it has gotten progressively worse. In talking with the teacher, we discovered that her most common reactions to Barry's behaviors were to first ignore them and, if they did not cease, to send him to the principal's or the counselor's office, or to a desk in the hall. As a result of these disciplinary practices, Barry often fails to complete his assignments, which in turn worsens his grade in math. The trigger, or antecedent, for these behaviors is fairly obvious: math worksheets or any type of math instruction. What is not so well understood is why, especially after being punished for engaging in these behaviors, Barry's behavior has not only persisted but actually worsened. In looking more closely at the behavior, we see that all of the consequences for Barry's behavior result in him being able to *avoid* or *escape* his math assignments. Thus, we say that Barry's behaviors are *negatively reinforced* because whenever he is sent out of the room, whether to the principal, the counselor, or a desk in the hall, each of these consequences result in him not having to do his math or listen to math instruction. In essence, these behaviors are "working" for Barry because they result in him not having to do math. A simple concept? Most definitely. Well understood by most in the school system? Definitely not. It does not matter whether a person intends for a particular consequence to be a punishment or not, as in the case of Barry's teacher. What matters is the effect the consequences have on behavior. In this example, Barry's behaviors are caused by the consequences that follow the behavior and are operant behaviors.*

---

*This story was told here with the permission of Barry (a pseudonym but a real kid).

From these two examples, we see that behavior can be caused by events that precede it (i.e., respondent conditioning) and by events that follow it (i.e., operant conditioning). In some instances, behavior is a function of both respondent and operant conditioning. In such instances, the behavior may be referred to as "two-factor" behavior. To illustrate two-factor learning, let's return to Mackenzie from the respondent conditioning example (see the accompanying box below).

A REAL-LIFE EXAMPLE OF TWO-FACTOR LEARNING

Recall that Mackenzie exhibited running, crying, and screaming behavior when she observed a wasp (respondent behavior). This behavior resulted from her being stung by a wasp some days earlier. The most immediate result of her running, crying, and screaming was avoiding another sting from a wasp (the operant element). Thus, we can say that these behaviors were negatively reinforced and are controlled partly by their consequences (avoidance of a sting) and partly by the stimuli that precedes them (sight of the wasp).

One of the obvious criticisms of Thorndike's and Skinner's work is that they used animals—and not humans—to scientifically study behavior. Certainly the behavior of humans is much more complex than that of cats or rats because humans can think, reason, talk, develop morals, make laws, and the like. Or is it? Beginning in the early-to-middle 1950s and throughout the 1960s, applied researchers began using Skinner's principles to solve problems presented by humans. One early study examined the effects of using positive reinforcement on cooperation in children ranging in age from 7 to 12 years (Azrin & Lindsley, 1956). It was found that, even in the absence of instructions to cooperate, positive reinforcement was effective for developing and maintaining cooperative behavior. Likewise, discontinuing reinforcement for cooperative behavior resulted in elimination of cooperation. In perhaps one of the most interesting early behavior modification studies, Flanagan, Goldiamond, and Azrin (1959) demonstrated that stuttering could be instituted in otherwise fluent speakers by making escape from mild shock contingent upon nonfluent speech. That is, stuttering was negatively reinforced because it resulted in the termination of a painful stimulus. Please remember that this study was conducted more than 40 years ago when different ethical standards were in place for experimental studies using human subjects. Putting that consideration aside for the moment, we note that this study was a powerful demonstration of the effects that consequences have on human behavior.

In another study, Azrin (1960) used contingent rest breaks (a form of negative reinforcement because the person got to take a break from working) to increase work output by 50%, despite reports that the individual had reached his or her physical limit. (*Does this type of procedure ring a bell for anyone trying to increase the amount of work that a student produces in class? If not, it certainly should!*) Ayllon (1960) and Ayllon and Azrin (1965, 1968) used basic reinforcement procedures such as a token economy and desirable activities (e.g., going for a walk, watching a movie, and attending a music session) to modify the psychotic and social behaviors of patients in a mental hospital ward. Baer and Sherman (1964) and Baer, Peterson, and Sherman (1967) demonstrated that the imitative behaviors of young children and children with mental retardation could be altered using social reinforcers. The effects of time-out from positive reinforcement (a procedure that is alive and well today and is considered to be one of the most effective, nonintrusive means for changing a variety of behaviors) were experimentally investigated by Holz, Azrin, and Ayllon (1963) and Azrin (1961). Their findings influenced the development of proper use of time-out and the ancillary procedures that are often used to augment the effects of time-out. Even cigarette smoking, which is considered to be one of the most difficult behaviors to modify, was significantly decreased by using stimulus control (Azrin & Powell, 1968) and punishment (Powell & Azrin, 1968) procedures.

In the studies cited above, the common thread was that each used procedures derived from Skinner's principles of operant conditioning. Collectively, the science of behavior change that grew from these and numerous other studies was known as *behavior modification*. Although function was not specifically addressed in behavior change studies at that time, there was tacit acknowledgment and demonstration that consequences exert tremendous influence on human behavior.

In 1968, Bijou, Peterson, and Ault were among the first applied researchers to conduct what would later become known as descriptive functional analyses to derive interventions. They argued that, instead of merely answering the question "How?," applied psychology should concern itself with answering the question "Why." In a layperson's language, "why" is synonymous with the "function" or the "motivation" behind a behavior. In other words, the science of human behavior could only advance when the individual's interactions with the environment were clearly delineated so that the "purpose" or function of the behavior could be discerned. To that end, Bijou and his colleagues advocated that an A-B-C (i.e., *antecedent–behavior–consequence*) system be used when one is directly observing and recording behavior and they demonstrated the procedure using a case example. From these relatively humble beginnings, the A-B-C procedure has become the basis for FBAs/ analyses. This recording procedure has persisted for almost four decades, a testament to its applied value and its usefulness for helping to understand the "whys" of human behavior.

Throughout the 1970s and early 1980s, applied researchers continued to refine existing techniques and develop new strategies for changing human behavior, all of which were based on operant principles. These techniques were applied to a wide range of human problems across a wide span of settings, particularly educational settings. In 1977, Carr published a seminal article on identifying the "motivation" for self-injurious behavior (SIB). Carr reviewed the extant studies on SIB and concluded that, across studies, one of five hypotheses consistently emerged to explain SIB, with four of the five actually having an empirical basis. These four hypotheses were as follows:

1. SIB is maintained by some type of socially mediated *positive reinforcement*.
2. SIB is maintained by some type of socially mediated *negative reinforcement*.
3. SIB is maintained by the *sensory stimulation* produced by the behavior.
4. SIB is the by-product of an *aberrant physiological process*, that is, due to some biological or genetic disorder.

Although Carr further described a step-by-step methodology for determining the motivation (i.e., function) of SIB, he did not directly utilize the methodology he proposed.

Taking the mantle from Carr, Iwata and colleagues (1982) published the first study using an experimental method for determining function in nine participants with SIB. The methodology they employed was essentially the same methodology that Carr (1977) had laid out previously. Without going into undue detail (mainly because we explore functional analysis in greater depth in Chapter 9), we note that Iwata et al. systematically exposed participants to several experimental conditions designed to test each of the motivational hypotheses for SIB presented by Carr. To test the first (social attention) hypothesis, the experimenter provided a verbal reprimand and brief physical touch contingent upon SIB. To test the second (negative reinforcement) hypothesis, the experimenter terminated the presentation of a difficult academic task contingent upon SIB. To test the third (sensory stimulation) hypothesis, the experimenter placed the participant in a therapy room alone without any toys or other materials. An unstructured play condition was included to act as a control condition. Iwata et al. found idiosyncratic functions across the nine participants. That is, for four of the participants it appeared that the function of SIB was automatic reinforcement (i.e., sensory stimulation). For two of the participants, the function of SIB appeared to be escape from academic task demands. One participant's SIB seemed to be maintained by social attention. Three of the participants had high levels of SIB across all experimental conditions, perhaps suggesting that their SIB was maintained by multiple functions.

From the time of Iwata and associates' seminal publication, literally hundreds of studies utilizing some type of FBA procedure have been published in the professional literature. A great portion of these studies, admittedly, have very little applied value. That is, they were conducted using very lengthy and complex experimental functional analysis procedures, in settings that could best be described as contrived, and with participants with little or no decision-making or ambulatory ability. However, a number of studies have been conducted in applied settings using the natural consequences found in the environment with normal-functioning participants that have extended the ecological validity of FBA.

Since Ervin and Ehrhardt's (2000) review of FBA/analysis studies that have been conducted in educational settings, a number of additional studies have been conducted that address a wide range of topics related to FBA including:

- Models of brief functional analysis (Cihak, Alberto, & Frederick, 2007; Wilder, Chen, Atwell, Pritchard, & Weinstein, 2006).
- Training school personnel (Erbas, Tekin-Iftar, & Yucesoy, 2006; Kamps, Wendland, & Culpepper, 2006).
- Assessing the reliability and validity of various FBA procedures and the degree of convergence between FBA procedures (Berg et al., 2007; Borgmeier & Horner, 2006; Dufrene, 2005; English & Anderson, 2006; Kwak, Ervin, Anderson, & Austin, 2004).
- Comparing the effectiveness of function-derived versus topographically derived interventions (Newcomer & Lewis, 2004).
- The interaction between function of behavior and psychopharmacological medication (Kern, Bailin, & Mauk, 2003; Valdovinos, Ellringer, & Alexander, 2007; Zarcone et al., 2004).
- Assessing the acceptability of FBA procedures and the resulting interventions (Jones & Lugaro, 2000; Lockley, 2001; Weigle & Scotti, 2000).

Instead of boring the reader with an extensive literature review on each of these topics, we will instead note the primary, but general, findings for each of the above bulleted points:

- Brief functional analysis procedures can be highly effective for identifying function and appropriate interventions, particularly when multiple methods are utilized including indirect, direct descriptive, and functional analysis methodologies.
- With proper training, special education teachers can be taught to implement FBA procedures; general education teachers are also able to use FBA procedures with prompting from experienced examiners. Teacher attitudes toward FBA increases as a result of their learning and implementing the procedures.
- FBA procedures and paired-choice assessments can yield very similar results for identifying reinforcers; however, the reliability among different methods is a bit more tenuous as the data are mixed with respect to convergence among different methods of FBA; that is, some studies have found that different methods point to the same function, whereas other studies have found that the identified function for a particular individual may depend upon the method utilized.

• Interventions derived from an FBA are more effective than those based on topography, particularly for difficult cases or cases where the student has been labeled "intervention-resistant"; however, interventions that use very powerful differential reinforcement programs may be equally successful as those that are based on function.

• There is often an interaction not only between the presence or absence of psychotropic medication and function but also between function and varying dosage levels; the important point here is to assess function while considering medication status/dosage level as a unconditioned motivating operation.

• Although there are legitimate criticisms and limitations associated with making decisions about treatments based on *pretreatment acceptability* ratings (Sterling-Turner & Watson, 2002; Valleley, 2004), researchers have found that teachers rated classroom-based interventions that are based on FBA data more acceptable and more likely to be used than interventions that are not based on data derived from a FBA.

In part because of the vast amount of empirical literature that has accumulated on deriving interventions based on function since the early 1980s and partly because of the philosophical movement away from punishment-based interventions that were sometimes present in behavior modification programs, basing interventions on function has become best practice in the field of applied behavior analysis and, through federal legislation, has worked its way into the special education arena via the IDEA and the IDEIA. Many would say that its appearance in education is long overdue. We agree that it is long overdue because it took almost 15 years and a plethora of research before education "caught on" and embraced FBA as a way of designing maximally effective interventions. We also agree that it is possible that, in another 15 years, there will have been sufficient scientific and technological advances in the understanding of human behavior that functional methodology may be replaced by something more effective (we are not sure what it will be but we are willing to acknowledge the possibility). However, until other, more effective means of understanding and changing human behavior become available, it behooves all educators to become familiar with the rationale behind FBA and the associated terminology, procedures, and methodology to help ensure a better educational experience for the children they serve each day.

During the past 20 years, advances within the fields of applied behavior analysis, special education, developmental disabilities, and school psychology have established innovative technologies that are designed to improve our understanding of what problem behavior looks like, where and when it occurs, what might trigger it, and how to use this information to design behavioral support plans and document behavior change (cf. Dufrene, Doggett, Henington, & Watson, 2007; Hoff et al., 2005; LaRue & Handleman, 2006; Steege et al., 2002; Wilder, Harris, Reagan, & Rasey, 2007; Wright-Gallo, Higbee, Reagon, & Davey, 2006). Paralleling these technological advances have been legislative, regulatory, and legal decisions that have emphasized and, in some cases mandated, individualized assessment and intervention services for persons with disabilities. For example, in the late 1980s, the Association for Behavior Analysis and the National Institutes of Health both endorsed the use of FBA procedures to evaluate problem behavior, with the results used to design behavioral interventions with persons who display problem behavior. More recently, the IDEA

Amendments of 1997 and IDEIA required that school districts conduct FBAs and provide positive behavioral support interventions in cases where students are disciplined for problem behaviors. In addition, several states mandate that whenever restrictive interventions are used within school settings on a regular basis, it is required that the educational team examine the school environment to determine factors that may be contributing to the students' behavior problems and develop plans for teaching prosocial behaviors (Jones & Jones, 1998). Finally, several states (e.g., Minnesota, Florida, California, Utah, Washington, New York, and Maine) have developed laws or regulations requiring that FBAs be conducted and used as the basis for designing individualized behavioral programs (Hager, Slocum, & Detrich, 2007; Lewis-Palmer & Barrett, 2007; O'Neill et al., 1997).

Acknowledging that complicated or extended FBAs may not always be necessary, practical, or feasible in a school setting, there has been a focus on developing procedures that can be used in a concise, time-limited format. Collectively, these procedures may be referred to as "brief functional behavioral assessments."

A LOOK AHEAD

As this is a second edition, we have not only updated information from the first edition, we have also made the decision to add more advanced material that necessitated a reorganization of chapters. Chapter 3 is an update of legal issues affecting FBA and positive behavioral supports. Chapter 4 describes the basic principles upon which FBA is based, with Chapter 5 covering the key elements of FBA. Chapters 4 and 5 in this edition were constructed from Chapter 4 in the first edition. We have elaborated on key concepts and ideas and even revised our conceptual model. (*Remember, all models, procedures, and methodologies are a work in progress. When we discover something that is more effective for understanding and changing behavior, we pass it on to you.*) We have also added three completely new chapters: Chapter 9, Brief Functional Analysis of Behavior; Chapter 10, Behavior-Analytic Problem-Solving Model; and Chapter 13, Direct Behavioral Consultation. It is our hope that these additional chapters as well as the new information embedded in the other chapters will further enhance your knowledge, understanding, and ability to use FBA.

A Special Note

Before continuing, we would like to briefly describe the conceptual model to which we adhere that guides all of the activities associated with our FBAs. This is called the S-M-I-R-C model:

> *S:* Stimulus/discriminative stimulus
> *M:*Motivating operations
> *I:* Individual variables (e.g., observed individual differences, prior learning, affect, medical conditions) are those personal characteristics of the individual that contribute to the occurrence of the behavior

R: *R*esponse exhibited by the person

C: *C*onsequence variables are those events that occur contingently after a behavior and serve to strengthen and maintain the behavior.

Within this model, human behavior is considered to be the result of an interaction among variables that are both within an individual (the *I* in this model and sometimes the *M*otivating operations) and surrounding that individual (i.e., discriminative stimuli, motivating operations, and consequences). To gain a complete understanding of a student's behavior, the team needs to carefully consider each of these variables. The following chapters show you how to assess each of these variables in order to understand human behavior and then design positive behavioral supports to change behavior.

Good luck!

3

Legal Aspects of Functional Behavioral Assessment

The temptation to form theories based on insufficient data
is the bane of our profession.
—SHERLOCK HOLMES (by Sir Arthur Conan Doyle)

This chapter is intended to provide a brief overview and our opinion regarding some of the major legal issues and challenges related to FBA and positive behavior support plans (i.e., *Behavior Intervention Plans*, or BIPS). This is by no means an exhaustive treatment or definitive legal treatise on the topic of FBAs and BIPs.[1] There are several other sources that offer a more in-depth treatment of the legal aspects of FBAs. In an attempt to clarify what must be done according to the law, we will, however:

- Examine the pertinent sections of IDEIA that are related to FBAs and BIPs.
- Provide discussion of representative due process and/or administrative hearing decisions.
- Discuss relevant case law.
- Review Office of Special Education Programs (OSEP) policy statements.

Along with our review of the legal parameters of FBAs and BIPs, we will infuse (or confuse?) the discussion with best practice recommendations. In most instances, our recommendations for best practices will be consistent with the legal directives. At other times, the relationship between what we consider best practice and the letter or intent of the law may be a bit murky. In the final analysis, we contend that if practitioners utilize the procedures outlined in this book (which are best practices in the field of FBA) and observe the legal timelines and guidelines, they will be operating on safe ground relative to legal inquiries and questions about the appropriateness of the FBA.

---

[1]Throughout this book, we will use the terms "positive behavioral supports," "behavior intervention plan," and "function-based intervention" interchangeably. Use of one term in a particular context is not meant to convey any specific meaning or intent.

It is extremely important for readers to remember that we are not attorneys, we are not rendering expert opinions on matters of law, and our opinions are not legally binding. Furthermore, special education law is a complex and fast-changing field. It is complex because there are many different laws that govern the provision of services—laws that at times seem to contradict one another. Another reason behind this complexity is that different courts have yielded different rulings on the same issue. Thus, a school district's legal obligation may sometimes depend on the U.S. district court jurisdiction in which it resides. A third reason for the complexity of special education law is related to the hearing process. In some states, procedural matters may be heavily weighted, whereas in other states procedural issues are largely discarded. Hearing officers often have considerable leeway in interpreting state rules, regulations, and guidelines as they apply to individual cases. Hence, the decisions provided by hearing officers may at times seem inconsistent with case law regarding a particular issue.

In noting why FBAs and BIPs were proving to be onerous tasks for school-based practitioners, we noted the following in the first edition:

> From our collective professional experiences and reading of the literature in these areas, it seems that there are three primary sources for the asperity associated with FBAs and behavior intervention plans (BIPs). First, much of the difficulty may lie in the lack of clear direction provided by the IDEA. At times the language is ambiguous and allows for great latitude in interpretation of the law and the requirements for adherence. Second, perhaps some of the difficulty is attributed to the lack of appropriately trained school district personnel. We will discuss the skills that we think are necessary for conducting not only legally defensible FBAs but also "best-practice" FBAs. Each of these requires specific skills and a knowledge base that are not typically present in most educational systems. And, third, it may be that school districts and administrative personnel are unaware of their legal obligations to perform FBAs and design behavior plans that focus on positive instead of aversive consequences and the implications of not doing so.

Certainly, with respect to the lack of guidance and direction, this time from IDEIA, this argument still seems to be true. IDEIA itself, and various courts, have failed to define the procedures or methodologies that constitute a legal FBA.

With respect to the second argument, that schools lack appropriately trained personnel, we would like to think that this situation has markedly changed in the past 5 years. However, we can not find evidence that school districts are engaging in systematic training of personnel to guide the FBA/BIP process. Although the data are a bit outdated, a recent analysis of FBAs and BIPs in Wisconsin reveals many errors in the FBA process. For instance, over 60% of FBAs conducted in a 3-year period did not include a clearly defined target behavior. Other notable findings:

- In only 50% of cases was the teacher behavior included in the FBA.
- The BIP was based on the FBA in only 50% of cases.
- In 73% of cases the BIP contained only a general list of options, not options geared toward the specific student.

- A list of teacher and student supports was included in the BIP in only 30% of cases.
- Sixty-seven percent of the cases failed to include a plan to monitor/evaluate the BIP (Van Acker & Boreson, 2008).

We are certainly not saying that the data from the Wisconsin analysis are representative of data from any other state. Indeed, this analysis was completed in 2001. Since that time, great strides may have occurred there and elsewhere in terms of remedying the problems identified from the analysis. The problem, at least from our scientific perspective, is that there are limited data showing that the situation of training personnel is improving on a wide-scale basis. Two notable examples are the Maryland statewide initiative (Lewis-Palmer & Barrett, 2007) and Utah's alternate assessment model (Hager et al., 2007).

Finally, regarding the third issue—that school districts and administrative personnel are unaware of their legal obligations to perform FBAs and design behavior plans that focus on positive instead of aversive consequences and the implications of not doing so—we believe that school personnel are indeed aware of their legal obligation to conduct FBAs and design BIPs. The question then becomes, in the face of inadequate, less than best practice, or just nonexistent FBAs/BIPs, was the problem a skill deficit (did not know how to conduct a "good" FBA or design a "good" BIP) or a performance deficit (basic know-how is present, but for a variety of reasons the team failed to conduct a thorough FBA). It has been our collective experience that teams often fail because of lack of expertise, lack of time, lack of clear guidance, and various building-internal reasons. None of these reasons, however, mitigates a team's responsibility from implementing FBAs and BIPs.

THE INDIVIDUALS WITH DISABILITIES EDUCATION IMPROVEMENT ACT

Shortly after publication of the first edition of this book, President George W. Bush reauthorized a major revision of IDEA, the Individuals with Disabilities Education Improvement Act (Public Law 108-446), which went into effect on July 1, 2005. This new law preserved many of the relevant principles from IDEA, at least as it relates to FBA and positive behavior supports. One of the most significant parts of IDEIA is:

A child with a disability who is removed from the child's current placement under subparagraph (G) (irrespective of whether the behavior is determined to be a manifestation of the child's disability) or subparagraph (C) shall—

(ii) receive, as appropriate, a functional behavioral assessment, behavioral intervention services and modifications, that are designed to address the behavior violations so that it does not recur.

Note in this section that a manifestation determination is not necessary in order for a child to receive an FBA and resulting behavioral intervention, where appropriate, *if* the behavior resulted in a removal from the child's placement. It is our contention that, under these circumstances in which a behavior would be sufficiently severe or disruptive for a child's placement to be changed, that an FBA is always appropriate as is a behavior support plan. Having said that, we recognize that there are situations where bodily injury has occurred as a result of behavior or the safety of the classroom and/or school has been compromised. In cases such as these, the school must first act to restore safety and protection and then go about the process of systematically addressing the variables that are related to the destructive and/or injurious behavior.

In those cases where a manifestation determination has been conducted, IDEIA states the following:

> (F) DETERMINATION THAT BEHAVIOR WAS A MANIFESTATION.—If the local educational agency, the parent, and relevant members of the IEP Team make the determination that the conduct was a manifestation of the child's disability, the IEP Team shall—
>
>   (i) conduct a functional behavioral assessment, and implement a behavioral intervention plan for such child, provided that the local educational agency had not conducted such assessment prior to such determination before the behavior that resulted in a change in placement described in subparagraph (C) or (G);
>   (ii) in the situation where a behavioral intervention plan has been developed, review the behavioral intervention plan if the child already has such a behavioral intervention plan, and modify it, as necessary, to address the behavior; . . .

Notice that the language in this subparagraph says that an FBA *shall* be conducted; it does not say that "it would be a good idea" or "someone might want to consider" conducting an FBA. In legal vernacular, "shall" is a very strong word in that it compels the performance of a specific action. With regards to FBA, the law compels the school to conduct an FBA under certain circumstances. Although the law mandates FBA, there remain many problems related to carrying out correct and effective FBAs including:

- There are no legally mandated procedures for what constitutes a minimal standard or best practice criteria for an FBA.
- There are no qualifications or training criteria specified for those who are competent to conduct an FBA.
- There is no guidance on determining the "validity" of previously conducted FBAs, particularly with respect to the passage of time.

Under Public Law 108-446, the criteria for determining that a behavior is related to the student's disability (i.e., manifestation determination) are:

- If conduct was caused by, or had a direct and substantial relationship to, the child's disability or
- If conduct was direct result of the local education agency's (LEA's) failure to implement the IEP [615(k)(1)(E)(i)].

In our opinion, this second criterion has direct relevance for positive behavioral supports in that the district (LEA) must show that a behavioral plan, if one was included on the IEP, has indeed been implemented. Without data indicating the ongoing implementation and evaluation of a behavioral plan that was included on the IEP, the district would be unable to show that it was appropriately implementing an IEP. Further, we argue that monitoring a BIP should involve more than a checklist or something similar that a teacher completes each day. Rather, monitoring should involve brief observations to assess integrity (the degree to which staff implements the behavioral support plan in the way it was intended at the appropriate times), data collection and graphing, and/or permanent product measures of the student's behavior.

FUNCTIONAL BEHAVIORAL ASSESSMENTS

When Does the Law Require That We Conduct an FBA?

One of the major changes from IDEA to IDEIA was that Public Law 108-446 removed the requirement for an LEA to conduct an FBA or review and modify an existing BIP for *all* children within 10 days of a disciplinary removal, regardless of whether the behavior was a result of their disability. Now, under 34 CFR §300.530(f), an LEA must conduct an FBA and/or implement a BIP when:

- The LEA, the parent, and the child's IEP team determine that the child's behavior is a manifestation of his or her disability under 34 CFR §300.530(e).
- When a student is removed for more than 10 days for misconduct that *was not* (emphasis added) determined to be a manifestation of the child's disability.
- When an FBA was not conducted before behavior that resulted in a change in placement.
- When a student is placed in an interim alternative educational setting (IAES) for a weapons or drug offense.

Although these are pretty circumscribed circumstances in which an FBA *must* be conducted, there is nothing in the law that *prevents* an IEP team from concluding that an FBA and a BIP are appropriate supports for any child, whether or not they happen to be diagnosed with a disability. Best practices would suggest, particularly for children who are exhibiting repeated patterns of interfering behavior, that an FBA and BIP are indeed appropriate.

Neither IDEIA nor subsequent federal regulations identify specific "problem behaviors" that would result in an FBA. Yell (2006) presented a list of types of behaviors that probably should trigger an FBA based on his review of administrative hearings and court cases:

- Behaviors that preclude the teacher from teaching.
- Behaviors that prevent other students from learning.

- Noncompliance.
- Verbal aggression/abuse.
- Physical aggression/abuse.
- Property destruction.

Again, this list leaves a great deal of latitude to the IEP team to determine which behaviors trigger the FBA process. Historically, the U.S. Congress has given IEP teams a rather free hand to make individualized decisions for students with disabilities, which brings us to the next question.

Must We Conduct an FBA before Suspending a Student Receiving Special Services for Less Than 10 Cumulative Days in a School Year?

This one is easy. The answer is "no," you *musn't*, but you probably *should*. The only thing magical about the number 10 is that the IDEIA gives us this criterion. If you notice that a student is exhibiting behavior that is consistently disruptive and that has either already resulted in some type of disciplinary action or out-of-school suspensions, it is wise to go ahead and conduct the FBA even though the 10-day rule has not yet been met. There is one notable exception to this rule, however, and that is if there is a change in placement. If the school is considering any type of discipline-based change of placement *and/or* the behavior is judged to be related to the child's disability, then an FBA *must be conducted* and a positive BIP implemented prior to the change in placement. If a BIP was already in place, it must be reviewed prior to the change in placement (34 C.F.R. § 300.530 [f][1][ii]). The law is not really clear as to what constitutes a "review" of the behavior plan. It is our position that a review must explore and attempt to resolve the following questions to be legally defensible:

- Is the behavior plan tied to the results from the FBA?
- Is the plan primarily proactive in nature (i.e., skill building or accelerative) and not merely intended to eliminate an undesirable behavior?
- Are there data to show that the plan has actually been implemented as intended (i.e., treatment integrity)?
- Are there data to show the effectiveness or ineffectiveness of the plan (most likely if there is a review of the behavior plan prior to a possible change in placement, the plan has been judged to be ineffective)?
- If the plan was deemed ineffective, is there evidence that the team modified the plan at least once in an attempt to change the behavior in the current environment?
- Are there data to show that the modified plan was not working?

Answering the above questions not only provides substantial legal protection to the school district, it also ensures that the student is getting appropriate educational services.

Is Parental Consent Required for the District to Conduct an FBA?

Five years ago, our answer to this question would probably have been "No." Now, given a recent Office of Special Education (OSEP, 2007) opinion, our answer is " *Yes.*" According to OSEP, FBA is considered an evaluation if it is used to evaluate an individual student to assist in determining if the student has a disability and/or the nature and extent of the needs of that student. Although many of the FBA procedures that we describe in subsequent chapters may occur in the course of a regular school day for many practitioners (e.g., record reviews, review of disciplinary history, brief teacher interview), when information is systematically collected and analyzed for the express purpose of determining behavioral function and the development of a BIP, it should be considered an evaluation and parental permission obtained. The only exception here is that if the FBA simply consisted of reviewing existing data (which we know you would not do because that would be a very poor FBA), parental permission is not required. Further, if an FBA was conducted for the express purpose of designing or modifying a BIP for a particular student, parents who disagree with either the methodology or the results of the FBA have the right to obtain an IEE (*Independent Educational Evaluation*) at public expense! (This is but another excellent reason to use the procedures we outline, saving your district $$$$).

Do I Conduct FBAs Only for Children with Disabilities, or Do I Have to Use FBAs with Children in Regular Education?

The law is fairly clear about when an FBA must be conducted for children who are diagnosed with disabilities. For children without disabilities, the answer is a bit ambiguous and open to some degree of interpretation. However, our opinion on this issue is very unambiguous: *Whether a student is diagnosed with a disorder or not is of little consequence. If a student is exhibiting behaviors that are interfering with the educational process, then an FBA should be conducted and a BIP designed.* Consider two identical children who are exhibiting the same exact behaviors in the classroom resulting in the same amount of disruption. The only difference between the two is that one is diagnosed with a disorder and the other is not. How can any responsible and morally obligated educator provide effective services to one child but not the other? We vehemently contend that *both* children should receive an FBA and a BIP!

In addition, there is case law that has addressed issues related to this question and given some very solid guidance. In *Hacienda La Puente Unified School District v Honig* (1992), the Ninth Circuit Court ruled that the protections offered by the IDEA (in this case, the "stay-put" rule) extended also to those children who had not been previously identified by their LEA as having a disability. Although other courts supported this decision, *Rodiriecus L. v Waukegan School District No. 60* (1996) provided some limitations to the protections offered by the *Honig* case. The court ruled that in order for the stay-put rule to apply to students without identified disabilities, the LEA must have a reasonable suspicion that the student had a disability or that a school official must have known that the student had a disability. Public Law 108-446 delineates the standards that constitute a district's knowledge:

- The parent of the child expressed concern in writing to supervisory or administrative personnel of the appropriate educational agency, or a teacher of the child, that the child is in need of special education and related services;
- The parent of the child has requested an evaluation of the child pursuant to Section 614(a)(1)(B); or
- The teacher of the child, or other personnel of the LEA, has expressed specific concerns about a pattern of behavior demonstrated by the child, directly to the director of special education of such agency or to other supervisory personnel of the agency. (20 U.S.C. § 1415[k][5][B][iii])

If any of these conditions exist, then a student without a disability who evidences a pattern of interfering behavior should be considered, for all practical and legal purposes, as a child with a disability with all the associated procedural safeguards. Thus, the legal compulsion to perform an FBA for such students is clearly indicated. It is important to note that, with respect to the third criterion, the expression of concern about a pattern of behavior *does not* have to be in writing. Under 34 CFR §300.534(b)(3), there is no requirement that specific concerns about a child's behavior must be expressed in writing. However, LEAs may develop guidelines and procedures (and in our opinion, should) regarding how personnel are to express their concerns about a child's need for special education and related services.

It is our opinion that a number of instances that occur in schools satisfy the intent of this criterion. For instance, a student who is repeatedly disciplined by being sent to the office, being sent home, or whose parents are called by the teacher because of interfering behavior is known by the teacher and probably other supervisory personnel (e.g., a building principal) for having a repetitive pattern of interfering behavior. Let's take a look at an example to illustrate this point:

Divinia is a fifth-grade student who engages in a variety of behaviors that her teacher, Ms. Presley, has generically labeled as "odd." For instance, Divinia often speaks in very hushed tones punctuated by loud giggles, meows in class, yells obscenities at the teacher, scratches herself to the point of drawing blood, and calls other students names. All of these behaviors occur during class and often interfere with academic instruction or related activities. Ms. Presley has sent Divinia to the principal's office on a number of occasions for these and other behaviors because she was unable to teach with these behaviors occurring. In response, the principal, Mr. Martin, has suspended Divinia both in and out of school on several occasions. She is coming dangerously close to being suspended for more than 10 days because of these behaviors. Ms. Presley was overheard one day in the teacher's lounge telling the speech pathologist, a member of the building's teacher support team, that surely Divinia had some type of "emotional problem" that was causing these behaviors to occur. The speech pathologist correctly informed Ms. Presley that because she suspected that Divinia was suffering from an emotional problem, she should make a referral to the building's teacher support team for an FBA and positive behavioral intervention before any further disciplinary action was taken against Divinia.

It is also important to note that the interfering behavior does not have to be topographically identical across incidents for a pattern to exist. That is, although the student may exhibit a number of *different* behaviors, they all interfere with learning. In these cases, both best practice and the IDEIA would dictate that an FBA with a related BIP would be the most appropriate course of action.

Both case law and the IDEIA seem to protect students without disabilities if their behavior or performance (we take "performance" to mean either academic or behavioral performance) would reasonably indicate that a disability is present. For children whose behavior is of sufficient concern that teachers conference with parents, make repeated referrals to the principal's office or school counselor, or engage in other disciplinary procedures, an FBA should be conducted to protect the school district from legal action should the parents question what may seem to be excessive disciplinary action taken against their child. It never hurts anyone to conduct an FBA and implement positive behavioral supports. All it takes is time and effort, although both are sometimes in short supply for certain students.

We would be remiss if we did not mention that LEAs may document that they had no knowledge of a disability if they have met any of the following criteria:

- If the parent of the child has not allowed an evaluation pursuant to Section 614.
- If the parent has refused services under Part B.
- If the child has been evaluated and it was determined that the child was not a child with a disability under Part B (615[k][5][C]).

In cases where any of the above criteria are met, the LEAs may proceed with their normal disciplinary procedures.

Does the Law Specify the Length of Time for Which an FBA Is Considered "Current" or "Valid"?

This is a very interesting question as it probably stems from the diagnostic model of service delivery where the results of a "psychoeducational evaluation" were considered valid for 3 years. We have already addressed the limitations associated with using the diagnostic model for providing services in schools in Chapter 1 and will not readdress this issue here to avoid redundancy. Not surprisingly, the law nor subsequent regulations specify the amount of time for which an FBA is considered valid. Rather, "such decisions are best left to the LEA, the parent, and relevant members of the IEP team (as determined by the LEA and the parent). . ." (IDEIA 615[k][1][E]).

As an astute reader, you probably have already guessed our response to this question: *The validity of the FBA is not a function of the amount of time that has passed; rather it depends upon whether the results of the FBA have been used to make socially meaningful changes for the student.* As we have repeatedly stated, human behavior is a dynamic, not a static, interaction among many variables. Thus, the function of a behavior could change over the course of a month, a week, a day, or whatever. When the results of the FBA fail to result in intervention strategies that produce reductions in the interfering behavior and increases in appropriate replacement behaviors, it is no longer valid.

Must We Conduct an FBA Prior to Holding a Manifestation Determination Review?

Okay, this one is a bit tricky. Technically, we suppose, the answer is "No" because the law nor resulting federal regulations say that you must. In a roundabout way, however, the law says that you should! How can this be? Although it is highly unusual for federal laws to contain contradictory statements, this one certainly might. To conduct a manifestation determination, IDEIA states that the IEP team must determine if the behavior was " . . . caused by, or had a direct and substantial relationship to, the child's disability; or . . . the direct result of the local educational agency's failure to implement the IEP." So . . . how is this contradictory?

Follow our logic and see where it leads: To conduct a proper manifestation review, the IEP team must determine if the IEP has been implemented. In most cases involving discipline and student conduct, it is highly likely that there would be a behavioral component on the IEP. If there is a behavioral component on the IEP, it should have been developed from an FBA. Therefore, although there is no direct legal requirement to conduct an FBA *prior* to a manifestation review, you probably should. If there was not a behavior component on the IEP but there should have been, you will need to conduct an FBA anyway! In either case, an FBA is the most logical course of action.

We Often Remove Students to an Interim Alternative Educational Setting (IAES) and Then Conduct an FBA. Is This Legal?

Probably not. If the behavior that resulted in the removal to an IAES involved weapons or drugs, then the LEA has the authority to do so for purposes of safety for a period of up to 45 days without an *order* from an independent hearing officer. In such cases, the FBA process would involve indirect assessment procedures. In our collective experiences, however, most of the school districts that place students into an IAES prior to conducting an FBA are doing so without justifiable concerns for safety. In cases where safety is not an issue and the student has already been placed into an IAES without benefit of an FBA or a BIP, then the district would be considered to have made a change in placement without first adhering to the requirements of accommodating the student's interfering behaviors in the least restrictive setting. Furthermore, as we indicated earlier, failing to address a student's interfering behaviors before making a change in placement denies the student an appropriate education.

If a Student Has Already Been Suspended, Can We Conduct a "Post Hoc FBA"?

The obvious answer is "Well, sort of." You can conduct an FBA, but it would certainly not be a best practices approach. There may be circumstances in which the student has been suspended, and previously collected data (e.g., student attendance records, detentions served, discipline referrals, recordings of specific interfering behaviors) may be useful. In addition, interviews with key informants (e.g., teachers, guidance staff, administrators, family members) could also yield valuable information. Because the student is not present within the natural educational setting, however, direct observations and recordings of behaviors and related contextual variables cannot be conducted. Thus, the assessment is limited to recording reviews and interviews. In these types of situations, in which the practitioner is limited only to indirect FBA procedures, we recommend labeling the report as a "preliminary functional behavioral assessment."

We Have a Student with a Disability Who Is Having Difficulty on the Bus. Must We Conduct a Bus FBA?

The short answer is, "Yes." IDEIA does not relieve a district of the responsibility for conducting an FBA merely because a student is riding school-sponsored transportation. If disciplinary decisions are being made with regard to a student with a disability that involves his or her transportation, then an FBA must be conducted in the setting where the interfering behavior is occurring: on the bus! This may be more difficult than it sounds even with the use of indirect assessment procedures like the ones we have described in this book and video technology, which would allow for a modified (i.e., removed in time) direct descriptive assessment. Two recent cases that we were involved with highlight many of the issues that are covered not only in this chapter but throughout the book:

Jack was an 18-year-old male with multiple disabilities including cerebral palsy, severe mental retardation, and blindness. He was attending a self-contained class for students with multiple disabilities in a small rural school. Jack engaged in mild SIB during the day but especially on the bus. In an attempt to modify his bus-related SIB, the school district modified the seat in several ways, made certain his protective helmet was in place prior to getting on the bus, and had him strapped upright to the seat with a harness that buckled in the back. Jack's mother requested that the district not use the harness because that was not teaching him to sit in the seat without banging his head on the glass window (in our opinion Jack's mother was absolutely right in this case). In other words, she was asking for a more proactive approach. Because of the size of this school district, it contracted with consultants to provide their FBA services. The problem was that district policy did not allow nonemployees to ride the bus! Therefore, how was the district going to conduct the FBA? Could it use videotapes to record Jack's behavior? Possibly, but videotapes might not capture all of the stimuli that could be functionally related to Jack's SIB (e.g., rough roads, comments from others, bumps in the road). In this particular case, the solution involved getting special permission from the school board to allow the consultants on the bus to complete the FBA that was required by law. Allowing the consultants to ride the bus and directly observe Jack's behavior also served to prevent the mother from filing a threatened suit against the district for not adhering to the IDEA and failing to provide her son with the appropriate accommodations.

The next case was a bit different in that it did not involve a student with an identified disability but rather a student for whom school personnel *suspected* that she had a disability.

LaTarsi was a 5-year-old female kindergarten student who had been warned by the principal several times not to "stand up" on the bus while it was in motion. Concurrently, her teachers noted on an internal written progress form that she was "slow in her schoolwork and would probably need to be tested for special education at some point" and that "she had difficulty remembering classroom rules." After being written up once more by the bus driver for standing up while the bus was moving, LaTarsi was removed from her class by the principal, who swatted her buttocks seven to nine times with a wooden paddle to "try and help her remember to remain seated on the bus." Whether or not you personally or philosophically agree with corporal punishment, there are two issues involved here: (1) LaTarsi was suspected of having a disability as evidenced by the written note of the teacher, and thus IDEA protections extend to her as if she indeed had been diagnosed with a disability; (2) the principal engaged in a very negative behavior reduction technique without first conducting an FBA and trying a more positive, proactive approach. In a school board hearing regarding the matter, the principal was demoted and transferred and the school was ordered to perform an FBA and implement a positive behavior support plan.

Both of these cases, although a bit extreme, highlight the necessity of performing FBAs for "on-bus" behavior. Positive proactive behavioral intervention strategies do not need to cease at the schoolhouse door; they can be extended to any part of the student's educational experience.

Does FBA Apply to Extended Day Programs and Summer School?

Yes and yes, the requirements to conduct an FBA extend to after-school programs as well as summer school programs. Part of the reason this is so is because a school day is defined as "any day, including a partial day, that children are in attendance at school for instructional purposes" (34 C.F.R. §§ 300.9, 300.519–300.529). Furthermore, neither IDEA nor any supporting regulations define a "school year." Thus, the school year does not merely encompass the traditional 9-month school calendar. A recent U.S. district court decision (in the Eastern District of New York) affirmed that "summer school education for struggling students is intrinsically related to the ability to receive a free appropriate public education" (*LIH v New York City Board of Education*, 2000). Therefore, students with disabilities or those who are suspected of having a disability are afforded the same protections under IDEA during these two activities as they are during the regular school day and school year.

If There Is No One in Our School District Qualified to Conduct and Interpret FBAs, What Do We Do Then?

First, let us state unequivocally that neither IDEA nor IDEIA relieves a district from the responsibility of conducting an FBA simply because of lack of personnel with the appropriate training or expertise. Because it is the LEA's "burden" to conduct an FBA in certain circumstances, there are actually several options of which the LEA can avail itself. The first is to train school-based teams of personnel to conduct FBAs, although this option has some limitations that we have already discussed. The second option is to contract with someone on a case-by-case basis who does have expertise in conducting FBAs. And a third option is to hire someone whose sole responsibility is to conduct FBAs. There are a number of advantages and disadvantages associated with each of these options, which means that each district must decide on which is most workable for its specific circumstances. Some very small school districts, for example, may find it more economically feasible and realistic to hire a qualified person on a case-by-case basis. A larger district, on the other hand, may receive such a large number of referrals that training school-based teams or hiring a full-time behavior specialist, or several, can best meet its needs. We believe that all of these are viable options and are consistent with the IDEIA. In an ideal situation, each school would have a behavior specialist on staff that has graduate education and training on functional assessment and applied behavioral interventions.

BEHAVIOR INTERVENTION PLANS

What Is a BIP?

Behavioral intervention is defined as an "intervention based upon the methods and empirical findings of behavioral science and designed to influence a child's actions or behaviors positively" (23 Ill.Adm.Code 226.75). Thus, a behavior intervention plan (BIP) is not one that the IEP team selects because of familiarity, relative response effort, the fact that it was found in an intervention manual, and so on. An appropriate BIP is one that has a basis in empirical science and has been shown to positively impact the interfering behavior.

Does the Law Specify the Substantive Components of a BIP?

This one is relatively easy to answer: "*No!*" Neither Congress nor the Department of Education (DOE) has specified what should be included in a BIP. In addition, recent court cases have ruled on *procedural* aspects of BIPs, but not on anything to do with their substantive content. For instance, the Seventh U.S. Circuit Court of Appeals rejected a parent's claim that her child's BIP was substantively insufficient because there do not exist any substantive criteria for purposes of comparison (*Alex R. by Beth R. v. Forrestville Valley Community Unit School District #221*, 2004).

How Do We Demonstrate the "Sufficiency" of a BIP?

In what might be considered a court's closest decision related to some of the more substantive aspects of a BIP, in *Mason City Community School District* (2001), the review panel put forth a four-part test for determining the sufficiency of a BIP:

1. The BIP must be based upon assessment data (we conclude that this means data from an FBA although it is not specified).
2. The BIP must be individualized to meet the child's unique needs.

3. The BIP must include positive behavioral change strategies (we interpret this to mean that positive, accelerative-based procedures must appear whether or not "disciplinary" or negative consequences are included).
4. The BIP must be consistently implemented and monitored (again, there must be a system in place to track the "integrity" of the BIP).

Although this case was conducted at the time of IDEA and not IDEIA, the basic components of a sufficient BIP would appear to be roughly the same, at least according to the specifications as outlined in this case.

Is It Really Important That the Positive Behavior Intervention Be Implemented as Indicated on the IEP? (This Roughly Translates to: Is It Enough for Us to Just Have This Plan on the IEP with No Evidence of Implementation?)

We just love the easy questions, and this is another one of those. No! It is not enough merely to have documented that a positive BIP was designed. If school-based teams do not implement positive behavioral supports and do not have evidence indicating that they have done so, they are guilty of failing to provide a "free and appropriate public education" (FAPE). FAPE is one of the cornerstones of the original IDEA (Public Law 94-142) and stresses that education must be individualized to meet the unique needs and challenges of the student with a disability. Failure to implement this individualized plan denies the student of an "appropriate" education. Therefore, school districts should develop some mechanism to demonstrate that they are indeed addressing interfering behaviors identified on the IEP. This mechanism should involve, at the very least, all of the following:

- Some type of intervention checklist (i.e., procedural integrity or treatment integrity).
- A means to graphically illustrate student performance.
- A criterion against which the student's behavior is evaluated.
- Evidence that the plan has been modified based on the student's performance.

Is There a Potential Relationship between FBA/BIP and FAPE?

According to *Grayslake* (2002), the answer is *Yes*. In this case, it was ruled that a child diagnosed with autism spectrum disorder was denied a FAPE because the district conducted an insufficient and untimely FBA/BIP and the staff lacked sufficient expertise to conduct an appropriate FBA. Even in the face of this lack of expertise, the district did not contract for the outside services of someone with more experience and skill in conducting an FBA for children with autism. Because of these factors, the child was denied a FAPE.

What about Changes in Placement? Is an FBA/BIP Needed Before a Change in Placement Occurs?

Results of three other cases indicated the importance of FBA and BIP when considering placement decisions. The first of these, *Oak Park and River Forest H.S. District #200* (2001), noted that a valid FBA/BIP was needed *prior* (emphasis added) to moving a child to a more restrictive placement. Relatedly, *Sandwich Community Unit School District No. 430* (2001) asserted that, before a child who was truant could be moved to a more restrictive placement, a BIP was needed to address the truant behavior. Finally, in *District No. 211 v. Michael R.* (2005), it was held that when a district wishes to move a student to a more restrictive setting, BIPs that have been revised and monitored are important elements that support the district's decision.

SUMMARY

As previously stated, we are not attorneys and are not rendering expert opinions on matters of law. Practitioners who have legal questions or predicaments need to seek the services of a legal professional. Quite obviously, the above questions do not represent *all* of the issues that arise when FBAs and BIPs are addressed. They are instead a sampling of cases across a wide range of domains to give you a "feel" for the legal landscape. Perhaps the best advice we can give regarding FBAs and BIPS is this: *If you think an FBA might be needed (for best practice purposes or for legal purposes) go ahead and do it without spending undue time trying to determine exactly how much (or how little) you and your school district must do to stay out of legal hot water.* Conducting an FBA and implementing a positive intervention certainly carries no harm and provides students with state-of-the-art educational services. In the end, who knows, you might just make a significant difference in the lives of the kids with whom you interact.

4

Everything You Always Wanted to Know about the Conceptual Foundations of Functional Behavioral Assessments . . . but Were Afraid to Ask

Or, Basic Principles of Functional Behavioral Assessment

The external variables of which behavior is a function provide for what may be called a causal or functional analysis. We undertake to predict and control the behavior of the individual organism. This is our "dependent variable"—the effect for which we are to find the cause. Our "independent variable"—the causes of behavior—are the external conditions of which behavior is a function. Relationships between the two—the "cause–effect relationships" in behavior—are the laws of a science. A synthesis of these laws expressed in quantitative terms yields a comprehensive picture of the organism as a behaving system.
—B. F. SKINNER (1953, p. 35)

ANTECEDENTS AND CONSEQUENCES

At its most basic level, FBA is a rather simple concept. The purposes of all activities within the FBA domain are to determine under what conditions a behavior is most likely to occur (*antecedents*) and what happens in the environment as a result of that behavior and maintains that behavior (*consequences*). When an evaluator is conducting an FBA, it is critical that he or she differentiate among antecedents and consequences that are *associated* with interfering behavior and those variables that are *functionally related* to interfering behavior (see the accompanying box). Essentially, a functional relationship is a *cause–effect* relationship. Put another way, events can be viewed as being either *molar* or *molecular* in nature.

43

A "molar event" refers to associated relationships, while "molecular events" refer to those that are functionally related to interfering behavior. Casual, anecdotal observations tend to yield information regarding molar variables. Perhaps the best example of a molar event is the widely held notion that odd behavior occurs more frequently during a full moon. That is, although there may be an association between some behaviors and the lunar cycle, the moon is not *causing* odd behavior. A more systematic analysis of behavior typically uncovers the molecular variables that trigger and/or reinforce behavior. Consider the case of a student who frequently engages in disruptive behavior when the teacher provides verbal instruction. At a molar level, we might say that verbal instructions serve as an antecedent to disruptive behavior. Further assessment showed that it was the length of verbal instructions that triggered disruptive behavior and not verbal instructions per se. This is an important distinction because of the direct implications for intervention. If the school staff merely altered the content of the verbal instruction without altering its length, there would likely be a minimal effect on the disruptive behavior. As it turned out, the staff reduced verbal instructions to one- to three-word cues, which eliminated disruptive behavior and prompted the student to participate in instructional programming. Identifying these molecular influences on behavior requires considerable knowledge, time, expertise, a degree of experience with FBA, and skill in observing behavior.

An *antecedent* is any event or stimulus that occurs before a behavior occurs. For any behavior there may be one or numerous antecedents. The dual purpose of an FBA is first to identify these antecedents and then to determine which are directly related to *triggering* the target behavior.

A *consequence* is any event or stimulus that occurs after a behavior. Again, there may be many things that happen after a behavior. The purposes of an FBA are to identify what actually happens after the target behavior and then determine which one or combination of these events are maintaining (i.e., reinforcing) that behavior.

Before discussing methodology or FBA procedures, we think it is essential that the same basic terminology be understood and used by everyone who is conducting and talking about FBAs. You will have noticed by now that we use italics to highlight words that we think are especially important. Words or concepts of even greater import get their own box with a more in-depth description. Therefore, the first section of this chapter describes some of these vital principles of FBA. As the book progresses, however, we hope to introduce more complex topics and procedures associated with FBAs.

Consider the case of a student who was referred for disruptive behavior during math class. During the initial anecdotal observation, the student was observed to display verbal opposition (e.g., verbally refusing to complete assignments) and property destruction (e.g., tearing up worksheets and books) when he was directed by the classroom teacher to complete math worksheets. Following the occurrence of these interfering behaviors, the teacher provided a verbal reprimand and then asked the student to leave the classroom. Subsequent interviews with the teacher and the student and additional observations during math class revealed that interfering behaviors were not predictable. For example, when presented with math worksheets and verbal directions, the student did not always exhibit verbal opposition and property destruction. In fact, the range of *student responses* following the initial directives from the teacher to complete math worksheets were inconsistent. Sometimes the student:

- Completed the math worksheets with no verbal opposition or property destruction.
- Completed portions of the worksheets, and then displayed verbal opposition.
- Completed portions of the worksheets, and then displayed verbal opposition *and* property destruction.
- Displayed verbal opposition, but following verbal reprimands and verbal redirection prompts from the teacher, complied and completed the worksheets.
- Displayed verbal opposition, but following verbal reprimands and verbal redirection prompts from the teacher, engaged in additional verbal opposition and then property destruction.
- Exhibited property destruction and no occurrences of verbal opposition.

In addition, further analysis revealed that the worksheets varied in terms of:

- Length (i.e., number of problems to solve).
- Complexity (i.e., computation vs. story problems).
- Skill level (i.e., mastery, instructional, frustration).

To complicate matters, the classroom teacher provided varying degrees of feedback to the student. Sometimes the teacher:

- Provided verbal praise when the student initiated the worksheets.
- Did not provide any feedback, regardless of the student's behavior.
- Delivered a verbal reprimand and asked the student to leave the classroom when the student exhibited interfering behaviors.
- Delivered a verbal reprimand, but did not ask the student to leave the room.
- Provided verbal praise when the student initiated the worksheets, but when subsequent interfering behavior occurred, she delivered a varying combination of verbal reprimands, verbal redirection, and directions for the student to leave the classroom.

Interviews with the student revealed a number of variables that influenced his behaviors. On some days:

- He arrived at school with a headache, had difficulty concentrating, and "would rather just be left alone."
- The math worksheets followed the completion of other difficult assignments and "that was the straw that broke the camel's back."
- He arrived at school in a "good mood and didn't mind doing the work."

- He arrived at school after having an argument with his parents and was "pissed off at the world."
- He smoked marijuana before coming to school, had the "munchies," was very sleepy, and "just felt like chilling."

Identification and analysis of the variables that contribute to the occurrence of interfering behaviors requires the consideration of an array of interacting variables. Remember the case of Mackenzie . . . the sting of the wasp (the stimulus) caused her to flinch and run away (the response). With Mackenzie, the stimulus predictably produced the response (a cause–effect relationship) and we say that the stimulus *elicited* the response. However, for the vast majority of the behaviors addressed in an FBA, this simple cause–effect relationship does *not* exist and interfering behaviors do not predictably occur when a specific stimulus is presented. Moreover, reinforcing consequences are not always delivered consistently. When conducting an FBA, it is critical that we examine and understand the relative contributions of a host of variables that influence occurrences of interfering behavior. In the following sections, we begin to discuss models for assessing and analyzing the amalgam that constitutes human behavior.

ANTECEDENTS OF BEHAVIOR

Antecedents are stimuli that occur prior to a behavior and that influence its occurrence. There are two types of learned antecedents that increase the probability of interfering behavior (1) discriminative stimuli and (2) motivating operations.

Discriminative Stimuli

Behaviors occur in the presence of specific stimuli. Eventually, the stimuli regularly associated with a behavior (we call this repeated association a "learning history") serve as cues and increase the probability that the behavior will be performed (Kazdin, 2001). These stimuli that precede the occurrence of behavior and signal that reinforcement following the behavior is likely to occur are called *discriminative stimuli* (SDs). Unlike respondent conditioning, in which a stimulus elicits a response in operant conditioning the SD *sets the occasion* for a subsequent response, or increases the probability of a behavior. As one typical example, Sam is a sophomore in high school who has difficulty completing assignments at home (e.g., reading assigned chapters, writing papers, doing math computation assignments). Sam typically completes homework in her bedroom. Sam's bedroom does not include a desk or chair, but does have a TV. Several times a week, Sam goes to her bedroom with the best intentions of studying. In fact, she carries in her school books, paper, pens and pencils, and study guides (all of these items *may be* SDs for studying). However, after a few minutes she turns on the TV, "channel surfs," and spends much more time watching TV than studying. With Sam, the TV is an SD for watching television. Removing the TV from her bedroom and adding a desk (an SD for studying) resulted in decreased TV watching and increased studying behaviors.

A behavior that occurs more frequently in the presence of one stimulus condition than it does in others is called a *discriminated operant*. A behavior is said to be under *stimulus control* when responses emitted in the presence of the stimulus produce reinforcement more often than responses that occur in the absence of the stimulus. Or, stated in a slightly different way, a behavior that occurs at a higher rate in the presence of a given stimulus than it does in its absence is said to be under stimulus control (Cooper et al., 2007). For example, we answer a phone when it rings, but not when it is silent; when driving, we stop the car more often at an intersection in the presence of a red traffic light or a stop sign than in their absence (Cooper et al., 2007). When a behavior is under stimulus control, it is highly probable (but not automatic) that given a particular stimulus, a specific response will occur.

Motivating Antecedents of Behavior

Antecedents other than SDs can influence the occurrence of behavior (Iwata, Smith, & Michael, 2000). Laraway, Snycerski, Michael, and Poling (2003) used the term *motivating operation* (MO) as the overarching term to describe those antecedent variables that influence behavior change by *momentarily* altering the effectiveness of reinforcing consequences. Essentially, MOs influence behavior change in numerous ways. A stimulus, object, or event may have:

Value-Altering Effects

- Increases the reinforcing effectiveness (or value) of a stimulus, object, or event (i.e., an establishing operation).
- Decreases the reinforcing effectiveness (or value) of a consequence (i.e., abolishing operation).

Behavior-Altering Effects

- Increases the frequency of behavior that has been reinforced by a stimulus, object, or event (i.e., an evocative effect).
- Decreases the frequency of behavior that has been reinforced by a stimulus, object, or event (i.e., an abative effect).

MOs are both unlearned (i.e., *unconditioned*) and learned (i.e., *conditioned*). Table 4.1 lists examples of several unconditioned MOs and both their *reinforcer-establishing* effect and their corresponding *evocative* effect. Table 4.2 lists examples of several unconditioned MOs and both their *reinforcer-abolishing* effect and their corresponding *abative* effect.

Table 4.3 provides examples of conditioned MOs, the reinforcer-establishing effect, and the evocative effect that the MO has on the occurrence of interfering behaviors. Table 4.4 provides examples of conditioned MOs, the reinforcer-abolishing effect, and the abative effect on interfering behaviors.

MOs are *momentary* and a single MO may affect *multiple behaviors and consequences simultaneously* (Mace, Gritter, Johnson, Malley, & Steege, 2006). For example, Mace et al.

TABLE 4.1. Unconditioned Motivating Operations: Reinforcer-Establishing Effects

Unconditioned motivating operation	Reinforcer-establishing effect	Evocative effect on interfering behaviors
Food deprivation	*Increases* the effectiveness of food as a positive reinforcer.	Increases the frequency of *behaviors* that have previously been reinforced with food (e.g., taking foods from others that are not on the student's approved diet).
Fluid deprivation	*Increases* the effectiveness of fluids as a positive reinforcer.	Increases the frequency of *behaviors* that have previously been reinforced with fluids (e.g., tantrum to obtain a drink).
Activity deprivation	*Increases* the effectiveness of an activity as a positive or negative reinforcer.	Increases the frequency of *behaviors* that have previously been reinforced by participation in the activity (e.g., self-injury reinforced by sensory input).
Increase in physically irritating/ painful stimulus	*Increases* the effectiveness of a reduction in pain as a negative reinforcer.	Increases the frequency of *behaviors* that have previously been reinforced with reduction of irritation/pain (e.g., scratching an itch until it bleeds).
Sleep deprivation	*Increases* the effectiveness of sleep as a positive reinforcer.	Increases the frequency of *behaviors* that have previously been reinforced with being able to sleep (e.g., laying down in class and taking a nap).

Note. Based on Cooper, Heron, and Heward (2007).

(2006) offer an illustration in which an individual who really enjoys cooking accidentally touches a hot pan. In this example, upon touching the hot pan, the effectiveness of cooking as a positive reinforcer is *temporarily abolished,* while at the same time the effectiveness of dropping the hot pan and obtaining ice as a negative reinforcer is temporarily *established.* Behaviors related to these consequences either decrease (the chef stops cooking) or increase (she drops the pan and opens the freezer and grabs some ice) accordingly.

HOW MOTIVATING OPERATIONS INFLUENCE DISCRIMINATIVE STIMULI

Not only do MOs increase the value of the reinforcing consequence, they also increase the effectiveness of SDs in occasioning behavior. For example, consider the case of a student who exhibits swearing behavior that has been reinforced by social attention from parents, teachers, siblings and classmates. This behavior usually produces a response from others (e.g., verbal reprimands, facial grimaces, moans, groans, laughter). The IEP team decided to put this behavior on extinction (i.e., provide no reaction when the behavior occurs). This deprivation of attention temporarily increases the value of attention as a reinforcer (an

TABLE 4.2. Unconditioned Motivating Operations: Reinforcer-Abolishing Effects

Unconditioned motivating operation	Reinforcer-abolishing effect	Abative effect on interfering behaviors
Food ingestion	*Decreases* the effectiveness of food as a positive reinforcer.	Decreases the frequency of *behaviors* that have previously been reinforced with food (e.g., verbal threats of aggression to obtain a snack from a classmate).
Fluid ingestion	*Decreases* the effectiveness of fluids as a positive reinforcer.	Decreases the frequency of *behaviors* that have previously been reinforced with fluids (e.g., student bolting from desk to obtain teacher's coffee).
Participation in activity	*Decreases* the effectiveness of an activity as a positive or negative reinforcer.	Decreases the frequency of *behaviors* that have previously been reinforced through participation in the activity(e.g., physical stereotypy reinforced by arousal reduction).
Decrease in physically irritating/ painful stimulus	*Decreases* the effectiveness of escape/ avoidance as a negative reinforcer.	Decreases the frequency of *behaviors* that have previously been reinforced with reduction of irritation/pain (e.g., aggression that is followed by removal from a loud and aversive classroom).
Sufficient sleep	*Decreases* the effectiveness of sleep as a positive reinforcer.	Decreases the frequency of *behaviors* that have previously been reinforced with being able to sleep (e.g., disruptive behavior that has been followed by opportunities to lay on the floor, cover up with a blanket, and sleep).

Note. Based on Cooper, Heron, and Heward (2007).

establishing effect). Not only does that increase the probability of "attention-seeking" interfering behaviors (an evocative effect), this deprivation also increased the likelihood that the student would engage in interfering behaviors in the presence of parents, teachers, siblings and classmates. Thus, within the classroom setting, when the classroom teacher ignores swearing behavior, the value of reactions from classmates has temporarily increased *and* the effectiveness of classmates as discriminative stimuli to occasion swearing behavior has increased.

Likewise, consider the case of Bud, an adolescent with autism who resides in a group home. Bud has gained a considerable amount of weight over the past 18 months. Due to health concerns, the IEP team decided to put him on a restrictive diet designed to help Bud to lose one-half pound per week. In addition to reducing his portions and switching him to a low-fat diet, the team changed Bud's reinforcement program from edible reinforcers such as chocolate chips, raisins, and chocolate-covered peanuts to a reinforcer menu that included carrots, celery, and radishes. The team reported that Bud, after being on the diet for 2 months, had not lost any weight. In fact, he had gained 3 pounds. Moreover, Bud had

TABLE 4.3. Examples of Conditioned Motivating Operations: Reinforcer-Establishing Effects

Conditioned motivating operation	Reinforcer-establishing effect	Evocative effect on interfering behaviors
Deprivation of social attention	*Increases* the effectiveness of social attention as a positive reinforcer.	Increases the frequency of *behaviors* that have previously been reinforced with social attention (e.g., inappropriate social comments in class that are followed by peer attention).
Difficult tasks	*Increases* the effectiveness of escape/avoidance as a negative reinforcer.	Increases the frequency of *behaviors* that have previously been reinforced with avoiding or terminating difficult tasks (e.g., verbal opposition and swearing that results in the cessation of tasks).
Aversive (nonpreferred) social interactions	*Increases* the effectiveness of escape/avoidance as a negative reinforcer.	Increases the frequency of *behaviors* that have previously been reinforced with avoiding or terminating nonreinforcing social interactions (e.g., looking away to avoid eye contact; not returning a phone call).
Deprivation of a reinforcing tangible (e.g., token, money)	*Increases* the effectiveness of a tangible as a reinforcer.	Increases the frequency of *behaviors* that have previously been reinforced with access to a tangible (e.g., stealing money).
Deprivation of a reinforcing activity	*Increases* the effectiveness of participation in the activity as a reinforcer.	Increases the frequency of *behaviors* that have previously been reinforced with participation in the activity (e.g., bullying to get into a game; bolting to playground).

increasingly been exhibiting food-stealing behaviors (e.g., taking food from others, raiding the refrigerator, rummaging through the garbage).

Question: So, what's going on here?

Answer: Bud is in a state of food deprivation and the value of food items has increased.

Because of his increased *motivation* to obtain food, Bud is now much more observant of his environment and is constantly "on the lookout" for food. In fact, stimulus items that had never previously occasioned food-stealing behavior were now serving as "triggers." For example, when Bud sees the refrigerator, the food pantry, staff member's backpacks, dining plates of housemates, the trash container in the kitchen, and the garbage cans in the garage, he is much more likely to engage in food-stealing behaviors.

Thus, in this example, the deprivation of food increases:

- The effectiveness of discriminative stimuli (refrigerator, backpack, etc.) in occasioning foraging/food-stealing behaviors.
- The value of food as a reinforcer.
- The probability of foraging/food-stealing behaviors.

TABLE 4.4. **Examples of Conditioned Motivating Operations: Reinforcer-Abolishing Effects**

Conditioned motivating operation	Reinforcer-abolishing effect	Abative effect on interfering behaviors
Noncontingent social attention	*Decreases* the effectiveness of social attention as a reinforcer.	Decreases the frequency of *behaviors* that have previously been reinforced with social attention (e.g., decreases aggression directed at classmates that was followed by teacher attention).
Reduction of task demands	*Decreases* the effectiveness of escape/avoidance as a negative reinforcer.	Decreases the frequency of *behaviors* that have previously been reinforced with avoidance of or escape from task demands (e.g., decreases aggression and self-injury that were followed by the cessation of tasks).
Reduction of aversive components/features of social interactions	*Decreases* the effectiveness of escape/avoidance as a negative reinforcer.	Decreases the frequency of *behaviors* that have previously been reinforced with avoidance of or escape from social interactions (e.g., decreases screaming at peers that was followed by unwanted social feedback).
Increased access to reinforcing tangibles	*Decreases* the effectiveness of tangibles as a positive reinforcer.	Decreases the frequency of *behaviors* that have previously been reinforced with access to reinforcing tangibles (e.g., decreases verbal threats and aggression that were followed by access to magazines and catalogs).
Increased access to reinforcing activities	*Decreases* the effectiveness of activities as a positive reinforcer.	Decreases the frequency of *behaviors* that have previously been reinforced with opportunities to participate in activities (e.g., decreases pushing a classmate off of the swing that was followed by getting on the swing and swinging for 10 minutes).
Reduction of aversive components/features of activities	*Decreases* the effectiveness of escape/avoidance as a negative reinforcer.	Decreases the frequency of *behaviors* that have previously been reinforced with avoidance of or escape from nonpreferred activities (e.g., decreases tantrum behaviors that previously had resulted in the avoidance of haircuts).

FUNCTIONAL ANTECEDENTS VERSUS NEUTRAL STIMULI

Remember, a wide array of stimuli occur *prior* to occurrences of interfering behavior. Some of these stimuli are functionally related to the interfering behavior while others are not. For example, during the first few moments of an anecdotal observation of a student with a history of disruptive behaviors (e.g., swearing, arguing), the school psychologist noticed that immediately prior to the onset of disruptive behaviors, a classmate began humming the tune to a disco song. Does this mean that the classmate's humming is a functional antecedent that triggered the interfering behaviors? Perhaps, but not likely.

(continued)

(box continues)

Read On

Based on interviews with the teacher and the student and the subsequent observations, it was determined that just prior to the school psychologist entering the classroom and the humming of the disco song, the classroom teacher had delivered the third verbal and gestural cue for the student to disengage from socializing with a peer and to begin an assignment.

In this case, the humming was a *neutral stimulus* and the redirection cues offered by the teacher were the *functional antecedent*.

As you might guess, distinguishing neutral from functional cues may at times be difficult and perplexing and at other times quite obvious. One of the purposes of a thorough FBA is making such a distinction. The implications for intervention planning should be apparent.

STIMULUS DELTA: THE OTHER DISCRIMINATIVE STIMULUS

Stimulus delta (S^Δ) is a stimulus in the presence of which a given behavior has not produced reinforcement in the past (Cooper et al., 2007). Suppose you are driving on a turnpike and are approaching the toll booth in which there are six lanes. Three lanes are lighted (indicating that they are open) and the other three are not (indicating that they are closed). Each of the lighted lanes is an SD that signals the availability of reinforcement (i.e., continued passage), whereas the dark lanes are an S^Δ signaling "the end of the line." Likewise, suppose you are very thirsty and are "dying" for a soda. You walk by a series of soda ("pop" for those from the Midwest) machines and find that one is lighted and that the others are all dark. The lit machine is an SD signaling that soda is available, while the other machines are an S^Δ signaling that soda is not available.

In order for a stimulus to function as an SD, an S^Δ must also be available. The S^Δ not only signals a condition of the unavailability of reinforcement, but also denotes a condition that provides a lesser quality of reinforcement than the SD condition (Michael, 1993).

For example: Pain is an unconditioned motivating operation (UMO). It is not an SD because in order for a stimulus to function as an SD, an S^Δ condition must be observable where the unavailability of reinforcement is a possibility. Specifically, if the onset of pain in a toothache were an SD that led to "pain-relieving behavior" (e.g. rubbing one's jaw, taking aspirin), there would need to be an S^Δ condition to contrast with the SD condition. There is no S^Δ condition because it would require that negative reinforcement (pain relief) be available when there is not pain. Therefore, it is illogical to assume that a condition exists where the cessation of pain is differentially available in the absence of pain. Therefore, we would conclude that the painful stimulus is a UMO, not an SD.

An MO does not require this two-factor test. Rather an MO is a "stand-alone" stimulus that evokes behavior.

DISCRIMINATIVE STIMULI AND MOTIVATING OPERATIONS

SDs and MOs share three important similarities:

- Both events occur before the behavior of interest.
- Both are operant (learned) responses.
- Both events have evocative functions (i.e., they both produce, or occasion, behavior).

(continued)

(box continues)

An SD controls the occurrence of behavior because that stimulus has been differentially reinforced (i.e., the reinforcing consequence has been available in the presence of the stimulus and unavailable in its absence). An SD constitutes a high probability that the relevant consequence will follow the response. While the SD signals the *availability* of the reinforcing consequence, an MO alters the *value* of the reinforcing consequence. The real-world distinction may be stated as:

MOs change how much people want something; SDs change their chance of getting it (McGill, 1999). For example, the ringing of the phone is an SD for answering the phone. When the phone rings and you answer it, there is a high probability that someone will talk to you. Suppose you have a headache and are trying to take a nap and the phone rings. The headache functions as a UMO that increases your motivation to cover your head tightly with a pillow until the ringing of the phone stops. Now suppose that your headache is gone and it is late at night and you have not heard from your teenage son since early evening. To complicate matters, it is starting to snow and this will be his first attempt at driving in inclement weather. You call his cell phone, but he does not pick up. You place your own cell phone on your lap and anxiously await his return call. The lack of contact with your son is an MO that increases your motivation to pick up the phone the moment it rings.

Thus, in these examples the behaviors you exhibit when a phone rings are altered because of antecedent stimuli. The stimulus change may occasion responses (stimulus control) or evoke responses (MOs) (Thompson & Iwata, 2005).

ALTERED STATES

Altered states are specific antecedent events that are either chemically induced or cognitively induced changes within the individual that increase the value of a stimulus/event as a positive reinforcer or a negative reinforcer. For example, a student who smokes marijuana is experiencing an *altered state* that affects her motivation (e.g., increases the value of munchies as a reinforcer, increases the value of sleep as a reinforcer, increases the value of escape from class as a reinforcer). Likewise, a student who experiences cognitively mediated test anxiety is experiencing an altered state that affects his motivation (e.g., increases the value of escape from multiple-choice exams). Also, a student with cognitively mediated depression and who has difficulty concentrating on assignments is experiencing an altered state that affects his motivation to engage in interfering behaviors (e.g., increases the value of social reinforcement from preferred peers, increases the value of avoiding challenging reading assignments). *We assert that these types of altered states are antecedent events that influence the occurrence of interfering behavior.*

Caution: It may be tempting to attribute the causes of interfering behavior only to these altered states and to incorrectly conclude that "there's nothing we can do about this." Altered states interact with environmental antecedents and consequences to induce interfering behavior. Therefore, variables such as anxiety and depression *do not cause* interfering behavior. Also, events in the environment may heighten or moderate internal states.

Interventions addressing interfering behavior need to address the interactive impacts of these altered states.

THE THREE AMIGOS

There are three types of conditioned MOs, all of which were motivationally neutral prior to their repeated pairing with another MO or reinforcing/punishing consequences (Cooper et al., 2007). The three types of conditioned MOs are classified as:

- *Surrogate conditioned MO (CMO-S):* a stimulus that has been paired within another MO.
- *Reflexive conditioned MO (CMO-R):* a stimulus that has systematically preceded some form of worsening or improvement.
- *Transitive conditioned MO (CMO-T):* a stimulus that alters the value of another stimulus).

For additional reading on MOs, see the following:

Carbone, Morgenstern, Zecchin-Tirri, and Kolberg (2007).
Cooper, Heron, and Heward (2007).
Langthorne, McGill, and O'Reilly (2007).
Mace, Gritter, Johnson, Malley, and Steege (2006).
Michael (1993).
Michael (2000).
Ray and Watson (2001).

REINFORCING CONSEQUENCES OF BEHAVIOR

Consequences are those events that follow behavior and either increase or decrease the behavior. Consequences that follow and strengthen a behavior (i.e., increase in frequency, duration, and/or intensity) are called *reinforcers.* The process by which a behavior is strengthened when it is followed by a stimulus/event is called *reinforcement.* In contrast, consequences that follow and weaken behavior (i.e., decrease in frequency, duration, and/or intensity) are called *punishers.* And the process by which a behavior is weakened when it is followed by a stimulus/event is called *punishment.*

FUNCTIONAL CONSEQUENCES VERSUS NEUTRAL CONSEQUENCES

Remember, a wide array of stimuli occur *following* the occurrences of interfering behavior. Some of these stimuli are functionally related to the interfering behavior, while others are not. For example, during the first few moments of an anecdotal observation of a student with a history of disruptive behaviors (e.g., swearing, arguing) during a sustained silent reading session the school psychologist noticed that immediately following the occurrence of these behaviors several classmates laughed, snickered, and/or guffawed. As the classmates' laughter was fading, the classroom teacher directed the student to put down his book and to report to the guidance office. An educational assistant next escorted the student from the classroom.

(continued)

(box continues)

In this case, it might be tempting to conclude that social attention from peers (positive reinforcement) and termination of an academic task (negative reinforcement) are maintaining disruptive behaviors.

However, based on interviews with the student and the classroom teacher, it was discovered that the student considered the laughter from peers to be aversive ("They're always making fun of me. I hate those snob bastards and just want to get away from those assholes") and reading was a highly preferred activity. Moreover, disruptive behavior occurred immediately after a classmate handed the student a piece of paper with a lewd drawing in which the student was depicted as half-person and half-animal. This was found to be a consistent pattern that occurred during multiple stimulus conditions (e.g., most notably during cooperative learning activities).

In this case, the functional consequence was escape from peers (negative reinforcement). The termination of reading was a neutral consequence.

There are three forms of reinforcement:

1. Positive reinforcement
2. Negative reinforcement
3. Automatic reinforcement

Each of these categories includes a number of subcategories. Before looking at the various possibilities within each, however, let's discuss them in a very broad sense. The first set, social attention and access to activities and tangibles, is referred to as *positive reinforcement*. Humans, by their very nature, are social beings. Thus, attention from others is often a powerful positive reinforcer for behavior.

Let's take a look at two examples whose circumstances are probably familiar to most readers to illustrate the power of social attention as a positive reinforcer:

Kent is a seventh grader of average-to-above average ability. His daily classroom performance and test grades do not reflect his true potential, according to his teachers. In fact, they often report that Kent is quite annoying in the classroom. When asked to describe what he does that is so annoying, his teachers uniformly report that he makes numerous wisecracks each day in response to lecture material or class discussions. His teachers feel that he spends more time thinking about what he is going to say than in listening to either the lecture or doing his work. On a side note, they do report that his comments are often quite funny and evoke at least mild chuckles from classmates. Direct observations of Kent's behavior confirm the teacher's reports of his wisecracking behavior, the inherent humor in what he says, and—perhaps most importantly—the response of his classmates: laughter or groans.

In this example, the response from his classmates (i.e., laughter or groans) is positively reinforcing Kent's wisecrack remarks. Thus, his wisecracking has increased in frequency and is likely to continue for as long as his peers respond in this manner.

Let's now look at the other example:

> Teresa is a 5-year-old who had moved from her mother's home to live with her grandmother. Many adults around Teresa considered the move to be quite traumatic, as her mother was being investigated for child neglect and endangerment and her grandmother lived over a thousand miles away. Shortly after the move, Teresa began kindergarten. During the first few days, Teresa cried when she entered the classroom. The teacher, Ms. Rob, who was a very competent, loving, nurturing teacher, took extra care to make sure that Teresa felt safe in her new environment by greeting her with a hug in the morning and a hug whenever she cried. This was a strategy this particular teacher had successfully used on new kindergarteners for more than 20 years. In addition, Ms. Rob often paired Teresa with a sympathetic classmate when she noticed Teresa becoming tearful during a class activity or at a media center. In this particular case, however, Teresa's crying did not abate within a couple of days. In fact, her crying became worse in terms of intensity (louder) and duration (longer crying periods). To the teacher's dismay, Teresa's behavior even took a turn for the worse: she began to behave in an aggressive manner toward the teacher and her classmates. When she exhibited aggressive behavior, Ms. Rob removed her from the classroom to the assistant principal's office, where the assistant principal talked to her to discover what she was so "angry about" or "afraid of."

In this example, social attention from the teacher and peers, and possibly from the assistant principal, seems to be the function maintaining Teresa's crying. What is not clear at this point is whether it is the teacher's attention, the peer's attention, the assistant principal's attention, or any combination that are functional for Teresa's crying.

The second function, escape or avoidance of unpleasant events or painful stimulation, is called *negative reinforcement*. Humans find some activities fun and enjoyable and other activities boring, painful, too difficult, or otherwise aversive in some way. Activities that are sufficiently unpleasant without having any, or minimal, reinforcing value are those that we tend to shy away from. Most adults, for instance, do not engage in behaviors that they do not find fun in some way (perhaps one of the best examples is exercising). Below is an example of how negative reinforcement operates in the classroom:

> Creed is an 8-year-old male who exhibited disruptive behavior (e.g., throwing materials, yelling at the teacher, climbing on desks, running out of the room) throughout the day. His teacher, Ms. Timmerman, had not noticed a pattern to his behavior and noted that his outbursts seemingly occurred at random times. She tried every trick in her disciplinary bag from a "corner time-out" to keeping him in the classroom during recess. As the number of incidents began to pile up during the day, she resorted to sending Creed to the principal's office where corporal punishment had been administered on multiple occasions. Ms. Timmerman, in a somewhat bewildered tone, offered the observation that Creed's behavior had not gotten any better. After conducting some FBA using a time-based scatterplot and the A-B-C recording form, the school practitioner noticed that Creed's outbursts did indeed have a pattern. In fact, almost all of his outbursts occurred when writing was part of the assignment. He used a pencil

to fill in ovals on his spelling tests without incident, but any time he was required to actually produce written work, regardless of the subject matter, an outburst occurred. Thus, the antecedent was identified (i.e., assignments that required writing), as was the consequences (i.e., all of the consequences implemented by the teacher resulted in his either completely avoiding or escaping the assignment). As a result, Creed learned through numerous interactions in the classroom that anytime an assignment was given that involved writing, a disruptive outburst allowed him to either escape or avoid that assignment. Thus, his outbursts were being *negatively reinforced*. In addition, his grades were suffering in some subjects because he was not producing the required written work.

One component of the third function, *automatic reinforcement*, is typically regarded as behavior that, when performed, results in some type of physiological sensation. One example of this is a young girl who twirls her hair because the sensations produced by having the hair in her hands and by the feeling in her scalp is positively reinforcing. Thus, this type of automatic reinforcement is called *automatic positive reinforcement*. Conversely, there are some behaviors that, when performed, result in the lessening of painful or aversive physiological stimulation. For instance, scratching an area on your arm that itches reduces the "amount" of itch. Thus, scratching has been *automatically negatively reinforced* because that behavior (i.e., scratching) resulted in the person reducing an itching sensation. In both examples, the behaviors were not socially mediated behaviors; they did not require the presence of anyone else to be either positively or negatively reinforced. This point is critical for understanding the experimental conditions associated with an extended functional analysis because an "alone" condition is often included to determine if the student will perform the behavior without anyone or anything present. Performance of the behavior while alone points to the possibility of an automatic reinforcement component. It is also important to note that the types of behaviors that are most likely to be maintained by some type of automatic reinforcement are self-injurious behaviors (SIBs), stereotypies, and certain habits (e.g., thumb sucking, nail biting, hair pulling/twirling).

The foregoing discussion addressed those behaviors that have social or sensory consequences. But what about behaviors that *do not appear* to be related to these functions and appear to be related to "private events" such as thoughts and feelings? For example, consider the case of an adolescent who exhibits bullying behavior within the school setting. As part of an FBA for bullying behavior, team members report that these behaviors are motivated by power and control. Issues of power and control suggest cognitively mediated events. From our perspective, placing the emphasis on cognitively mediated events is a molar level of analysis. As stated earlier, a molecular-level analysis involves identifying how these variables serve to directly reinforce bullying behavior. A molecular analysis would involve asking questions such as the following:

- How might power and control impact this student's opportunity to receive attention from others?
- How might these behaviors impact this student's ability to obtain tangibles?

- How might these behaviors impact this student's ability to avoid social and/or academic situations?
- How might these behaviors result in the student's increased perception of self-esteem?

Assessing the bullying behaviors from this angle allows a more precise delineation of the observable variables that are serving to maintain bullying. Consider the case of Steve, an 11-year-old male who bullies his male peers in the hallway during class changes. He typically bullies them by bumping into them, calling them names, and using verbal threats. The interdisciplinary team to which he was referred conducted interviews with Steve and his victims and concluded, prematurely and incorrectly, that the primary function of his bullying behavior was to gain power for himself and control over his peers. A closer look yielded a remarkably different picture. Careful observations indicated that a small circle of friends provided both immediate and delayed positive reinforcement for Steve's bullying by laughing at him (immediate social reinforcement) and by talking at length about his bullying several hours after the event (delayed social reinforcement). In addition, the observations indicated that the victims exhibited behavior that Steve reported in an interview to be reinforcing (e.g., looking scared, moving away from him, avoiding him in the hallway). Steve also reported that he "liked" the reputation of being a "tough guy" and was especially pleased when he overheard someone say that about him. Thus, the molecular analysis indicated a much clearer picture than the molar analysis of *why* Steve was engaging in bullying behavior. In this case, the molecular analysis resulted in a deeper understanding of the critical issues that reinforced bullying behavior and consequently identified the specific variables to be addressed in interventions.

CONCEPTUAL MODELS

Three-Term Contingency: The ABCs of FBA

In 1968 Bijiou et al. were among the first researchers to examine the contextual variables that trigger and reinforce interfering behaviors. Their A-B-C (i.e., antecedent–behavior–consequence) method for understanding the function(s) of behavior continues to be used by practitioners. Within this A-B-C model, *antecedents* are stimuli that occur prior to a behavior and that influence its occurrence. *Behavior* refers to the response of the individual (i.e., functional or interfering behavior). *Consequences* are those events that follow behavior and either increase or decrease the behavior. Only those stimuli that occur prior to the behavior that influence its occurrence are functional antecedents. Also, only those events that follow behavior that influence its occurrence are functional consequences. The following table illustrates the three-term contingency:

Antecedent	Behavior	Consequence
A cell phone rings.	The student answers the phone.	Voice of classmate on the line.
A teacher instructs students to begin an assignment.	The student begins the assignment.	Teacher provides verbal praise.
A parent verbally directs a child to clean her bedroom.	The child complies and picks up her toys.	Parent provides verbal praise and a hug.
A student is on a low-calorie diet imposed by caregivers.	During lunch, the student takes food from classmates.	The student eats the food items.
A teacher instructs all students to read silently from their book.	One student engages in "goofy" joking behavior directed at classmate.	Classmate laughs, smiles, and nods.
A student arrives at school with a headache and attending to class discussion heightens the pain.	The student engages in disruptive behavior.	The student is directed to the office (quiet area) and then to the school nurse (aspirin).
Teacher directs student to complete a series of steps within a tooth-brushing behavior chain.	Student screams, throws the toothbrush, and slap self on the leg.	Teacher offers the student a "break" and directs the student to a preferred activity.

Note. Based on Kazdin (2001).

The S-O-R-C Model

Goldfried and Sprafkin (1976) and later Nelson and Hayes (1981) expanded the A-B-C model by including organism (or individual) variables within the analysis of behavior. They supported the concept of *interactionism,* wherein behavior is best viewed as a function of both immediate environmental and organism variables (Nelson & Hayes, 1981). They described a model in which the *r*esponse (i.e., the interfering behavior) was viewed as the result of an interaction among the following variables:

1. Stimuli (e.g., noise, classroom setting, presentation of math worksheets, etc.).
2. *O*rganism (e.g., those individual differences the student brings to the current environmental situation such as past learning, genetic factors, medical issues, physiological states, etc.) and
3. *C*onsequence (e.g., environmental events that occur following a response that influence its frequency).

The following table illustrates the S-O-R-C model:

Stimulus	Organism	Response	Consequence
The teacher verbally directs a student to complete a math worksheet containing 20 long division problems.	The student has a history of difficulties with following oral instructions, completing math worksheets, and "math anxiety."	The student displays verbal opposition (e.g., "This is stupid. I won't do it").	The student is directed to leave the classroom and report to the in-school suspension classroom for the remainder of the class.
Following a student's nonresponding to verbal direction to complete a prevocational task, the teacher provides physical prompts in an attempt to evoke an appropriate response.	The student has a history of difficulties following oral directions and is very sensitive to touch by others.	The student pulls away and simultaneously hits the teacher on her arm using a closed fist.	The teacher immediately discontinues instruction and ignores the student for 5 minutes.
During a small-group social skills training activity, the school psychologist verbally cues a student to practice conversations with a classmate.	The student has significant delays in initiating and maintaining reciprocal social interactions with classmates.	The target student screams and covers her ears with cupped hands.	The teacher ignores the student and directs other students in the group to participate in the activity.

Limitations of the A-B-C and S-O-R-C Models

Both the A-B-C and the S-O-R-C models tend to be used in a linear fashion (i.e., first the antecedent, then the behavior, then the consequence; first the stimulus, then consideration of individual variables, then the behavior, then the consequence, respectively). Critical shortcomings of these models are (1) the lack of consideration of the influences of motivating operations on both discriminative stimuli and reinforcing consequences and (2) such a linear analysis underestimates the dynamic, transient, and metamorphic nature of human behavior. We propose the following model:

The S-M-I-R-C Model

The S-M-I-R-C model includes the following components:

- S: stimulus/discriminative stimulus
- M: motivating operations
- I: individual (organism) variables
- R: response
- C: consequence

Unlike the consideration of behavior using a linear model (i.e., A-B-C or S-O-R-C models), the S-M-I-R-C model considers the *dynamic* interaction among antecedent (SDs and MOs), individual variables, and reinforcing consequences. The following figure illustrates the dynamic nature of these interactions:

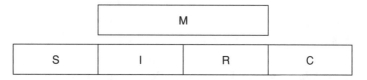

Within the S-M-I-R-C model, interfering behavior is considered to be a complex interaction involving all or some of the five components. Consider the case of Will, a student with a diagnosis of mild mental retardation with a history of self-injury (e.g., slapping self on the face/ear with an open hand). A comprehensive FBA revealed that self-injury resulted from a *dynamic interaction* of the following variables:

M (Motivating Operations)

• *Unconditioned M.* aversive auditory stimuli in the environment motivated self-injury by increasing the value of subsequent removal from the classroom (e.g., when a particular classmate exhibited loud screaming behaviors, Will often exhibited face-slapping behaviors and was directed to a small, quiet room across the hallway that contained several highly preferred toys).

• *Conditioned M.* difficult tasks motivated self-injury by increasing the value of "escape" from the tasks (e.g., when a teacher presented a complex, labor-intensive, and low-reward fine motor prevocational task, Will exhibited self-injury that typically resulted in the termination of the task demands).

DANGER . . . DANGER WILL ROBINSON: THE WARNING STIMULUS

The CMO-R is an environmental event that ultimately increases the value of conditioned negative reinforcement and therefore evokes any behavior that has lead to a reduction in the current aversive condition (Carbone et al., 2007). In the case of Will, the difficult task serves as a "warning stimulus" and establishes its removal as a reinforcer. Thus, when the classroom teacher presents the task, Will typically engages in interfering behavior.

S (Discriminative Stimuli)

• In this example, there are two discriminative stimuli (i.e., stimuli that signal the availability of reinforcement): (1) the classmate who screams and (2) the teacher who presents challenging tasks. The very presence of the student who exhibits screaming behavior signals the *availability* of both negative reinforcement (i.e., removal from the aversive screaming) and positive reinforcement (i.e., access to preferred toys). The presence of the teacher signals the availability of avoidance of and escape from difficult tasks.

I (Individual Variables)

- There are two types of individual variables that may contribute to the occurrence of interfering behaviors: (1) individual mediating and (2) individual skill deficits.

1. *Mediating variables*: personal characteristics, sensitivities, and/or internal states that when combined with various antecedent events increase the probability of interfering behavior. Will is very sensitive to sudden loud noises. For example, when the school bell rings, a classmate slides a chair across the floor, or a classmate screams loudly, Will almost always engages in self-injury.
2. *Individual behavior deficits*: delays or impairments in communication, academic, social, personal living, or community living skills that contribute to the occurrence of interfering behaviors. For example, Will evidences an orthopedic impairment. Tasks that require fine motor skills are very difficult for Will. Presenting tasks that require fine motor skills increases the probability of interfering behaviors. Moreover, Will has a severe articulation disorder and significant expressive language delays. He does not have the expressive language skills to request a change of tasks, a modification of tasks, assistance, or breaks during work sessions. These expressive communication delays contribute to the occurrences of interfering behaviors.

R (Response)

- Self-injury (i.e., face/ear-slapping behavior with an open hand).

C (Consequences)

- Positive, negative, and/or automatic reinforcement following the occurrence of interfering behaviors. For example, negative reinforcement (i.e., avoidance of or escape from aversive stimuli and difficult tasks) and positive reinforcement (i.e., access to a quiet room with preferred toys). It is also possible that SIB was reinforced by a second type of negative reinforcement (i.e., ear slapping buffered the aversive auditory stimuli).

ADDITIONAL TERMS AND CONCEPTS

Response Class (When It Rains, It Pours)

Sometimes behaviors of varying topographies have similar functional antecedents and consequences. (*This is just our cool way of saying that behaviors that look different may be very alike in that they share the same antecedents and consequences.*) In these cases, we say that these behaviors are members of the same response class. For example, behaviors such as hitting, kicking, slapping, and biting of others, while of different topographies, may be influenced by the same factors, occasioned by the same stimulus conditions (i.e., discriminative stimuli), and followed by the same reinforcing consequences. Often times, these behaviors occur as a *response set* (i.e., two or more of the behaviors of the response class occur within the context of a single behavioral episode) . . . *when it rains it pours.*

Response Class Hierarchies (First the Sky Darkens, Then There Is Thunder, Then Lightning, Followed by Light Rain, Then It Pours)

Sometimes, behaviors that are members of the same response class occur as part of a *predictable* behavior chain. Often, the initial response in the chain is a low-intensity behavior that is of minimal disruption. When this behavior does not result in reinforcement, the student may then escalate her behavior by exhibiting increasingly intense behaviors within the same response class. And when this behavior is not reinforced, she next displays a more intense behavior, and so forth and so on until a behavior results in desired reinforcement. This terminal behavior tends to be one of high intensity and robust disruption.

A Real-Life Example of Response Class and Response Class Hierarchies

Let's review the case of Michelle, a student with mild mental retardation who really likes attention from her teachers. Michelle has a variety of behaviors in her repertoire for obtaining teacher attention (a reinforcing consequence). For example, depending on the situation, she may exhibit a wide range of socially appropriate behaviors that are reinforced by social attention (e.g., asking for help, greeting her teacher, completing an assignment and bringing it to her teacher). She infrequently displays interfering behaviors (e.g., loud throat clearing, stating "Hey, Heyyy, Heyyyy," table slapping, and picking at scabs on her hands). These behaviors have been determined through a comprehensive FBA to be reinforced by intermittent social attention. These "attention-seeking behaviors" are members of the same response class. Due to an unexpected absence of two educational assistants and the unavailability of trained substitutes, the teacher-to-student ratio within the classroom has abruptly shifted from 4:10 to 2:10. Michelle, who typically displays few, if any, interfering behaviors, is receiving much less attention from the classroom teachers than which she is accustomed. (*Special Note:* This reduction of attention is a conditioned motivating operation that increases the value of teacher attention as a reinforcer.) On this particular school day, Michelle first displays appropriate behaviors to gain teacher attention (e.g., politely asking for assistance). She is told to wait her turn. She next gets up from her desk, walks to the teacher, and politely asks for help. She is told that she needs to " . . . wait just a minute more." Several minutes go by and Michelle has experienced no social interactions with teachers. Michelle then clears her throat three times and says, "I need help, please." Still no response from her teacher. She then loudly yells "Heyyy, Heyyyy, Heyyyyyyyy" and slaps the table six times. The teacher looks at Michelle and sternly says, "Michelle, you know better . . . now behave." Michelle pauses and stares, like a famished lioness studying her prey, and then begins to pick at some scabs on her hand until they bleed. At this point, her teacher runs over and says, "Michelle, don't do that . . . you're hurting yourself and making a mess."

In our role as consultants, we see this sequence played out many times across all types of classrooms, grade levels, and exceptionalities with all types of interfering behaviors.

Matching Law

The matching law (Herrnstein, 1961, 1970) states that the rate of responding typically is proportional to the rate of reinforcement available among choices. That is, when given a choice among various options, we typically opt for the option that is associated with the greatest amount of reinforcement. To illustrate the concept of the matching law using a very simple example, consider Bonita, a 12-year-old student diagnosed with a behavior disorder who spends most of her day in a regular education classroom. Over the course of her day, she has the *choice* between engaging in (1) appropriate, academically engaged behavior or (2) interfering behavior. This simple choice situation is ongoing as many hundreds of opportunities are presented to Bonita each day. Now, no matter how disruptive Bonita can be, she does not display interfering behavior 100% of the school day. The percentage of time that Bonita could be expected (predicted) to engage in both appropriate and interfering behaviors, according to the matching law, is based primarily on the rate of reinforcement associated with these behaviors. Because neither interfering behavior nor appropriate behavior results in reinforcement 100% of the time, Bonita must engage in both behaviors to maximize the amount of reinforcement she receives. Therefore, sometimes she will engage in appropriate social and academic behaviors and *switch* to interfering behaviors, or vice versa. It is very important to remember that the goal of Bonita, and indeed any student, is to *maximize* the rate of reinforcement he or she receives for his or her responding. The matching law has been shown to explain and predict rates of both interfering and appropriate behavior in the classroom (Billington & DiTommaso, 2003; Martens, Halperin, Rummel, & Kilpatrick, 1990; Martens & Houk, 1989; Shriver & Kramer, 1997).

Although rate of reinforcement is a primary variable in influencing which option a student will choose among two or more concurrently available choices, there are other variables that directly impact choice behavior in the matching law (Cooper et al, 2007; Hoch, McComas, Johnson, Faranda, & Guenther, 2002; Mace & Roberts, 2003; Volkert, Lerman, & Vorndran, 2005):

- Quality of reinforcement (i.e., the degree with which the stimulus is preferred; e.g., a cola drink vs. water)
- Magnitude (i.e., the number, duration, or intensity of reinforcement; e.g., getting an entire piece of pie vs. a tiny bite of pie)
- Timing of reinforcement (i.e., immediate or delayed access to reinforcement; e.g., getting a break now vs. getting one 2 hours later)
- Response effort (i.e., the amount of effort required to exhibit the behavior; e.g., carrying an empty box to the dumpster vs. carrying a box loaded with paper to the dumpster)

It is important to consider each of these factors, including the rate of reinforcement, during the analysis of interfering behavior as they have direct implications for designing effective treatment plans. Consider the case of Rachel, a student with reading delays who rarely completes homework assignments across all subject areas. In an effort to increase Rachel's homework completion, both her English and math teachers develop separate intervention plans. Ms. Contingent, the English teacher, sets up a plan that gradually increases the length of assignments and consistently provides Rachel with (1) verbal praise and (2) five tokens each morning that Rachel brings to class completed homework assignments. Tokens may later be exchanged for reinforcing activities within the classroom. Ms. Guided, the math teacher, makes an effort to praise Rachel at the end of each week for her completion of homework assignments. However, Ms. Guided sometimes forgets to deliver verbal praise to Rachel. It is not surprising that over time Rachel consistently completes reading homework and fails to complete her math assignments. The following table illustrates the use of the matching law to analyze Rachel's behaviors:

	Math assignments	Reading assignments	Analysis
Schedule of reinforcement	Fixed-ratio 5 and sometimes variable-ratio 15	Fixed-ratio 1	Much higher density of reinforcement for completing reading assignments
Quality of reinforcement	Low	High	Tangible and activity reinforcement higher preference than praise
Magnitude of reinforcement	Small	Large	Larger amounts/durations of reinforcement strengthens behaviors
Timing of reinforcement	Delayed (praise)	Immediate (praise and token) Delayed (activity)	Immediate contingent reinforcement strengthens behaviors
Response effort	High	Initially low and gradually increasing the task demands	Initially reducing the length of assignments reduced the response effort

SUMMARY

Wow! Clearly the analysis of human behavior is not simplistic. Rather, behavior is often the result of a complex interaction of multiple variables. This interaction is not necessarily a linear process and behavior certainly is not static. Conducting an FBA requires the consideration and assessment of each of the potentially controlling variables. In the following chapters we discuss several methods that may be used to tease out the variables that influence and maintain human behavior.

5

Key Elements of
Functional Behavioral Assessment

What is a scientist after all? It is a curious man looking through
a keyhole, the keyhole of nature, trying to know what's going on.
—JACQUES COUSTEAU

As you probably have gathered from reading the previous chapters, FBA is both (1) a theoretical framework for understanding human behavior and (2) a set of assessment procedures. From a best practices perspective, an FBA involves the use of a multimethod, multisource, and multisetting assessment process (Knoff, 2002; Steege & Watson, 2008). Within this model, information is gathered using several assessment procedures (e.g., interviews, observations), across informants (e.g., teachers, parents, students), and in various environments (e.g., classrooms, home, school, and community) to plan the most effective interventions. Unlike traditional standardized assessment, which is very static, FBA is a dynamic process in which both sequential and simultaneous activities occur throughout the assessment. It is sequential in the sense that most FBAs involve using a set of preestablished methods and procedures. It is simultaneous in that the examiner often moves back and forth between procedures based on the information gathered at a particular point in time.

FUNCTIONAL BEHAVIORAL ASSESSMENT:
INDIVIDUALIZED ASSESSMENT
RESULTING IN INDIVIDUALIZED FUNCTION-BASED INTERVENTIONS

Conceptual models describing the use of FBA procedures have often relied on a multistage model of assessment. For example, Steege and Northup (1998) described a sequential three-stage process involving (1) interviews and record review, (2) direct observations, and, finally, (3) functional analysis of behavior. In practice, however, the use of FBA procedures is not

(continued)

(box continues)

so linear. Rather, FBA is a dynamic process in which the evaluator uses a blend of assessment procedures with the results of one assessment often directing and informing subsequent assessment procedures. For example, the initial interview may lead to anecdotal observations within the classroom setting, which then leads to additional interviews, then to more observations, then to a brief functional analysis, followed by additional interviews, and so on. Conducting an FBA is an investigative process that is driven by the information obtained as opposed to any prescribed assessment protocol. Thus, the FBA is conducted on a case-by-case basis and is individualized to address the unique presenting behaviors and contributory variables specific to the individual. The results of the FBA are then used to design individually tailored function-based behavioral support plans.

DECISION TREES

Before discussing the basic elements involved in conducting an FBA, we think it is important to understand the deductive process that best embodies school-based FBA. We have included "decision trees" (see Figures 5.1 and 5.2) that we use in our understanding of human behavior, but also for expanding and describing the process and results of the FBA to parents and school personnel.

KEY ELEMENTS

FBA involves a range of assessment strategies that are used to identify the motivating operations (MOs), antecedents, individual variables, and consequences that set the occasion for problem behaviors and maintain them. It is also a process of gathering information that can be used to maximize the effectiveness and efficacy of behavior support plans. O'Neill et al. (1997) specified that an FBA is complete when:

- The interfering behavior is defined operationally.
- The interfering behavior can be predicted to occur.
- The function of the interfering behavior is defined.

Although all three of these are indeed essential for an FBA, we maintain that there are additional activities that comprise a *complete* FBA:

- Identifying and describing of motivating operations.
- Identifying and describing of antecedent variables.
- Identifying and describing of individual variables.
- Identifying and describing of consequence variables.
- Recording the occurrence of interfering behaviors.
- Matching recommended interventions to the results of the FBA, which constitute the basis of a positive behavior support plan.

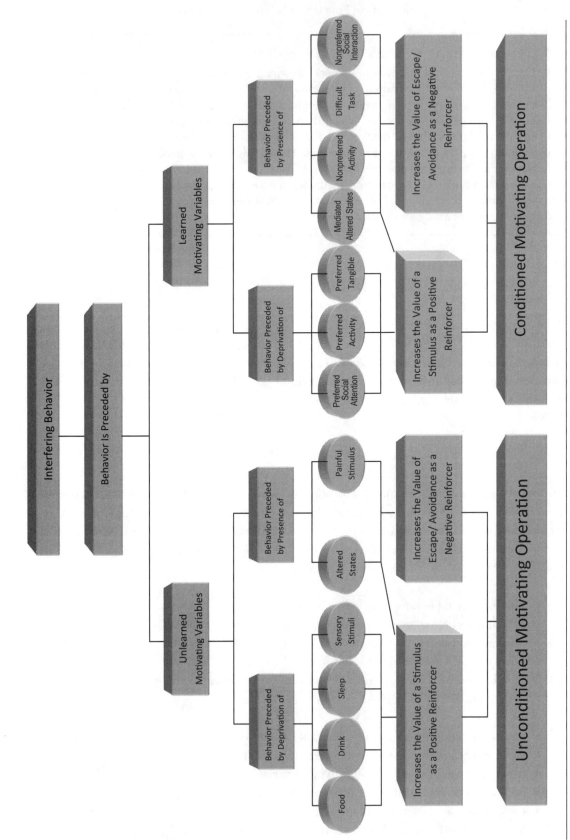

FIGURE 5.1. Motivating antecedents of behavior.

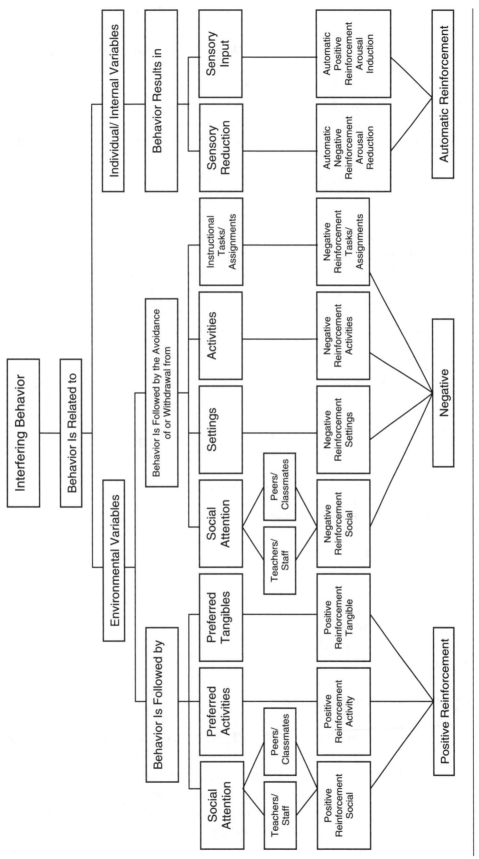

FIGURE 5.2. Reinforcing consequences of behavior.

69

Relatedly, we assert that the general components of a comprehensive FBA are:

- Identifying behaviors that interfere with a student's acquisition or display of skills.
- Describing interfering behaviors in objective, concrete terms.
- Measuring the magnitude of interfering behaviors.
- Identifying the antecedent, individual, and consequence variables that contribute to the occurrence of interfering behaviors.
- Developing hypotheses regarding the function(s) of interfering behaviors.
- Identifying function-based interventions to address interfering behaviors.

Although conceptualizing and conducting an FBA and implementing positive behavioral supports may at first seem like a daunting task, there are a number of considerations that, if observed, will make the process operate more smoothly. Table 5.1 should serve both as a guide and as a reminder as you work your way through the FBA/PBS process.

Although many activities and procedures may be considered to be an FBA, there are three categories of FBA into which all procedures fall:

- Indirect FBA.
- Direct descriptive FBA.
- Functional behavioral *analysis*.

Each of these categories is described in detail in the following paragraphs.

Indirect Functional Behavioral Assessment

Indirect methods involve a variety of procedures including:

- Review of records.
- Behavior rating scales.
- Adaptive behavior scales.
- Interviews.
- Social skill assessments.
- Assessment of academic skills.
- Semistructured interviews.

The primary purposes of indirect FBAs are to:

- Identify the behaviors that interfere with the students' academic or social development.
- Describe interfering behaviors in clear, unambiguous terms.
- Identify environmental variables that appear to trigger interfering behavior.
- Identify environmental variables that occur after an interfering behavior has occurred and that appear to serve to reinforce the behavior.
- Identify possible individual differences that may contribute to the occurrence of interfering behavior.

TABLE 5.1. What to Be Thinking about as You Complete the FBA Process

- Identify those behaviors that interfere with the person's acquisition or performance of skills/behaviors.
- Identify and describe the behaviors in concrete terms.
- Use a hypothesis-testing approach. In the early stages of the FBA process any and all ideas, suggestions, and explanations should be considered tentative and must be verified through further assessment.
- Use a multimethod, multisetting, multisource assessment model: indirect FBA procedures, direct descriptive FBA procedures, and functional analysis procedures.
- When directly recording behaviors, make sure that the recording procedure is matched to the dimensions of the behavior and that adequate resources are available to record accurately.
- Consider the full range of potential functions of behavior: positive reinforcement, negative reinforcement, automatic reinforcement.
- Note that a single behavior may have multiple functions.
- Use the S-M-I-R-C model to identify and describe all relevant setting variables, antecedent variables, individual (organism) variables (including skill deficits), and consequence variables.
- Note that a setting variable is the immediate environment in which the interfering behavior occurs, while an antecedent variable is the specific event within the environment that triggers the interfering behavior.
- Consider the possible effects of UMOs and CMOs in motivating behavior.
- Consider the effects of SDs in occasioning behavior.
- Note that an identified consequence may be delivered consistently or intermittently.
- Provide examples that clearly illustrate the behavioral principles involved.
- Attempt to identify those situations in which problem behavior does not occur.
- Consider the results of adaptive behavior and social–emotional and academic assessments.
- Consider modifying triggering environmental antecedents to reduce the probability of occurrence of the interfering behavior.
- Link assessment to intervention: Remember, the ultimate utility of the FBA process is directly related to the design and ultimate effectiveness of individually tailored intervention strategies. Always be thinking about possible interventions.
- Consider the logical replacement behavior(s) for each interfering behavior and to what degree the replacement behavior is incompatible with the interfering behavior, is within the student's repertoire of skills, is useful and practical for the student, and results in similar and comparable levels of reinforcement in the natural environment.
- Consider modifying environmental consequences that are reinforcing interfering behavior.
- Identify reactive procedures, the procedures to use if interfering behavior does occur.

- Identify possible replacement behaviors.
- Identify possible interventions.

Review of Records

Many students with whom school practitioners come into contact have mountainous cumulative folders. Unfortunately, much of the information contained in these folders is either irrelevant for FBA or the relevant information is buried among the scree. Therefore, it is wise to be selective and purposeful about the type of information that one is attempting to cull from such folders. You may find the book *School Archival Records Search* (SARS; Walker, Block-Pedego, Todis, Severson, & Pedego, 1991) a useful guide to systematically collecting and synthesizing information found in a student's cumulative folder. See Chapter 7 for a more in-depth discussion of what to look for during a record review.

Behavior Rating Scales

There are a multitude of parent, teacher, and student self-report versions of behavior rating scales available. Although most of these won't be particularly useful for identifying function, they can help to identify behaviors of concern and perhaps identify *functionally equivalent behaviors* (see the accompanying box).

FUNCTIONALLY EQUIVALENT BEHAVIORS

These are behaviors that look different on the surface but have the same function. For example, a boy may call out in class, walk around the room, bother his neighbors, and quietly make rude remarks to the girls because of the attention those behaviors gain him. Even though they are very different behaviors, they all serve the same function. Identifying functionally equivalent behaviors is especially important in the FBA process because intervening with one behavior may have positive effects on all the other behaviors, thus precluding the need for designing separate interventions for each of the behaviors. The trick is to identify the one behavior that, when reduced or eliminated, will result in the reduction of functionally equivalent inappropriate behaviors.

Adaptive Behavior Scales, Academic Assessments, and Social Skills Assessments

You may be asking, "Why adaptive behavior, academic, and social skills assessments? I thought these were part of a traditional standardized assessment. Don't these deal primarily with personal living, social, communication, leisure, vocational, community living, and self-help skills?" *Precisely!!* Many problem behaviors are directly related to specific skill deficits. By assessing these skill domains, one may identify critical variables related to interfering behavior. For example, some problem behaviors are often directly related to communication skill delays. In such cases, teaching functionally equivalent communication skills eliminates the targeted problem behaviors. Moreover, in schools, problem behavior is often motivated by avoidance of or termination of academic assignments or tasks. Modifying academic tasks often results in an increase in active participation within academic situations *and* a decrease or elimination of problem behavior. Teaching prosocial behaviors is often a critical component of a positive behavioral intervention. Finally, social skills deficits are often directly related to the occurrence of interfering behaviors. In short, assessment of adaptive behavior, academic skills, and social skills is often an essential component of the comprehensive FBA process.

Interviews

One of the most frequently used types of indirect FBA methods involves either clinical or semistructured interviewing. Every school practitioner is probably familiar with conducting some type of clinical interview with teachers, parents, and/or the referred student but may be less familiar with semistructured interviews associated with ascertaining function. Sattler's (2001) book is an excellent resource that includes three chapters covering issues related to (1) clinical assessment interview techniques; (2) interviewing children, parents, teachers, and families; (3) reliability and validity of interview procedures; (4) self-evaluation of interviewing; and (5) advantages and disadvantages of different interview techniques. Interviews can be valuable sources of information during the FBA process. Several available semistructured interviews have been demonstrated to be quite useful in helping to identify salient antecedents and consequences. Two of the most promising semistructured interviews are the Functional Assessment Interview Form (FAIF) provided in O'Neill et al. (1997) and the Functional Assessment Informant Record—Teacher (FAIR-T) provided in Edwards (2002) (see also Figure 7.10).

As with other forms of assessment, it is important to conduct reliable and accurate behavioral interviews. A couple of the main advantages of semistructured interviews are that they are designed to decrease subjective responding by interviewees and to increase accuracy of secondhand information. In subsequent sections of this book, we have included examples of semistructured interview forms that we have found to be effective when conducting FBAs.

Direct Descriptive Functional Behavioral Assessment

Direct descriptive FBA provides data on the occurrence of the behavior within the context of the natural environment in which it occurs (e.g., classroom, home, cafeteria, media center) and also on the environmental events that surround it (McComas & Mace, 2000). This procedure involves all of the following:

- Generating an operational definition of the behavior.
- Determining an appropriate behavior-recording procedure.
- Observing and recording the behavior.
- Observing and recording the associated antecedent and consequent variables.

One of the primary advantages of direct observation of target behaviors and related conditions/events within the natural environment is that school practitioners and educational teams can use the data to construct applied interventions that are clearly indicated by the observational data (cf. Skinner, Rhymer, & McDaniel, 2000). There are a variety of direct descriptive FBA methods. The selection of the most appropriate method typically depends on several factors including the topography of the behavior and the skills and/or resources of those who are conducting the assessment. Each method of assessment is conducted by observing and recording behavior as it occurs in the *natural* environment. At the most basic level, direct descriptive FBA involves identifying and describing the behavior, designing appropriate behavior-recording procedures, and observing and recording the behavior and associated antecedent and consequent variables.

Note: These procedures are particularly useful for assessing low-incidence behaviors, behaviors difficult to observe due to unpredictable occurrence, and those behaviors that are dangerous to the individual or others.

There are four basic ways of conducting a direct descriptive FBA:

1. Anecdotal record keeping (e.g., McComas & Mace, 2000).
2. Antecedent–behavior–consequence (A-B-C) assessments (Bijou et al., 1968; O'Neill et al., 1997).
3. Scatterplot assessments (Touchette, MacDonald, & Langer, 1985).
4. Descriptive assessments (Lalli, Browder, Mace, & Brown, 1993; Mace & Lalli, 1991).

In the following subsections, we provide brief descriptions of each of these procedures.

Anecdotal Record Keeping

Anecdotal record keeping involves observing the individual within natural settings and writing down specific behaviors and relevant associated variables. This type of recording tends to be narrative in nature and can be quite informative *if* followed up with an interview and/or with an analysis of the information using a behavioral stream procedure or an A-B-C procedure.

A-B-C Assessment

Examples of standard and extended A-B-C assessments are shown in Figure 5.3. With the extended version, the evaluator observes and records the interfering behavior and related variables (i.e., date, time of day, variables occurring prior to the interfering behavior, the interfering behavior itself, variables that occurred following the interfering behavior, and the resulting change in the frequency, duration, or intensity of the interfering behavior).

Scatterplot Assessments

The most basic type of scatterplot assessment involves recording the time of day at which problem behavior occurred across several days. With this type of assessment, visual inspection of the data sheets allows one to identify possible associations between the interfering behavior, the time of day, and related tasks and/or activities. By correlating the target behavior with the time of day, tasks, activities, staff, and other variables, one is able to identify those variables associated with the occurrence of interfering behavior and to form hypotheses regarding the possible cause–effect relationships.

Descriptive Assessments

Descriptive assessments involve the real-time recording of variables that trigger interfering behavior, the interfering behavior, and consequent variables. Descriptive FBA is conducted by directly observing the referred student within natural settings. By recording the target behavior and related antecedent and consequence variables, one can compute conditional probabilities of behavior in relationship to these variables. For example, if a student calls out in the middle of the teacher's lecture 20 times during an observation session and the teacher

A: Antecedent	B: Behavior	C: Consequence

Date/Time	Setting	Antecedent	Behavior	Consequence	Effect
When did the interfering behavior occur?	**Where** did the interfering behavior occur?	What happened immediately **prior** (i.e., triggered) to the interfering behavior?	Describe the interfering **behavior.**	What did you do or what happened **after** the interfering behavior occurred?	What **effect** did the consequence have on the frequency, duration, and/or intensity of the interfering behavior?

FIGURE 5.3. Examples of A-B-C and extended A-B-C assessment procedures.

verbally reprimands the student following 15 of those instances, the probability that the student's calling-out behavior will result in some form of teacher attention is .75. Conversely, if the student raised her hand to speak 10 times and was only acknowledged once by the teacher, her probability of gaining teacher attention for a more appropriate behavior is only .10. Relative to the interfering behavior, the student is engaging in a behavior that is very effective for her, at least in terms of gaining teacher attention.

These probabilities, like the information derived from other methods of direct observation, are used to generate hypotheses about what appears to trigger and reinforce interfering behavior. The primary purpose of direct FBA procedures is to identify those variables that are associated with the target behavior(s). Although valuable in identifying these relationships, information gathered without systematically isolating and manipulating environmental variables is only *suggestive* of functional relationships (McComas & Mace, 2000).

TREATMENT VALIDITY
OF FUNCTIONAL BEHAVIORAL ASSESSMENT

It is important to note that ultimately the utility of FBA is the degree with which the results of assessment are used to design effective interventions. The "treatment validity" of FBA refers to whether the assessment results contribute to effective intervention. In other words, even if an FBA may have yielded reliable and accurate assessment results, if the data do not contribute to the development of effective interventions then the assessment method is not considered useful (Shriver, Anderson, & Proctor, 2001). This is an extremely important point. FBAs should be conducted not only to understand and predict behavior but to lead to the development of effective interventions. FBAs that result in the writing of a comprehensive report that, after being shared with team members, is simply filed away do not meet the standard of treatment validity. The ultimate value of the FBA is subsequent interventions that result in meaningful and lasting behavior change. Clearly, many factors influence the efficacy of interventions (e.g., resources, treatment integrity, trained staff) as well as inaccurate FBAs. It is critical, then, that in addition to conducting sound assessments, practitioners need to systematically evaluate the effectiveness of the interventions that were based on the assessment results. Only by formally evaluating interventions can we demonstrate the treatment validity of the assessment results.

SUMMARY

It is probably safe to say that many school practitioners subscribe to the empirical rigors of behavioral assessments that include a *functional behavioral analysis*. The implementation of these procedures within school settings, however, is an arduous process that is impractical (and perhaps unnecessary) in many circumstances. Moreover, although functional behavior analyses may be highly accurate at the time of assessment, their temporal stability may be in question due to the tendency of behavioral function to change across time, situations, and people. In addition, whereas indirect FBAs are practical and efficient, they often yield inaccurate findings. The same can be said of direct descriptive FBA procedures. What is a practitioner to do?

A NOTE ABOUT FUNCTIONAL ANALYSIS OF INTERVENTIONS

Another model of functional analysis involves the systematic evaluation of the effectiveness of interventions. When we formally evaluate the degree with which an intervention causes a change in behavior(s), a functional relationship between the intervention and the resulting behavior change is demonstrated. A functional relationship is established when (1) the target behavior changes when an intervention is implemented while all other variables are held constant and (2) the process is repeated one or more times and the behavior changes each time (Miltenberger, 1997). The best practices approach to the evaluation of interventions involves the use of single-case experimental design methodologies. Using single-case experimental designs, we can demonstrate that the intervention was responsible for the observed behavior change and rule out the influence of extraneous variables (confounding or irrelevant variables). Steege, Brown-Chidsey, and Mace (2002) describe single-case experimental design methodology and the best practices approach of evaluating the effectiveness of interventions.

The Solution: Within this book, we endorse an FBA model that is procedurally rigorous and practical for implementation by school psychologists and related professionals. We propose a hypothesis-testing approach that incorporates a combination of interviews and direct observation procedures that are used at a minimum to:

- Identify and describe interfering behaviors.
- Document the relative occurrence of interfering behaviors.
- Identify variables associated with the occurrence of interfering behaviors.
- Identify hypotheses regarding the function of these behaviors.
- Identify function-based interventions.
- Design and evaluate the effectiveness of interventions.

It is important to recognize that in most cases comprehensive indirect FBA and direct descriptive FBA procedures will yield accurate data that are useful in designing and evaluating socially valid and effective positive behavioral support interventions. In some cases, however, practitioners may find that these procedures are insufficient. In such cases, practitioners may need to reevaluate the accuracy of their assessments and conduct more in-depth assessments (e.g., extended or brief functional behavioral *analyses*; see Chapter 9). It is our expectation that this volume will be useful for addressing a wide range of target behaviors and referral questions faced by practitioners within school settings.

A FINAL ELEMENT: THE FUNCTIONAL BEHAVIORAL ASSESSMENT RATING SCALE

Our experience has shown that the methodologies described in this book have been applicable for assessing a wide range of populations (e.g., students with autism, mental retardation, attentional deficits, behavioral disabilities, and specific learning disabilities, as well as typically developing students) and behaviors (e.g., aggression, self-injury, oppositional–defiant behavior, tantrums, disruption, and habits), in a variety of settings (e.g., special education classrooms, regular education classrooms, private homes, clinics, hospitals, inpatient facilities, and group homes). It is also our experience that many factors contribute to the accuracy of the FBA and the effectiveness of subsequent interventions (e.g., knowledge and experience of teachers, school resources, and administrative supports). Although you may not be able to control all of these variables, you are in a position to conduct a best practices FBA. You also have a professional responsibility and an ethical obligation to conduct an FBA that is technically sound and sufficiently comprehensive to result in an understanding of the variables that contribute to the occurrence of problem behavior and that lead to interventions that result in socially meaningful behavior change. To assist you with conducting meaningful and best practices FBAs, we have designed the Functional Behavioral Assessment Rating Scale (FuBARS) to measure the quality of FBAs (see Figure 5.4).

The FuBARS may be used:

- As a formative assessment guide when conducting an FBA.
- As a summative assessment tool to evaluate the completed FBA.

We have also provided an alternative checklist (see Figure 5.5) that we have used to guide and self-monitor the FBA process.

Functional Behavioral Assessment Rating Scale (FuBARS)

The Functional Behavioral Assessment Rating Scale (FuBARS) is designed to measure the quality of assessments of interfering behaviors. The FuBARS may be used:

- As a formative assessment guide when conducting an FBA.

- As a summative assessment tool to evaluate the completed FBA.

Functional Behavioral Assessment Procedures

An FBA may include some or all of the following procedures:

- Indirect assessment (e.g., record review, interviews, parent/teacher rating scales, checklists, adaptive behavior assessments).

- Direct descriptive assessment (e.g., direct observation, FBAOF recordings, IRP recordings, self-report rating scales, curriculum-based measurement).

- Functional analysis (e.g., structural FA, brief FA, extended FA).

(continued)

FIGURE 5.4. Blank Functional Behavioral Assessment Rating Scale (FuBARS).

FuBARS

Student _____ Date of birth _____

Grade _____ School _____

FBA completed by _____

Date completed _____

Person using the FuBARS _____

Use the following rating scale to evaluate the quality of the FBA:

1. **Functional Behavioral Assessment Procedures**
   0 = functional behavioral assessment of problem behavior not conducted
   1 = unstructured and/or indirect assessment only
   2 = a combination of indirect and direct descriptive assessment
   3 = a combination of indirect, direct descriptive and functional analysis (brief or extended)

2. **Identification and Description of Interfering Behavior(s)**
   0 = interfering behavior not identified
   1 = area of concern is identified (e.g., social problem), but specific target behavior is not identified
   2 = specific behavior is identified, but it is described in ambiguous and non-behavioral terms
   3 = behavior is identified and described in clear, unambiguous terms
     - 0= if multiple interfering behaviors, response class hierarchy not addressed
     - 1 = if multiple interfering behaviors, response class hierarchy considered and, when applicable, described
     - 0 = response effort not considered
     - 1 = response effort evaluated and measured/estimated

3. **Current Levels of Occurrence (CLO) of Interfering Behaviors**
   0 = CLO not reported
   1 = CLO estimated
   2 = CLO reported, but CLO based on limited data (e.g., 1-2 observations)
   3 = CLO reported and CLO based on multiple observations and recordings (e.g., use of the IRP)

4. **Identification and Description of Antecedent Variables: Discriminative Stimuli**
   0 = discriminative stimuli that occasion interfering behavior not assessed
   1 = discriminative stimuli that occasion interfering behavior identified
   2 = discriminative stimuli that occasion interfering behavior identified and described
   3 = discriminative stimuli that occasion interfering behavior identified and described, clear example provided
   NA: discriminative stimuli not applicable to the interfering behavior

5. **Identification and Description of Antecedent Variables: Unconditioned Motivating Operations (UMOs)**
   0 = unconditioned motivating operations that temporarily alter the value of a reinforcing consequence not assessed
   1 = unconditioned motivating operations that temporarily alter the value of a reinforcing consequence identified

(continued)

2 =   unconditioned motivating operations that temporarily alter the value of a reinforcing consequence identified and described

3 =   unconditioned motivating operations that temporarily alter the value of a reinforcing consequence identified and described, *clear example provided*

NA: UMO not applicable to the interfering behavior

6. **Identification and Description of Antecedent Variables: Conditioned Motivating Operations (CMOs)**

0 =   conditioned motivating operations that temporarily alter the value of a reinforcing consequence not assessed

1 =   conditioned motivating operations that temporarily alter the value of a reinforcing consequence identified

2 =   conditioned motivating operations that temporarily alter the value of a reinforcing consequence identified and described

3 =   conditioned motivating operations that temporarily alter the value of a reinforcing consequence identified and described, *clear example provided*

NA: CMO not applicable to the interfering behavior

7. **Identification and Description of Individual Mediating Variables that Contribute to the Interfering Behavior**

0 =   mediating individual variables that contribute to interfering behavior not assessed

1 =   mediating individual variables that contribute to interfering behavior identified

2 =   mediating individual variables that contribute to interfering behavior identified and described

3 =   mediating individual variables that contribute to interfering behavior identified and described, *clear example provided*

8. **Identification and Description of Individual Behavior Deficits**

0 =   behavior deficits that contribute to interfering behavior not assessed

1 =   behavior deficits that contribute to interfering behavior identified

2 =   behavior deficits that contribute to interfering behavior identified and described

3 =   behavior deficits that contribute to interfering behavior identified and described, *clear example provided*

   - Skill vs. Performance
     0 =   behavior deficit as a skill or a performance issue not identified
     1 =   behavior deficit as a skill or performance issue is identified and described

9. **Identification and Description of Reinforcing Consequences and Parameters of Reinforcement**

0 =   consequence variables that reinforce the occurrence of interfering behavior not assessed

1 =   consequence variables that reinforce the occurrence of interfering behavior identified

2 =   consequence variables that reinforce the occurrence of interfering behavior identified and described

3 =   consequences variables that reinforce the occurrence of interfering behavior identified and described, *clear example provided*

   - Schedule of Reinforcement
     0 =   schedule of reinforcing consequence not identified
     1 =   schedule of reinforcing consequence identified and described

(continued)

- Quality of Reinforcement
  - 0 = quality of reinforcing consequence not identified
  - 1 = quality of reinforcing consequence identified and described
- Magnitude of Reinforcement
  - 0 = magnitude of reinforcing consequence not identified
  - 1 = magnitude of reinforcing consequence identified and described
- Timing of Reinforcement
  - 0 = timing of reinforcing consequence not identified
  - 1 = timing of reinforcing consequence identified and described

10. Hypothesis Statement
0 = hypothesis statement not included
1 = hypothesis statement included, but written in ambiguous, non-behavioral terms (e.g., motivated by frustration)
2 = hypothesis statement written in behavioral terms, but does not consider all factors contributing to problem behavior (e.g., only describes antecedents to interfering behavior and fails to mention individual and consequence variables)
3 = hypothesis statement written in behavioral terms and considers the full range of antecedent, individual, and consequence variables associated with the occurrence of the problem behavior

11. Evidence-Based Interventions
0 = evidence-based interventions not included
1 = interventions are recommended, but they are not based on empirical research
2 = evidence-based interventions are recommended, but the research was conducted with populations that differ markedly from the individual
3 = evidence-based interventions are recommended and have been validated with similar clinical populations as the individual

12. Function-Based Interventions
0 = function-based interventions not included
1 = interventions are recommended, but they are not directly linked to the results of the assessment
2 = interventions are recommended and are function-based, but they only address one aspect of the referral question (e.g., interventions are designed to *reduce* interfering behavior only, interventions focus on modifying reinforcing consequences only)
3 = interventions are recommended and are function-based. Interventions address each of the controlling variables (e.g., discriminative stimuli, conditioned and unconditioned motivating operations, individual variables, and consequences)

Score: _____ Total points possible: _____

Percent score: _____

Functional Behavioral Assessment Checklist

Student _____ Grade _____ Date _____

1. **Functional Behavioral Assessment Procedures**
   _____ indirect assessment
   _____ direct descriptive assessment
   _____ functional analysis (brief or extended)

2. **Identification and Description of Interfering Behavior(s)**
   _____ behavior is identified and described in clear, unambiguous terms
   _____ response effort considered

3. **Current Levels of Occurrence (CLO) of Interfering Behaviors**
   _____ CLO reported

4. **Identification and Description of Antecedent Variables**
   _____ discriminative stimuli that occasion interfering behavior considered
   _____ unconditioned motivating operations that temporarily alter the value of a reinforcing consequence considered
   _____ conditioned motivating operations that temporarily alter the value of a reinforcing consequence identified and described

5. **Identification and Description of Individual Variables**
   _____ mediating individual variables that contribute to interfering behavior considered
   _____ behavior deficits that contribute to interfering behavior considered

6. **Reinforcing Consequences**
   _____ positive reinforcement considered
   _____ negative reinforcement considered
   _____ automatic reinforcement considered

7. **Parameters of Reinforcement**
   _____ schedule of reinforcement considered
   _____ quality of reinforcement considered
   _____ magnitude of reinforcement considered
   _____ timing of reinforcement considered

8. **Hypothesis Statement**
   _____ hypothesis statement included

9. **Evidence-Based Interventions**
   _____ evidence-based interventions are identified

10. **Function-Based Interventions**
    _____ function-based interventions are identified

FIGURE 5.5. Functional Behavioral Assessment Checklist.

6

Observing and Recording Behavior

Behavior is a difficult subject matter, not because it is inaccessible, but because it is extremely complex. Since it is a process, rather than a thing, it cannot be held still for observation. It is changing, fluid, evanescent, and for this reason it makes great technical demands upon the ingenuity and energy of the scientist. But there is nothing essentially insoluble about the problems which arise from this fact.

—B. F. SKINNER (1953, p. 15)

Conducting a complete FBA is a process that involves several interrelated stages. This process is usually initiated by a referral for assessment and intervention and begins by defining and recording behaviors.

DEFINING AND RECORDING BEHAVIOR

As we have noted in other chapters, the initial step in conducting an FBA involves identifying and describing target behaviors. In most cases, this involves a two-stage process of interviews and direct observations for the purpose of clarifying and describing target behaviors. This is a critical step because the accuracy of the FBA is dependent upon precise definitions of behaviors. When behaviors are precisely defined, we say that they have been "operationally" defined or defined in "concrete, observable terms."

Consider the case in which a classroom teacher referred a student with concerns regarding what was labeled as "aggressive behavior." Based solely on this information, the school psychologist conducted an observation within the classroom setting. The school psychologist used a frequency-recording procedure to measure the occurrences of aggressive behavior. After 45 minutes of careful observations, she had recorded no occurrences of aggressive behavior. She did note, however, that the student on several occasions had engaged in a behavior that she labeled "inappropriate verbal behaviors directed toward classmates." Following the observation session, the school psychologist and the classroom teacher met and reviewed the observation results. The classroom teacher was amazed when the school psychologist reported that she had not observed any occurrences of "aggressive behavior." Only after several minutes of discussion did they realize that they had not been talking a common language. Although both had indeed been observing the same behaviors (e.g., swearing at classmates, derogatory remarks directed to classmates), the teacher labeled them "aggressive" while the school psychologist labeled them "inappropriate verbalizations." Based on their discussion of the characteristics of the behaviors exhibited by the student and by reviewing several examples of the behaviors, they mutually decided to change the description of these verbalizations from "aggressive behavior" to "verbal aggression directed toward classmates."

In short, behaviors need to be described in a way that is understandable to all members of the team. Behavioral definitions need to be unambiguous and concise. Specifically, this means that behaviors should be described in such a way that after reviewing a written description of a target behavior, two observers should be able to observe a student and agree that the target behavior has or has not occurred. As a general rule, a description of behavior should meet three criteria (Kazdin, 2001):

- Objectivity
- Clarity
- Completeness

To be *objective*, the description of behavior should refer to observable features and not to internal characteristics, traits, intentions, meanings, and so on. To be *clear*, the definition should be so unambiguous that it can be accurately repeated and paraphrased by others. To be *complete*, the definition must delineate the observable characteristics of the behavior. We recommend a two-stage process for defining behaviors: (1) interviews and (2) observations.

STAGE 1: THE INTERVIEW

The interview should be conducted with persons very familiar with the student referred for evaluation. At this point in the FBA process, the interview should focus on identifying *observable* behavior-relevant characteristics displayed by the referred student. For example, in the previous case of aggressive behavior, the school practitioner would ask the teacher to clearly describe the observable characteristics that constitute aggressive behavior. Specific questions such as the following could be asked during a semistructured interview:

SCHOOL PRACTITIONER: You have indicated that Bob frequently displays aggressive behaviors in the classroom. What do you mean by the word "aggressive"?

CLASSROOM TEACHER: Well, he is often mean-spirited. He is aggressive with his classmates.

SCHOOL PRACTITIONER: You said that he is mean-spirited and aggressive. Could you give me an example of these behaviors?

CLASSROOM TEACHER: Yes. He says nasty things to classmates as if to provoke them.

SCHOOL PRACTITIONER: Give me some examples of the nasty things he says to classmates.

CLASSROOM TEACHER: Sure. Just yesterday during a group discussion in social studies class, one of the other students, Cindy, asked a question. Bob called Cindy "a stupid moron." When I asked him to apologize for his comment, he responded, "Cindy, I'm so sorry that you're such a stupid moron."

SCHOOL PRACTITIONER: In this example, the aggressive behavior exhibited by Bob is a form of verbal aggression. Does Bob display any other forms of aggressive behavior. For example, is he physically aggressive with others (e.g., hits, kicks, pushes, or scratches)?

CLASSROOM TEACHER: Oh, no. He's never been assaultive. Bob's aggressive behavior only involves verbal aggression.

SCHOOL PRACTITIONER: Let's further define what is meant by verbal aggression. Verbal aggression includes statements such as "stupid moron." What other things does Bob do that are verbally aggressive?

CLASSROOM TEACHER: Well, he might also swear at another student or refer to someone in a derogatory way such as "You loser," "You jerk," "What an idiot," "Screw you, asshole."

SCHOOL PRACTITIONER: OK. Aggressive verbal behavior also includes derogatory and inappropriate verbal comments directed to classmates.

CLASSROOM TEACHER: Yes. And toward teachers as well. For example, yesterday in class I had a little difficulty setting up my PowerPoint presentation. He called me a "technologically challenged idiot."

SCHOOL PRACTITIONER: Ouch! So verbal aggression may also be directed at teachers. How about other school staff?

CLASSROOM TEACHER: Yes, he does it to other staff, including Ms. Adams. She's the principal, you know.

SCHOOL PRACTITIONER: The first step of the FBA process involves clarifying and describing the target behaviors. With Bob, we have identified verbal aggression as the behavior of concern. Let's consider these possible definitions of verbal aggression:
    Verbal aggression directed to classmates (VBC): Bob directing derogatory comments (e.g., "You idiot") and/or inappropriate language (e.g., swearing) to classmates.
    Verbal aggression directed to staff (VBS): Bob directing derogatory comments (e.g., "You idiot") and/or inappropriate language (e.g., swearing) to school staff.
    Are these clear and unambiguous definitions?

CLASSROOM TEACHER: Yes. I think we've nailed it. This is very clear.

SCHOOL PRACTITIONER: Great! What I am planning to do next is to conduct a classroom observation. I will use these definitions to record occurrences of VBC and VBS behaviors. Are there days, times of day, or class sessions that you recommend I conduct the observations where the behaviors are most likely to occur?

In this example, both the school practitioner and the teacher are clear about what constitutes aggressive behavior. Making sure that the behavior is operationally defined prior to conducting the first observation will probably save the school practitioner time and a bit of frustration. In addition, something else was gleaned from the above interview that has particular relevance for the FBA. Want to take a guess as to what it is? For the answer, see the accompanying box. To assist both school practitioners and teachers in this first stage of the FBA process, we have included a representative listing of some of the most common referral problems and examples of their corresponding "operational" definitions; see the accompanying table. This is by no means a comprehensive list. Rather, it is a set of exemplars to serve as a prompt for writing clear behavioral definitions. The words that are underlined in the "Referral problem" column are "red-flag" words that should immediately be clarified.

Referral problem	Sample operational definition
Carter is off task	When given a written assignment to complete at his desk, Carter looks out the window, walks around the class, or walks over to the free-reading center.
Jeremy shows disrespect toward his teachers	When given a direction or command, Jeremy tells his teachers to shut up, stop telling him what to do, and get off his back. He then refuses to do the work by putting his head down on his desk or leaving the classroom.
Wilson has an attitude problem	When spoken to by an adult, Wilson frowns and turns away and does not do what has been asked or directed.
Nyetha is very sad and depressed	During times when she is working or playing alone, Nyetha often cries quietly.
Craig has a learning disability in math calculations	Craig is able to complete 1×1 multiplication problems with 20–30% accuracy.

> During the interview, the teacher noted that the verbally aggressive behavior occurs toward both peers and adults in the school environment. That piece of information is especially relevant for FBA because, although the same types of behaviors are occurring, they may have very different functions. For instance, the function of verbal aggression toward classmates may be to attract attention from peers, whereas verbal aggression toward adults may be maintained by escape/avoidance from academic instruction. Given that the functions may be different, the resulting interventions will likely look different as well. In addition to the implications for treatment, realizing that the verbally aggressive behavior may have different functions across targets also allows one to understand that successfully treating verbally aggressive behavior toward peers may not result in reductions in verbally aggressive behavior toward adults.

STAGE 2: THE DIRECT OBSERVATION

Following the interview, the next step in the FBA process typically involves a direct observation of the referred student. Direct observation of behavior is the core of behavioral assessment and is one of the most commonly used behavioral assessment techniques for addressing student's behaviors (C. H. Skinner, Dittmer, & Howell, 2000).

Generally, we recommend that the initial observation take place within naturally occurring settings and circumstances (e.g., with a student in her class while she is engaged in naturally occurring tasks/activities). At the most basic level, the direct observation involves no more than recording target behaviors. Observers could also conduct more comprehensive observations and record not only the target behaviors but contextual variables associated with the occurrence of target behavior (i.e., antecedents and consequences). Regardless of the FBA procedure used, the same behavior-recording procedures apply.

There are several methods for collecting and recording direct observation data (e.g., frequency recording, duration recording, and interval recording). No one procedure is necessarily superior to another. The selection of a measurement procedure should be driven by each of the following:

1. The dimensions of behavior (e.g., topography, frequency, duration).
2. The goals of the intervention.
3. Pragmatic considerations such as time, resources, and competency of observers.

The subsections below include descriptions and examples of data-recording procedures that are commonly used within an FBA. These procedures may be used by the evaluator to record behavior during a planned observation. These procedures are also routinely used by teachers and staff to record behavior both prior to the intervention (i.e., the FBA process) and during the intervention to measure the effectiveness of the treatment strategies. Figures 6.1, 6.2, 6.3, and 6.4, in addition to illustrating typical data-recording procedures, provide examples of clear, unambiguous descriptions of behaviors.

Frequency Recording

Frequency recording involves observing, counting, and recording the number of times a behavior has occurred. This procedure typically is used to record occurrences of discrete, low-rate behaviors (i.e., behaviors that have a definite beginning and end and that do not often occur). Although frequency recording is often a very accurate method for recording discrete behaviors, it tends to provide an underestimate of sustained behaviors (e.g., time on task), an inaccurate record of very high-rate behaviors, and the potential unreliability of observations when behavior onset and cessation are difficult to discriminate.

Figure 6.1 illustrates the application of a frequency-recording procedure. In this example, verbal aggression directed to classmates (VBC) was recorded using a frequency-recording procedure. The recording of behavior was conducted by an educational technician who was assigned to the special education program in which Bob received services. Twelve (12) occurrences of VBC were recorded. Because the length of observations may vary across days, due to shortened school days or to the unavailability of an observer/recorder, raw data (i.e., 12) were converted to rate per hour of VBC. Thus, the number of

Target Behavior:	Verbal aggression directed toward classmates (VBC)
Definition:	Verbal statements directed at classmates that include swearing, insults (e.g., "You're ugly," "I hate your guts"), or threats (e.g., "I'm going to hit you"). <u>Note:</u> record as discrete episodes when occurrences of VBC are separated by 15 seconds of no VBC.
Procedure:	Using a tallying system, record each occurrence of VBC.
Rationale:	VBC behaviors occur singularly (obviously a discrete event) or as a group (a response set, or episode). Recording each VBC statement may be unwieldy.
VBC:	⊬⊬⊬ ⊬⊬⊬ II
Frequency:	12
Program hours:	6
Rate:	2 occurrences per hour

FIGURE 6.1. Example of frequency-recording procedure.

occurrences, 12, in a 6-hour school day is converted to a rate of two occurrences of VBC per hour.

Duration Recording

This procedure involves observing, timing, and recording the total amount of time a behavior has occurred. It is most applicable for recording continuous behaviors (i.e., sustained behaviors such as on-task activity and stereotypy). Duration recording is typically done through use of a stopwatch and can be expressed as a percentage of time. It is difficult to use in measuring high-rate, short-duration behaviors or multiple behaviors.

Figure 6.2 illustrates the use of a duration-recording procedure. In this example, each tantrum was recorded using both frequency and duration-recording procedures. The recording of behavior was conducted by an educational technician who was assigned to the preschool special education program in which the student received services. The educational technician counted and recorded the number of times that Bob exhibited tantrums. During a 6-hour program day, five occurrences of tantrum behavior were observed and recorded. Why record duration when frequency is so simple? With this type of behavior, frequency is less accurate than duration. There is a big difference between 10 tantrums that last 5 seconds each time compared to one tantrum that lasts 50 minutes. Thus having both frequency and duration data provides a clearer picture of the tantrum behavior than either one alone. In addition to recording the frequency of behavior, the observer also used a stopwatch to record the length of each tantrum. Tantrum behaviors ranged in duration from a low of 3 minutes and 4 seconds to a high of 12 minutes. The cumulative duration of tantrum behaviors (i.e., 36 minutes and 53 seconds) was determined by adding the respective timed lengths of each of the five tantrum behaviors. Similar to the issues discussed with frequency recording, it is often more accurate to convert and report data in terms of rate as opposed to raw numbers. In this case, tantrum behavior could be reported as occurring at a rate of 0.8333 times per hour, with an average duration (i.e.,

Target Behavior:	Tantrum behavior
Definition:	A response set including two or more of the following behaviors: screaming, crying, throwing objects/materials, flopping to the floor, and/or kicking objects.
Procedure:	Using a stopwatch, record the length of time from the onset to the end of the tantrum behavior.
Rationale:	By recording the length of each tantrum, the recorder is measuring both the frequency of the tantrums and their duration. Frequency recording alone would be very misleading. For example, one (1) tantrum of 30-seconds duration is very different from one (1) tantrum of 1 hour duration.
Tantrum (T):	3' 4"; 8' 10"; 9' 00"; 12' 00"; 4' 39"
Frequency:	5
Program hours:	6
Rate:	0.833 times per hour
Cumulative duration:	36 minutes
Average duration:	6.67 minutes per occurrence

Percent duration (i.e., percentage of time in which person displayed tantrum behavior):

$$\frac{36'\ 39''}{360\ \text{program minutes}} = 11\% \text{ of the program day}$$

FIGURE 6.2. Example of duration-recording procedure.

the mean duration of tantrums) of 6.661 minutes per occurrence, or a duration of 11% of the program day.

Interval Recording

This procedure involves observing and recording the occurrence and nonoccurrence of behaviors at predetermined units of time (i.e., intervals ranging from several seconds to several minutes or even hours). There are three types of interval-recording procedures, each with its own advantages and disadvantages:

- *Whole interval*—in which a behavior is recorded only if it was observed to occur during the *entire* interval.
- *Partial interval*—in which a behavior is recorded if it was observed for *any part* of the interval.
- *Momentary time sampling*—in which the observer looks at the student only at predetermined points in time and notes if the target behavior is occurring at the precise moment the observation occurs.

The accompanying table gives direction as to which recording procedure to use in a particular circumstance.

If . . .	Then choose this recording procedure
Continuous performance of a behavior is desired (e.g., on-task behavior)	Whole-interval recording
The behavior occurs at a very high frequency and very rapidly (e.g., talking, head banging, hand flapping)	Partial-interval recording
It is difficult to continuously monitor the student	Momentary time sampling or performance-based recording
The teacher desires a low-effort method for collecting data	Momentary time sampling or performance-based recording

Of these three methods, whole-interval recording is recommended when continuous occurrence of the target behavior is expected (e.g., when recording sustained attention to a task). Partial-interval recording is preferred for measurement of high-frequency and rapidly occurring (e.g., self-injurious head banging) behaviors. Momentary time sampling is useful when continuous observation of a student is not practical or when an observer is monitoring and measuring target behaviors with several students in one setting. This procedure may underestimate the occurrence of low-rate behaviors. Note that interval-recording procedures provide only estimates of rate and duration of occurrence of target behaviors. The results of observations are reported in terms of the number or percentage of intervals in which target behaviors occur. Of the interval-recording procedures, partial-interval recording is the most frequently used.

Figure 6.3 displays a 6-second whole-interval recording procedure that was used to measure the on-task behavior of a student with a history of attentional deficits who had been referred to a behavioral consultant for FBA. The behavioral consultant initially attempted a partial-interval recording procedure, but she found that even a split second of on-task behavior was recorded within each 6-second interval, resulting in an overestimation of on-task behavior. She selected the whole-interval recording procedure because the student would need to exhibit on-task behavior throughout the entire interval to be recorded. Because the goal of the assessment and subsequent positive behavioral support intervention was to increase *sustained behavior*, the whole-interval recording procedure provided a more sensitive and accurate measure of behavior. In this example, on-task behavior was recorded only when it was observed to occur during the entire 6-second interval. The nonoccurrence of on-task behavior was also recorded. Nonoccurrence was recorded when on-task behavior did not occur for the whole interval. This could include either the student not exhibiting the defined behavior or exhibiting an inappropriate behavior (e.g., talking out, tossing a pencil) The behavioral consultant conducted several observations during different classroom settings (e.g., group math instruction, spelling examination, independent reading, completion of math worksheets, afternoon recess). For purposes of illustration of whole-interval recording, Figure 6.3 shows the data collected during the first 5 minutes of one of

Target Behavior: *On-task behavior*

Definition *Visual, motor, and/or verbal attention to and/or within tasks and activities.*

Procedure: *6-second whole-interval recording procedure. Record a "+" in each 6-second interval if on-task behavior occurred for the entire interval. Record a "O" in each 6-second interval if on-task behavior did not occur during the whole interval (e.g., O seconds or 1–5 seconds).*

	6	12	18	24	30	36	42	48	54	60
1 minute	+	0	+	0	0	+	+	0	0	+
2 minutes	+	+	0	+	+	0	0	+	+	+
3 minutes	+	0	+	+	+	0	0	0	+	+
4 minutes	0	0	0	+	0	+	+	+	+	0
5 minutes	+	+	+	+	+	+	+	0	0	0

$$\text{Percent occurrence} = \frac{\text{number of "+" intervals}}{\text{total number of intervals}} \times 100$$

Example: $\dfrac{30}{50} \times 100 = 60\%$ occurrence of on-task behavior

FIGURE 6.3. Example of whole-interval recording procedure.

the observations. During this observation, on-task behavior was recorded 30 times out of 50 intervals (60%) in which behavior was recorded.

The following case example illustrates the use of a partial-interval recording procedure. The psychologist conducted an FBA of a child with developmental disabilities who exhibited SIB (e.g., hand biting, face slapping, and head banging). Direct descriptive FBA involved direct measures of each of the target behaviors within school (e.g., academic instruction, functional life skills instruction, leisure skills instruction, recess, self-help skills instruction, and vocational skills instruction) and home (e.g., hanging out with siblings, dinner, dinner cleanup) environments. During these observations, antecedent and consequent variables were not manipulated. School personnel and family members were asked to carry on with typical routines and to act natural. Because there were multiple target behaviors and each one could be very brief (e.g., 1–2 seconds), the psychologist decided to use a 6-second partial-interval recording procedure to record each behavior. The psychologist considered recording SIB only when any of the three target behaviors occurred. However, anecdotal observations and interviews with school staff and family indicated that these behaviors did not occur as a response set, and that often only one behavior occurred during a behavioral incident whereas at other times two or three of the behaviors were exhibited. The psychologist also decided to record the occurrence of active participation. Active participation was recorded to (1) identify levels of occurrence of appropriate behavior within each setting/ activity and (2) to compare the occurrence of appropriate behavior and interfering behaviors across the various settings/activity.

For ease of recording and to increase the accuracy of data collection, the psychologist developed a behavior-recording data sheet that included each of the behavioral codes within each 6-second interval. Each time that any of the behaviors occurred, the psychologist circled the corresponding code. Figure 6.4 shows a completed partial-interval recording sheet for one observation conducted during an academic leisure task within the school setting. The results of the observation showed that self-injurious hand biting occurred during 48% of the intervals observed, self-injurious face slapping occurred during 22% of the intervals observed, and self-injurious head banging occurred during 12% of the intervals observed. Active participation was recorded for 21% of the intervals observed. Note that in several intervals there was no occurrence of any of the target behaviors.

Permanent Product Recording

Another aspect of a behavior that may be recorded is its product. Permanent product recording is used when a behavior results in specific *tangible* outcomes (Miltenberger, 1997). This procedure involves recording the number of products (e.g., number of math problems completed, number of bottles sorted accurately, number of letters written on a bathroom wall). It is used to record a wide range of products, or outcomes, of behavior. One advantage of this method is that the observer need not be present when the behavior occurs. One possible drawback to this procedure is that practitioners cannot always determine who exhibited the behaviors that led to the product recorded. For example, a teacher cannot determine whether a student completed his or her own homework, whether assistance was provided, or whether someone else completed the assignments.

Performance-Based Behavioral Recordings

These procedures involve observing and rating a behavior according to a predetermined scale as an estimate of occurrence, duration, and/or intensity of behaviors. This procedure is typically used when frequency, duration, partial-interval, or whole-interval procedures are not practical given the professional responsibilities, resources, and experience of the observers. Performance-based interval-recording procedures can be used simultaneously to record multiple behaviors (both adaptive and interfering). A particular advantage of this procedure is the capacity simultaneously to provide direct instructional/behavioral supports and to record data.

Although performance-based assessment procedures have been widely used within the field of education to evaluate student academic performance, their use within behavioral assessments is relatively recent. For example, Iwata, Pace, Kissel, Nau, and Farber (1990) used a performance-based assessment procedure to rate the intensity of SIB. Steege, Davin, and Hathaway (2001) developed a performance-based behavioral assessment procedure to record behaviors, including low-rate and sustained behaviors. Steege et al. (2001) first identified and described specific behaviors and then developed a rating scale that included assigned values corresponding to specific dimensions of behavior. Target behaviors were observed and recorded based on the rating scale. These procedures were demonstrated to have acceptable levels of reliability and validity. However, it should be noted that these

Procedure: Partial-interval recording procedure

Circle the number corresponding to the behavior in each 6-second interval in which the behavior occurred.

(Note: record even if the behavior occurred only for a split second.)

Target Behaviors	Number of Intervals	Percent Occurrence
(A) Self-injurious hand biting	48	48%
(B) Self-injurious face slapping	22	22%
(C) Self-injurious head banging	12	12%
(D) Active participation	21	21%

Grid (circled items shown in parentheses; each cell lists two rows: "A B" over "C D"):

	6	12	18	24	30	36	42	48	54	60
1	(A) B / C D	A (B) / C D	A (B) / C D	A (B) / C D	A B / C (D)	A B / C (D)	A B / C (D)	A B / C (D)	A B / C (D)	A B / C (D)
2	A B / (C) D	A B / C (D)	(A) (B) / C D	(A) (B) / C D	(A) (B) / C D	(A) B / C D	(A) B / C D	(A) B / C D	(A) B / C D	(A) B / C D
3	(A) (B) / C D	(A) (B) / C D	(A) (B) / C D	(A) (B) / C D	(A) (B) / C D	(A) B / C D	(A) B / C D	A B / C (D)	A B / C (D)	A B / (C) D
4	A B / (C) D	A B / (C) D	A B / C D	A B / C D	A B / C (D)	A B / C (D)	A B / C (D)	A B / C (D)	A B / C (D)	A B / C (D)
5	A B / C D	A B / C D	A B / C D	A B / C (D)	(A) (B) / C D	(A) (B) / C D	(A) (B) / C D	(A) (B) / C D	(A) (B) / C D	(A) B / C D
6	(A) B / C D	(A) B / C D	A B / C (D)	A B / C (D)	A B / C D	A B / C D	A B / (C) D	A B / (C) D	A B / (C) D	A B / (C) D
7	A B / (C) D	A B / C D	(A) B / C D	(A) B / C D	(A) B / C D	(A) B / C D	(A) B / C D	A B / C D	A B / C D	(A) B / C D
8	(A) B / C D	(A) B / C D	(A) B / C D	A B / C D	A B / C D	(A) B / C D	(A) B / C D	(A) B / C D	(A) B / C D	(A) (B) / C D
9	(A) (B) / C D	(A) (B) / C D	(A) (B) / C D	(A) (B) / C D	(A) (B) / C D	A B / C D	A B / C D	(A) B / C D	(A) B / C D	(A) B / C D
10	(A) B / C D	(A) B / C D	A B / C (D)	A B / C (D)	A B / C (D)	A B / C (D)	A B / (C) D	A B / (C) D	A B / (C) D	A B / (C) D

FIGURE 6.4. Example of partial-interval recording procedure.

methods may yield inaccurate results, especially with novice evaluators. Therefore, the precision of these procedures is maximized when

1. Behaviors are defined in explicit and unambiguous terms
2. Rating scales are clearly defined for each behavior
3. Adequate training and support are provided to staff prior to and during the initial phases of implementation
4. Ongoing follow-up is provided to check on the reliability and accuracy of behavior recordings

Figure 6.5 illustrates a performance-based recording procedure to record appropriate behaviors (e.g., active participation) and interfering behaviors (e.g., stereotypical behaviors of a student with developmental disabilities within a functional life skills program).

Target Behaviors
  Active Participation (AP): visual, verbal, motor, on-task responding; engaged in the task activity
  Stereotypy (S): waving hands in face, repetitive rocking, and/or repeated spinning/twirling/ tapping of objects

Recording Procedure: Performance-Based Recording
  0 = NO AP or S
  1 = 1" to 2' 59" of AP or S
  2 = 3' to 5' 59" of AP or S
  3 = 6' to 8' 59" of AP or S
  4 = 9' to 11' 59" of AP or S
  5 = 12' to 15' of AP or S

Time	Setting	Activity	Active Participation	Stereotypy	Staff Person
8:00 A.M. to 8:15	hallway, classroom	transition to class, hanging coat, backpack	4	1	MWS
8:15 to 8:30	special education classroom	morning circle time	2	2	MWS
8:30 to 8:45	special education classroom	morning circle time	1	3	MWS
8:45 to 9:00	second-grade classroom	reading group	1	4	MWS
9:00 to 9:15	second-grade classroom	reading group	2	3	MWS
9:15 to 9:30	second-grade classroom	snack	5	0	MWS

FIGURE 6.5. Example of performance-based recording procedure.

The performance-based recording procedure was used to estimate the relative occurrence of both active participation and stereotypy. At the end of each 15-minute interval, the staff person recorded the following:

- Setting.
- Specific activity.
- Rating of active participation.
- Rating of stereotypy.
- His or her initials.

These data show that both behaviors varied across times of day, settings, and activities.

Real-Time Recording

Although used mostly by researchers, real-time recording is likely to gain momentum in schools with the advent and availability of computer technology (e.g., personal digital assistants, laptops, handheld computers) and data collection software (e.g., Access CISSAR, Behavioral Evaluation Strategy and Taxonomy [BEST], Behavior Observation System [BOS], ODLog™, The Observer). There are a relatively large number of software applications to assist with real-time recording. For a review of these, the reader is referred to Kahng and Iwata (1998), Tapp and Walden (2000), and Tapp and Wehby (2000). Real-time recording is quite an easy concept; an observer merely marks the onset of a behavior (e.g., starting a timer) and the termination of a behavior (e.g., stopping a timer). This process of starting and stopping the timer occurs each time the behavior occurs without resetting the timer. The cumulative amount of time that the student engages in the behavior during an observation will yield a duration measure (e.g., Charlie was out of his seat for 468 seconds of a 900-second observation, 52% of the actual time), a frequency measure (how many times Charlie was in his seat and got out), and a timing measure (exactly when the behavior occurred during the observation period). Collectively, these dimensions—duration, frequency, and timing—are important for hypothesis development and intervention planning and provide a more accurate assessment of the interfering behavior than assessing a singular dimension.

Interobserver Agreement

An important consideration in measuring student behavior is the reliability of the recording method. Reliability of measurement is usually defined in terms of interobserver agreement. "Interobserver agreement" refers to common findings by two or more observers or raters on the occurrence and nonoccurrence of target behaviors, the ratings of behaviors, or the ratings of permanent products. There are several methods of determining the degree of interobserver agreement. The most commonly used method involves calculating the ratio of agreements to the total number of recordings of behavior (Steege et al., 2002). For example, suppose that while using an event-recording procedure to measure a student's calling-out behavior during teacher instructional time two observers simultaneously and independently observed and recorded target behaviors. The primary observer recorded 15 occurrences of the target behavior, while the secondary observer recorded 14 occurrences of the behavior. The total number of recordings of behavior was 15. The number of agreements was 14, resulting in the following ratio:

14/15, or 93% interobserver agreement

Generally speaking, an interobserver agreement percentage at or above 80% is considered the standard for concluding that the measurement of student behavior is reliable and valid (Miltenberger, 2001). Within research circles, it is recommended that interobserver agreement data be conducted for 25–30% of the sessions/samples (Steege et al., 2002). Within applied settings, when research outcomes are not expected, it is a good idea to intermittently use a second observer/recorder to measure interobserver agreement. How much is enough is highly dependent on the results of the observations. For example, if there is a high level of agreement between or among observers, fewer paired observations/recordings are necessary. On the other hand, if the level of agreement falls below 80%, then additional training, supervision, and monitoring needs to be offered. In situations in which a second observer/rater is unavailable, videotaping a sampling of sessions may be conducted. The videotape can then be viewed and behaviors recorded with a second observer.

SUMMARY

Remember the old adage, "Give a boy a hammer and he looks for a nail to pound"? Similarly, give a school practitioner a data-recording procedure and he or she looks for a behavior to record. If only it were that simple. Unfortunately, not every data-recording procedure fits every behavior: when a data-recording procedure is well matched to the characteristics of the behavior, it results in accurate and meaningful measurement; when there is a poor match between recording procedure and the behavior, the resulting measurement is often meaningless. One needs to be selective about the data-recording procedure that is chosen in a particular situation. The recording procedure should be matched to the dimensions of the behavior after the behavior has been operationally defined. Doing so will allow you to make more accurate estimates of behavior and meaningful decisions throughout the FBA process.

7

Indirect Functional Behavioral Assessment

Once you eliminate the impossible, whatever remains,
no matter how improbable, must be the truth.
—SHERLOCK HOLMES (by Sir Arthur Conan Doyle)

THE NEED FOR A GAME PLAN

Conducting an FBA is quite often a complex task, involving a wide range of variables to consider. As we initiate an FBA, it is important to recognize that it is really both a sequential and a simultaneous process. It is a sequential process in that we tend to assess behavior by marching through a set of preestablished investigative procedures. It is a simultaneous process in that we are continuously considering a host of variables that could be contributing to the occurrence of interfering behaviors. Consider the visual image depicted in Figure 7.1.

Here, as the school practitioner begins the FBA process, she is trying to remember to be sure to address each of the issues/variables one needs to consider when conducting a comprehensive FBA. She's finding this to be a daunting task that requires a tremendous amount of focus and organization. We've been there. In fact, in the old days, we often initiated an FBA armed only with a clipboard, graph paper, a pencil, and our own ingenuity. We invariably neglected to ask specific questions and missed potentially contributory variables. You've probably done that too. For example, 30 minutes after the initial interview with the classroom teacher and while you are driving to a student assistance team (SAT) at another school you think, "Hey! I forgot to ask about specific setting events," and then "It sounds as if disruptive behaviors are motivated by teacher attention. . . . But wait a minute, I forgot to ask how other students in the class respond when Jerry engages in disruptive behavior," and then (45 seconds later after you regained your composure after nearly running a red light because you were not concentrating on your driving behavior) "Holy cow! What about the difficulty of the tasks? Perhaps disruptive behavior is motivated by escape/avoidance of specific tasks due to an underlying specific learning disability?"

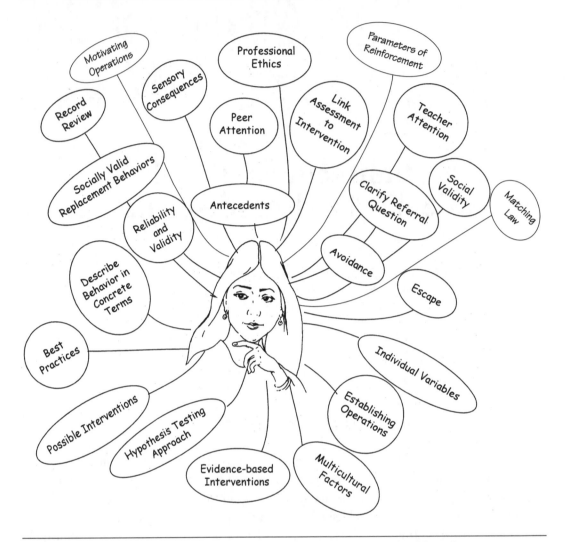

FIGURE 7.1. All things considered . . . in the professional life of a school-based practitioner.

In our experience in conducting hundreds of FBAs over the past 20 years, we have found that the accuracy of the FBA process is increased when we follow a collaborative problem-solving process that is based on a game plan that includes (1) a conceptual framework that is rooted in the principles of applied behavior analysis and (2) the necessary tools to conduct the assessment.

GUIDING CONCEPTUAL FRAMEWORK

We view the FBA process as an investigative journey that is based on the principles of applied behavior analysis. Essentially, from the initial record review or interview until the final evaluations of the effectiveness of the intervention, we are continuously assessing and reassessing behaviors against a backdrop of the S-M-I-R-C model. The basic premise used throughout the FBA process is that interfering behaviors are the result of an interaction among the following variables: (1) antecedent, (2) individual, and (3) consequence. We must also keep in mind that all behaviors are motivated by (1) positive reinforcement, (2) negative reinforcement, and (3) automatic reinforcement.

We use the decision trees (see Figures 5.1 and 5.2) in a linear fashion to consider the possible functions of behavior. It is important to refer to this model, or a similar model, and/ or to keep in mind all the various functions of behavior as you begin the FBA process. You need to keep an open mind and consider the full range of variables that influence behavior. We have found that the decision tree helps us both to "rule in" and to "rule out" the behavioral function(s) associated with referral behaviors.

Another important aspect of the game plan is having adequate resources, or tools to conduct the FBA. I (Steege) am reminded of one of the first school psychologists I met during the early stages of my career. Her name was Rosemary. My oh my, how she had resources! Because she traveled from school to school in rural Iowa, she bought an old postal Jeep that only had the driver's seat; she built custom-fitted shelves and cabinets in the remaining cavity of the Jeep, and she crammed it full of test equipment, protocols, materials, readings/handouts, supplies, and miscellaneous school psychology paraphernalia. As I said, she had resources. Rosemary had whatever she needed, and then some, to address any referral question, testing situation, intervention plan, or school psychology crisis situation. She had it all. Well, I have never replicated Rosemary's Traveling School Psychology Extravaganza. In my case, things like car seats, baseball equipment, basketball gear, golf clubs, sailing stuff, not to mention my wife and sons, took precedence. However, I have never forgotten the lessons I leaned from Rosemary: *Be prepared. Make sure you have the equipment and resources you need to get the job done efficiently and effectively.*

Just like with Rosemary's Jeep, we have crammed a lot of assessment protocols into this and the following chapters. These protocols are the tools that we use in conducting the FBA. Not every procedure is applicable to every case you encounter. Just as one needs to match the data-recording procedure to the dimensions of the behavior and the resources of the observers/recorders, one needs to be selective about the choice of FBA procedures. This is not a one-size-fits-all process. You need to carefully consider the referral behaviors and all available resources and develop a game plan that will allow you to conduct an efficient and effective FBA. In this chapter and Chapter 8 we offer several indirect FBA and direct descriptive FBA procedures that will give you, the practitioner, the tools necessary to conduct reliable and accurate assessments. It has been our experience that using the procedures described in the following sections will allow you to get the job done efficiently and effectively. This chapter includes examples and brief descriptions of several procedures that we use when conducting an indirect FBA. Chapter 8 includes examples and brief descriptions of several procedures that we use when conducting a direct descriptive FBA.

INDIRECT FUNCTIONAL BEHAVIORAL ASSESSMENT

"Indirect assessment" is so named because information regarding antecedents and consequences and other critical variables are gathered *indirectly* via interviews, rating scales, screening forms, and the like. The data obtained from these measures is generally not as reliable as those obtained from more direct procedures and are considered to be a useful *adjunct* to more direct measures. Indirect measures may be some of the first procedures used in an FBA because they allow one to construct more meaningful observations and to begin developing hypotheses about the function of behavior.

This chapter describes some of the most common methods of indirect functional behavioral assessment that we use and how they are related to the overall FBA process. All of these forms and the categories within them are merely examples. They may be used "as is" or may be modified to meet the demands of a particular assessment or situation. As explained previously, the reason for using the forms is that they "force" one to consider specific categories of variables, whereas an open-ended question such as "What are the triggers?" or "What are the consequences that reinforce the behavior?" often results in vague answers such as "I just don't know" or "We're not sure. The behavior just seems to happen out of the blue." We have found that the indirect FBA procedures described in the following subsections to be very useful in:

- Identifying and describing behaviors.
- Identifying and describing antecedent, individual, and consequence variables.
- Identifying hypotheses regarding the function(s) of behaviors.

We typically use the indirect FBA during the first stage of the FBA, with the results of the assessment used to inform and guide the next stage of the process, namely, direct descriptive FBAs.

Considerations for Evaluators
Conducting Indirect Functional Behavioral Assessments

The entire FBA process is a hypothesis-testing approach. It is an investigative process in which one is collecting information, identifying potential relationships, collecting more data, analyzing the influences of variables, and confirming or disconfirming hypotheses. Remember, hypotheses are not etched in stone. Many times they are more like drawings in the sand—with the next wave of data washing them away. We need to always keep in mind that indirect FBA procedures are based on information that is gathered from other sources. When conducting interviews, we need to exercise sound critical thinking skills. We need to actively listen to the interviewee and be acutely aware that any opinion, "fact," or "conclusion" offered by the interviewee may be inaccurate or biased. In short, information from interviewees needs to be considered with "a grain of salt"—and sometimes with a whole shaker full! On the other hand, there are many instances in which the interviewee offers information that is "right on." So don't prematurely throw out any ideas, suggestions, or opinions. Instead, consider *all the data* as you formalize your hypotheses.

Perhaps the easiest part of the FBA process is the identification of interfering behaviors. After all, interfering behavior is what prompted the FBA. Also parents, teachers, staff, and significant others are usually quite good at *identifying* behaviors that are problematic or just downright annoying. However, these informants often experience considerable difficulty in *describing* interfering behavior in concrete terms. The description of interfering behaviors is usually a fairly straightforward proposition. As previously discussed, it involves describing the behavior in behavioral terms. When informants are having difficulty verbally describing behavior, we sometimes ask them to model or "act out" the behavior. This provides us with a visual image of the behavior and often assists with the written description of the target behavior. A word of caution is needed here. We want to emphasize that we do not always ask the informant to act out the behavior in question. Some behaviors are either very difficult to replicate or—and probably most importantly—you would not want to have them performed. Why, you ask? Well, some behaviors may be dangerous to self or others (e.g., aggression, property destruction), may be inappropriate to model (e.g., sexual behaviors), or may be very difficult to replicate (e.g., manipulative soiling, ruminative vomiting). The key issue here is that it is critical to the accuracy of the entire FBA process that interfering behaviors are described in behavioral terms and that all members of the team agree that the definition of the interfering behavior reflects the actual behavior(s) of concern exhibited by the individual.

Following are descriptions of five structured indirect FBA procedures that we have developed, piloted, and recommend in conducting indirect FBAs:

- The Functional Behavioral Assessment Screening Form (FBASF).
- The Behavioral Stream Interview (BSI).
- The Antecedent Variables Assessment Form (AVAF).
- The Individual Variables Assessment Form (IVAF).
- The Consequence Variables Assessment Form (CVAF).

It is extremely important to remember that any FBA, whether indirect or direct descriptive, almost always involves a record review in the early stages of the process. The accompanying table can serve as a guide for information that is typically contained in a student's cumulative record and how that information may be pertinent to the FBA process.

Category	What to look for	Why important for FBA
Attendance history	Patterns of absences and total number of absences	May give clues about antecedents for problem behavior and possible skill deficits from lack of opportunity to receive instruction
Standardized test scores	Current and historical results of state standardized testing	May indicate academic subjects and activities that are most difficult for the student (skill deficits) and may be helpful for identifying at what age/grade the deficits became more pronounced (useful for planning curriculum-based measurements)

(continued)

Category	What to look for	Why important for FBA
Medical history	Vision and hearing problems as well as other problems that may be related to school performance (e.g., motor difficulties, head traumas, long-term illnesses, enuresis) and current medication use	Helpful for identifying conditions that may exacerbate existing problematic behavior or increase the likelihood of other problematic use behaviors
Social history	Frequent changes in address, foster home placement, recent occurrence of stressful events (e.g., parents' divorce, remarriage of parent, death in family, number of schools attended)	Points to possible establishing operations or setting events that may be impacting school behavior
Disciplinary history	Types of problematic behaviors, times at and locations in which they occurred, disciplinary penalty imposed, and increase/decrease in frequency/intensity of problem behavior	Helps to identify patterns of behavior (antecedents), effective and ineffective disciplinary strategies, and possible maintaining consequences, and helps chart the progression of problematic behavior
Previous FBA or related assessment results	Other assessments that have been conducted that focus on academic skills, behavioral functioning, language skills, etc.	Possible changes in function of behavior, previous antecedents, history of behavior and interventions, and programming decisions
Previous interventions	Formal and informal interventions that are documented in some way	Identify interventions that have been successful or unsuccessful and why they were or were not successful. If successful, why are they not currently being used? Likewise, why are unsuccessful interventions continuing to be applied?
IEP	Instructional goals and objectives, how/if they are being taught, how/if they are being monitored, and other data supporting student performance	Provides information on the degree to which the behaviors of concern are being addressed in the classroom and on the extent to which the teacher collects and records behavioral data

General Directions for Evaluators
Using Indirect Functional Behavioral Assessment Procedures

Other than the BSI, the remaining procedures include an assessment protocol (or form) that is designed to provide structure to the assessment process. There are two ways in which the evaluator can use these protocols. The first and most frequently used method involves employing the protocols within a semistructured interview. Providing the interviewee with a copy of the protocol during the interview often increases the fluency and accuracy of the interview. The second method involves providing the informant with copies of the forms and asking him or her to complete them. This latter method is only recommended in those cases in which the informant is well grounded in FBA principles and methodologies.

The Functional Behavioral Assessment Screening Form

Description

The FBASF is an FBA recording form that is used in the initial stages of the FBA process. The FBASF is used to record the following:

- Behavioral strengths (i.e., adaptive behaviors, skills, and characteristics that are functional and appropriate).
- Interfering behaviors (i.e., priority problem behaviors).
- Reinforcers (i.e., events, activities, objects, people, foods, situations, or stimuli that appear to be preferred by this person).
- Communication skills (i.e., verbal skills, signs, gestures, symbols, and/or electronic devices).

Because the focus of the FBA is on interfering behaviors, we have found that in the initial stages of the FBA process it is helpful to get a more balanced view of the individual. Identifying behavioral strengths, reinforcers, and communication skills provides us with valuable information that can be used in building behavioral support plans. Interviewees sometimes find it difficult to identify behavioral strengths. Behavioral strengths include both *interindividual* strengths (i.e., relative strengths compared to other people of the same age) and *intraindividual* strengths (i.e., behaviors that are personal strengths for the individual). A behavioral strength may be a mastered skill (e.g., above-grade-level reading skills), an emerging behavior (e.g., acquiring cooperative play skills), or a personal characteristic (e.g., a good sense of humor). Interviewees often report that the identification of potent and/ or consistent reinforcers is difficult. In these cases a more formal assessment of reinforcer preferences may be indicated.

Example of the Use of the Functional Behavioral Assessment Screening Form

Figure 7.2 is a copy of a blank FBASF, and Figure 7.3 includes an example of a completed FBASF. The FBASF was completed during an interview with the parents of a student with developmental disabilities who exhibited several interfering behaviors. Behavioral strengths were identified through both the interview and through review of recently completed adaptive behavior assessments. Three interfering behaviors were identified and described, several reinforcers were identified, and the methods of communication were identified and briefly described. The information gathered concerning interfering behaviors using the FBASF was used to guide the evaluator throughout the rest of the FBA process. Moreover, the information regarding behavioral strengths, reinforcers, and communication skills was useful in designing positive behavioral support interventions.

FUNCTIONAL BEHAVIORAL ASSESSMENT SCREENING FORM (FBASF)

Name _____ Date of birth _____ Grade _____

School/program _____ Date form completed _____

Person(s) completing this form _____

Behavioral Strengths: Identify and briefly describe adaptive behaviors, skills, and characteristics that are functional and appropriate.

1. _____

2. _____

3. _____

4. _____

5. _____

Interfering Behaviors: Identify and describe priority problem behaviors.

1. _____

2. _____

3. _____

4. _____

5. _____

Survey of Reinforcers: Describe events, activities, objects, people, foods, situations, or stimuli that appear to be preferred by this person.

1. _____

2. _____

3. _____

4. _____

5. _____

Communication Skills: Describe the primary methods the person uses to communicate (e.g., speech, signs, gestures, symbols, electronic devices).

_____

_____

_____

_____

_____

FIGURE 7.2. Blank Functional Behavioral Assessment Screening Form (FBASF).

FUNCTIONAL BEHAVIORAL ASSESSMENT SCREENING FORM (FBASF)

Name _Sandy_   Date of birth _5-15-1992_   Grade _10_

School/program _Sabre Island_   Date form completed _5-15-08_

Person(s) completing this form _John Halyard, School Psychologist_

Behavioral Strengths: Identify and briefly describe adaptive behaviors, skills, and characteristics that are functional and appropriate.

1. _initiaes social interactions with classmates_
2. _independent in all aspects of personal care_
3. _good sense of humor_
4. _math skills_
5. _peer relationships_

Interfering Behaviors: Identify and describe priority problem behaviors.

1. _verbal aggression (e.g., swears, screams, argues with teachers)_
2. _opposition (e.g., verbal refusal to complete tasks/assignments)_
3. _withdrawal (e.g., avoiding eye contact, refusing to respond, "sulking")_
4. _____
5. _____

Survey of Reinforcers: Describe events, activities, objects, people, foods, situations, or stimuli that appear to be preferred by this person.

1. _food (e.g., snacks, soda, gum)_
2. _sports (e.g., gym class, Special Olympics)_
3. _activities (e.g., movies, computer games, math games)_
4. _social interactions with classmates_
5. _____

Communication Skills: Describe the primary methods the person uses to communicate (e.g., speech, signs, gestures, symbols, electronic devices).

Sandy communicates with verbal speech. His receptive language skills appear to be much stronger than his
expressive language skills.

_____
_____
_____
_____

FIGURE 7.3. Example of a completed FBASF.

The Behavioral Stream Interview

Another form of interview involves identifying contextual variables associated with interfering behaviors. We refer to this type of interview as the Behavioral Stream Interview (BSI). This type of interview is based on the notion that there are many variables, among them antecedent, individual, and consequence variables, in the student's environment that impact challenging behavior and that these variables interact in some predictable manner. Moreover, these variables are not stagnant. The ongoing flow of behavior and related stimuli are comparable to a river—sometimes a stream that gently meanders through a meadow, and at other times a raging torrent rushing through mountainous canyons. The BSI helps to identify these patterns by determining the sequence in which the variables occur. Unlike a *photograph* in which we take a snapshot of a singular antecedent–behavior–consequence interaction (A-B-C), the BSI is similar to a *video* in which the entire sequence of events is captured.

> Consider the image of a single photograph of a canoeist paddling through a Class III rapids versus a 5-minute video of the same situation and you will understand the difference between a simple A-B-C analysis and a BSI.

Example of a Behavioral Stream Interview

In this case example of a BSI, the psychologist has worked with Bob for a number of years and is very familiar with his history, medical status, and the programming offered within the residential program.

PSYCHOLOGIST: Thanks for taking time out of your busy schedules to meet to discuss Bob. I understand that recently Bob has been displaying an increase in the frequency, intensity, and duration of aggressive behaviors. I've known Bob for several years, and it appears that there has been a marked increase in aggressive behaviors over the past few weeks. Could you briefly describe these behaviors?

ADMINISTRATOR: Sure . . . he has exhibited several occurrences of aggressive behavior.

PSYCHOLOGIST: Could you give me an example of what you mean by "aggressive behavior"?

ADMINISTRATOR: Well . . . his aggressive behavior involves the following: striking others with his fist, pushing others, and striking others with his forearm.

PSYCHOLOGIST: Are there any other forms of aggressive behavior?

ADMINISTRATOR: No . . . that's pretty much it.

PSYCHOLOGIST: I would like to review two to three recent examples of aggressive behavior with you and your staff. It will be helpful to interview the folks who have been working directly with Bob when these incidents occurred. The purpose of this interview is to gather as much information not only about the aggressive behavior but also about the variables that trigger and reinforce the behavior. My goal here is to evaluate Bob, not to evaluate the staff. But we all know that Bob's behavior is influenced by the environment in which he lives, so we need to look at the larger picture. As part of that assessment, one of the things I have found to be very useful is to conduct an interview called a Behavioral Stream Interview. I will be using this form [a copy of the form is then provided to each member of the team] to write down the critical variables that occurred during these incidents of aggressive behavior. This information will be very useful for us in determining why Bob has been displaying such high rates of severe aggression over the past few weeks. Does anyone have any questions before we begin?

ADMINISTRATOR: No . . . let's get started. . . . This looks like an interesting process that will lead to more effective interventions and supports for Bob.

PSYCHOLOGIST: That's the plan. . . . Let's start with a recent incidence of aggressive behavior. . . . Tell me what happened.

ADMINISTRATOR: Well, it happened out of the blue. Bob was having a really great day . . . and just before dinner . . . around 5:45 P.M. he hit Jeff [a staff member] on the back. This resulted in a 48-minute, three-person restraint.

PSYCHOLOGIST: Let's back up. . . . What was going on before the incidence of aggression? . . . What were the activities and interactions that occurred prior to the aggressive incident?

JEFF: Bob and I were outside playing pass with a football. He really likes to throw the ball around. . . . Sandy [another staff person] came to the backdoor and yelled, "It's time for dinner." I told Bob that we needed to go inside and wash our hands before dinner. That's when he hit me.

PSYCHOLOGIST: Did anything else happen before he hit you. Think back to that situation. . . . After you prompted Bob to go inside to wash hands before dinner, did anything else happen?

JEFF: Yes, now that I think of it . . . yeah . . . I told Bob that we needed to stop playing pass with the football. . . . He threw the ball over the fence into the neighbor's yard. I said, "We will have to get the ball after supper" and I put my arm on his shoulder and said "It's time for dinner. We need to go in and wash our hands." That's when he hit me.

PSYCHOLOGIST: Describe how he hit you.

JEFF: He screamed "AHHHH" and with his closed fist he used a chopping motion to hit me two to three times on the arm and chest areas. It wasn't very hard, but it met the criteria of aggressive behavior.

PSYCHOLOGIST: What did you do next?

JEFF: I followed the behavioral support protocol and first delivered a verbal reprimand—"Bob, no hitting"—and that's when he hit me again. . . . This time three to four times and much harder. That's when I began to use protective emergency restraints. . . . Within less than a minute Sandy and Jorge arrived and the three of us used the emergency restraint procedure. The entire restraint lasted 48 minutes.

In this example, it is clear that the aggressive behavior did not occur "out of the blue." In fact, behavior never occurs out of the blue, or randomly. It is caused by an interaction of antecedent–individual–consequence variables. We could hypothesize that the functions of Bob's aggressive behaviors were as follows:

- Positive reinforcement (i.e., Bob's interest in continuing to play with the football).
- Negative reinforcement (i.e., Bob's avoidance of washing his hands).
- Negative reinforcement (i.e., withdrawal from tactile contact and/or social disapproval).

When one is conducting an FBA, it is important not only to consider each of these variables but also to take into account the *stream* of antecedent, individual, and consequence variables that constitute a "behavioral incident."

For example, with a typical A-B-C assessment, upon the occurrence of interfering behavior the observer is expected to record the interfering behavior and the relevant immediate antecedent and consequence variables. Oftentimes, observers identify the one immediate antecedent and the one immediate consequence that occurred within a behavioral incident. Consider the following example in which a high school student displayed aggressive behavior toward a teacher within a classroom setting. The observer used an A-B-C interview procedure to record the following :

Antecedent	Behavior	Consequence
Teacher requested John to sit down and to be quiet.	John shoved the teacher.	Verbal reprimand; John was directed to the principal's office.

In this case, a singular A-B-C recording did not fully capture all of the relevant variables associated with this behavioral incident. In fact, there were several additional incidents that preceded this recording. When a series of behavioral incidents occur, it is our experience that observers often verbally report and/or record the final incident. In these cases, the observer is reporting only a small section of what we refer to as the "behavioral stream."

A behavioral stream involves the occurrence of a series of behavioral incidents—the unfolding of interrelated variables that constitute the continuous flow of antecedent, individual, interfering, and consequence variables. Indeed, when we consider a single A-B-C analysis, the behavioral incident appears to have a discrete beginning and end. However, the analysis of the flow of behavior and contextual variables provides a much richer and more comprehensive understanding of behavior. One also needs to consider that, when analyzing the stream of behavior, a variable that operates as a consequence for one behavior is an antecedent for a subsequent behavior. For example, consider the case in which a child exhibits interfering behavior within the home setting. In this example, the consequence of social attention (e.g., a verbal reprimand) delivered by the parent also served as the antecedent for a subsequent behavior (e.g., verbal opposition). Although one strategy might involve teaching observers and recorders to record each occurrence of interfering behavior and the relevant antecedent and consequence variables (i.e., a simple A-B-C), we have found it to be more informative and easier for the observers to record behavior using the following behavioral stream format.

Example of Behavioral Stream Recording

This example involves an elementary student diagnosed with emotional/behavioral disorders who displays a set of behaviors referred to as "tantrum behavior." *Tantrum behavior* is defined as a response set including two or more of the following: verbal opposition, swearing, screaming, and throwing or damaging materials. An incident of tantrum behavior was recorded using an A-B-C analysis as follows:

Antecedent	Behavior	Consequence
Teacher prompted Seth to participate in assigned task.	Seth exhibited tantrum behavior.	Seth was sent to time-out area for 5 minutes.

The behavioral stream recording of the same incident looked like this:

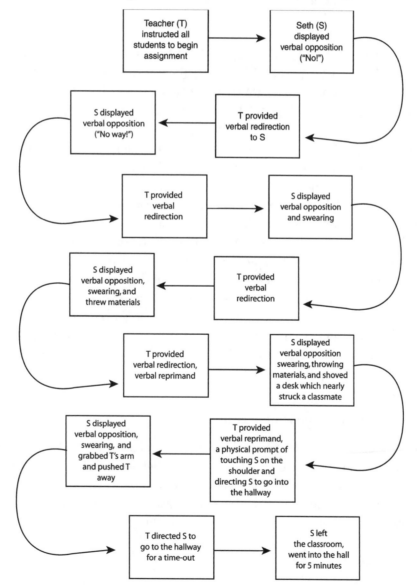

When one is conducting behavioral stream recording, it is not necessary to label stimuli or variables as antecedents or consequences while completing the recording. Instead, the focus is on describing the sequence of behaviors as the behavioral incident unfolds. It really is a matter of recording from a "he said/he did"—"she said/she did" perspective. Review and analysis of the behavioral stream recordings involves the identification of relevant triggers for problem behavior and the maintaining consequences. In the previous example, the A-B-C recording provided only a snapshot of what was otherwise a much more complicated scenario. The BSI captured the larger picture and provided details that allow for a more comprehensive understanding of the behavioral incident.

An additional advantage of using BSIs is that they are easily incorporated into the assessment report. Using the format in the written report and when describing the results of the observation allows others to see the complex relationships among a host of variables. As a result, more effective and efficient interventions can be designed.

CONSIDERATIONS WHEN EVALUATORS ARE USING THE ANTECEDENT VARIABLES ASSESSMENT FORM, THE INDIVIDUAL VARIABLES ASSESSMENT FORM, AND THE CONSEQUENCE VARIABLES ASSESSMENT FORM

The AVAF, IVAF, and CVAF procedures include a wide range of variables that have been found to trigger and reinforce interfering behaviors. Unlike a checklist where relevant variables are only identified, these procedures are designed to both *identify* relevant variables and to *describe* how those events serve to trigger or reinforce the interfering behaviors. When one is using these forms regarding the behavior of a specific individual, it is unlikely that all of the variables listed on the forms will be identified as contributing to the occurrence of interfering behaviors. In many cases, only a few variables will be identified. In cases where multiple interfering behaviors have been identified with one person, sequential review of potentially relevant antecedents on a "behavior-by-behavior" basis is recommended. In other words, we recommend using a new form for the assessment of each interfering behavior. For example, with an individual who displays aggressive, oppositional, and tantrum behaviors, we would recommend using a separate AVAF, IVAF, and CVAF recording sheet for the assessment of each behavior.

The Antecedent Variables Assessment Form

The AVAF is a recording form that is used in the initial stages of the FBA process. The AVAF is used to identify and describe the variables that set the occasion for, or "trigger," interfering behavior. The AVAF contains items across four variables that are typically related to interfering behavior in schools as well as one item prompting the evaluator to identify possible response chains. The four variables included on the AVAF are:

- Environmental
- Instructional

- Social
- Transition

Although there are other antecedent variables that may be related to interfering behavior, these are the ones most typically found in a school-based setting. Figure 7.4 is a copy of a blank AVAF, and Figure 7.5 includes an example of a completed AVAF.

The Individual Variables Assessment Form

The IVAF is a recording form that is used during the initial phase of the FBA process. The IVAF is used to identify and describe those individual variables (i.e., mediating and behavior deficits) that are associated with the occurrence of interfering behavior. Like the AVAF, the IVAF contains those individual variables that are most typically associated with interfering behavior. Therefore, there are undoubtedly other individual variables not accounted for by this form. Figure 7.6 is a copy of a blank IVAF, and Figure 7.7 is an example of a completed IVAF.

The Consequence Variables Assessment Form

The CVAF is also a recording form that is used during the initial stages of the FBA process. The CVAF is used to identify and describe those variables that typically follow the occurrence of interfering behaviors. The CVAF includes a set of supplementary questions that may be used to further clarify relationships between specific consequences and interfering behaviors. Figure 7.8 is a copy of a blank CVAF, and Figure 7.9 is an example of a completed CVAF.

Examples of the Use of the Antecedent Variables Assessment Form, the Individual Variables Assessment Form, and the Consequence Variables Assessment Form

Figures 7.5, 7.7, and 7.9 illustrate the application of the AVAF, IVAF, and CVAF during the FBA of a single interfering behavior. The student was a sophomore in high school who was referred for psychological evaluation, including an FBA, to address disruptive behaviors occurring within the school setting. This was the first time that this student had been brought to the attention of the SAT. The priority interfering behavior was "inappropriate verbal behavior." The behavior was defined as swearing (e.g., "F_____ you!" "Go to hell!") and/or name calling (e.g., "idiot," "bitch," "moron"). Because the classroom teacher was not experienced in conducting FBAs and was unfamiliar with these assessment forms, the school practitioner decided to use the AVAF, IVAF, and CVAF procedures as part of her semistructured interview. Because this behavior was reported to occur at the highest rates during English and geometry classes, the school practitioner arranged an interview simultaneously with both teachers. To assist with both interviewees' comprehension of the assessment items, blank copies of the forms were given to the teachers during the interviews.

(text continues on page 122)

ANTECEDENT VARIABLES ASSESSMENT FORM (AVAF)

Name _____ Date of birth _____ Grade _____

School/program _____ Date form completed _____

Person(s) completing this form _____

Interfering behavior _____

Environmental Variables: Briefly describe how the following variables trigger the occurrence of the interfering behavior.

Auditory stimulation (i.e., noise level) _____

_____

Visual stimulation _____

_____

Room arrangement _____

_____

Specific settings _____

_____

Time of day _____

_____

Instructional Variables: Briefly describe how the following variables trigger the occurrence of the interfering behavior.

Specific tasks/activities _____

_____

Task difficulty _____

_____

Errors or mistakes in responding _____

_____

Insufficient or inconsistent reinforcement _____

_____

Tasks not meaningful _____

_____

Pace of instruction (too fast or too slow) _____

_____

Lack of choice in tasks or activities _____

_____

Large-group instruction _____

_____

Independent seat work _____

_____

Cooperative learning or small-group tasks _____

_____

(continued)

FIGURE 7.4. Blank Antecedent Variables Assessment Form (AVAF).

ANTECEDENT VARIABLES ASSESSMENT FORM (AVAF)
(page 2 of 2)

Sequence of tasks/activities _____

_____

Correction or instruction following mistake(s)/error(s) _____

_____

Social Variables: Briefly describe how the following variables trigger the occurrence of the interfering behavior.

Specific people present _____

_____

Number of people present _____

_____

Proximity of others _____

_____

Interfering behavior of others _____

_____

Transition Variables: Briefly describe how the following variables trigger the occurrence of the interfering behavior.

Transitions to tasks/activities _____

_____

Transitions from tasks/activities _____

_____

Change in routine/schedule _____

_____

Change of staff/caregivers _____

_____

Transportation to or from school (e.g., bus, walking, car with friends) _____

_____

Interfering bahaviors often occur in a cluster or as part of a response chain. List and briefly describe those interfering behaviors that occur prior to and simultaneous with the priority interfering behavior.

Prior to _____

_____

Simultaneous with _____

_____

ANTECEDENT VARIABLES ASSESSMENT FORM (AVAF)

Name <u>Robert</u>   Date of birth <u>11-15-92</u>   Grade <u>10</u>

School/program <u>Oceanview High School</u>   Date form completed <u>11-17-08</u>

Person(s) completing this form <u>Pam Seacraft (School Psychologist)</u>

Interfering behavior <u>Inappropriate verbal behavior</u>

Environmental Variables: Briefly describe how the following variables trigger the occurrence of the interfering behavior.

Auditory stimulation (i.e., noise level) <u>N/A</u>

Visual stimulation <u>N/A</u>

Room arrangement <u>N/A</u>

Specific settings <u>English and Geometry classes</u>

Time of day <u>9:50 A.M. (English)   1 P.M. (Geometry)</u>

Instructional Variables: Briefly describe how the following variables trigger the occurrence of the interfering behavior.

Specific tasks/activities <u>N/A</u>

Task difficulty <u>N/A</u>

Errors or mistakes in responding <u>N/A</u>

Insufficient or inconsistent reinforcement <u>N/A</u>

Tasks not meaningful <u>N/A</u>

Pace of instruction (too fast or too slow) <u>N/A</u>

Lack of choice in tasks or activities <u>N/A</u>

Large-group instruction <u>Yes, especially if this involves interactions or cooperative work with classmates.</u>

Independent seat work <u>N/A</u>

Cooperative learning or small-group tasks <u>Yes! inappropriate verbal behaviors with peers.</u>

(continued)

FIGURE 7.5. Example of a completed AVAF.

ANTECEDENT VARIABLES ASSESSMENT FORM (AVAF)
(page 2 of 2)

Sequence of tasks/activities N/A

Correction or instruction following mistake(s)/error(s) N/A

Social Variables: Briefly describe how the following variables trigger the occurrence of the interfering behavior.

Specific people present specific classmates (i.e., Tom B., Pedro M., Drew P., Manny R., and Nomar G.)

Number of people present yes, especially when in a crowd, or unstructured situation

Proximity of others yes, when in a crowd and others are very close to Robert

Interfering behavior of others yes, if other students shout or swear at Robert

Transition Variables: Briefly describe how the following variables trigger the occurrence of the interfering behavior.

Transitions to tasks/activities yes. hallways; entering classes; between structured tasks or activities in
class

Transitions from tasks/activities yes. hallways; leaving classes

Change in routine/schedule N/A

Change of staff/caregivers N/A

Transportation to or from school (e.g., bus, walking, car with friends) not reported

Interfering bahaviors often occur in a cluster or as part of a response chain. List and briefly describe those interfering behaviors that occur prior to and simultaneous with the priority interfering behavior.

Prior to Robert often first exhibits facial tensing and agitated movements prior to engaging in
inappropriate verbal behaviors

Simultaneous with waving arms, stomping feet

INDIVIDUAL VARIABLES ASSESSMENT FORM (IVAF)

Name _____ Date of birth _____ Grade _____

School/program _____ Date form completed _____

Person(s) completing this form _____

Interfering behavior _____

Individual Variables: Briefly describe how the following variables appear to be related to the occurrence of the interfering behavior.

Receptive communication skills _____

_____

Expressive communication skills _____

_____

Academic skills _____

_____

Social skills _____

_____

Health issues (e.g., hearing, headache, bowel regularity) _____

_____

Sleep issues _____

_____

Prescribed medications _____

_____

Substance use/abuse _____

_____

Dietary issues _____

_____

Emotional states (e.g., anxiety, depression, anger) _____

_____

Cognitive skills _____

_____

Cognitive state (e.g., "thought disorders," "irrational thinking") _____

_____

Coping skills/strategies _____

_____

Personal sensitivities _____

_____

Relevant diagnoses _____

_____

Other individual variables _____

_____

FIGURE 7.6. Blank Individual Variables Assessment Form (IVAF).

INDIVIDUAL VARIABLES ASSESSMENT FORM (IVAF)

Name <u>Robert</u>   Date of birth <u>11-15-92</u>   Grade <u>10</u>

School/program <u>Oceanview High School</u>   Date form completed <u>11-17-08</u>

Person(s) completing this form <u>Pam Seacraft (School Psychologist)</u>

Interfering behavior <u>Inappropriate verbal behavior</u>

Individual Variables: Briefly describe how the following variables appear to be related to the occurrence of the interfering behavior.

Receptive communication skills <u>N/A</u>

Expressive communication skills <u>Robert has a mild speech dysfluency and a mild articulation disorder</u>

Academic skills <u>N/A</u>

Social skills <u>Robert has significant social skills delays, few friends, socially withdrawn</u>

Health issues (e.g., hearing, headache, bowel regularity) <u>N/A</u>

Sleep issues <u>N/A</u>

Prescribed medications <u>N/A</u>

Substance use/abuse <u>N/A</u>

Dietary issues <u>N/A</u>

Emotional states (e.g., anxiety, depression, anger) <u>Robert appears to be anxious when in large crowds and unstructured social situations</u>

Cognitive skills <u>N/A</u>

Cognitive state (e.g., "thought disorders," "irrational thinking") <u>N/A</u>

Coping skills/strategies <u>socially awkward; he appears to have great difficulty in initiating social interaction</u>

Personal sensitivities <u>he is sensitive to corrective feedback addressing speech difficulties</u>

Relevant diagnoses <u>NA</u>

Other individual variables <u>he seems to be interested in interacting with classmates and teachers, but lacks solid social skills; poor self-control</u>

FIGURE 7.7. Example of a completed IVAF.

CONSEQUENCE VARIABLES ASSESSMENT FORM (CVAF)

Name _____ Date of birth _____ Grade _____

School/program _____ Date form completed _____

Person(s) completing this form _____

Interfering behavior _____

The Consequence Variables Assessment Form (CVAF) is designed to identify variables that reinforce interfering behaviors.

Briefly describe situations in which interfering behavior results in:

    A. Social attention from teachers/staff: _____

    B. Social attention from classmates/peers: _____

    C. The individual obtaining objects: _____

    D. The individual obtaining activities: _____

Briefly describe situations in which interfering behavior results in the cessation of, withdrawal from, and/or avoidance of:

    A. Tasks or assignments: _____

    B. Activities: _____

    C. Settings: _____

    D. Social interactions (teachers/staff): _____

    E. Social interactions (classmates/peers): _____

Briefly describe those behaviors that appear to result in sensory consequences:

    A. Arousal induction (i.e., increases sensory stimulation): _____

        _____

    B. Arousal reduction (i.e., decreases sensory stimulation): _____

        _____

Briefly describe the following parameters of reinforcement:

    A. Schedule: _____

        _____

    B. Quality: _____

        _____

    C. Magnitude: _____

        _____

    D. Timing: _____

        _____

(continued)

FIGURE 7.8. Blank Consequence Variables Assessment Form (CVAF).

The Consequence Variables Assessment Form (CVAF) is designed to identify variables that reinforce interfering behaviors. The following questions may be used during an interview to elicit information regarding the motivating functions of interfering behaviors. This is especially helpful when one is attempting to "tease out" the variables that are reinforcing the problem behavior. Following is a list of questions that are matched to possible functions of interfering behaviors.

Positive Reinforcement Function

Positive Reinforcement: Social Attention (Teachers/Staff)

When the interfering behavior occurs, do teachers/staff give verbal or visual feedback, or respond in some way?

Does interfering behavior occur when the individual is not receiving attention from teachers/staff but a classmate/peer (or classmates/peers) is receiving attention?

When the interfering behavior occurs, do teachers/staff provide immediate attention to the individual?

Positive Reinforcement: Social Attention (Classmates/Peers)

When the interfering behavior occurs, do classmates/peers give verbal or visual feedback, or respond in some way?

Does interfering behavior occur when the individual is not receiving attention from classmates/peers but another classmate/peer (or classmates/peers) is receiving attention?

When the interfering behavior occurs, do classmates/peers provide immediate attention to the individual?

Positive Reinforcement (Objects):

Is the interfering likely to occur when the individual is told that he/she cannot have access to a preferred item?

Does the occurrence of interfering behavior result in the individual obtaining a preferred object?

Positive Reinforcement (Activity):

Is the interfering behavior more likely to occur when the individual is told that he/she cannot participate in a preferred activity?

Does the interfering behavior occur when the individual is told that a preferred activity is nearing completion or is finished?

Does the occurrence of interfering behavior result in the individual participating in a preferred activity?

Negative Reinforcement Function

Negative Reinforcement (Tasks/Assignments):

Does the interfering behavior occur when you request the individual to participate in a task/assignment that he/she has opposed (e.g., nonpreferred or difficult task/assignment)?

Does the interfering behavior occur when the individual is told that a nonpreferred or difficult instructional task/assignment will continue?

Negative Reinforcement (Activity):

Does the interfering behavior occur when you request the individual to participate in an activity that he/she has opposed (e.g., nonpreferred activity)?

Does the interfering behavior occur when the individual is told that a nonpreferred activity will continue?

Negative Reinforcement (Setting):

Does the interfering behavior result in the individual leaving (asking or being asked to leave) a setting that the individual finds uncomfortable (e.g., too loud, hot/cold, excess stimuli)?

(continued)

When the interfering behavior occurs, do teachers/staff/classmates/peers attempt to modify the environment (i.e., reduce environmental stimulation)?

Negative Reinforcement (Social: Teachers/Staff)

Does the interfering behavior result in the avoidance or termination of social interactions with teachers/staff?

When the interfering behavior occurs, do teachers/staff stop providing attention to the individual?

Negative Reinforcement (Social: Classmates/Peers)

Does the interfering behavior result in the avoidance or termination of social interactions with classmates/peers?

When the interfering behavior occurs, do classmates/peers stop providing attention to the individual?

Automatic Reinforcement

Arousal Induction

Does the interfering behavior appear to result in sensory input that the individual enjoys?

When the interfering behavior occurs, does the behavior appear to result in sensory consequences (e.g., visual, auditory, tactile) that are "self-stimulating"?

Arousal Reduction

Does the interfering behavior appear to result in the reduction of internal states of arousal (e.g., "venting")?

When the interfering behavior occurs does the individual appear to be agitated/frustrated?

When the interfering behavior occurs, does the behavior appear to result in sensory consequences that result in the release of "tension," "anxiety," and/or "frustration"?

Parameters of Reinforcement

Schedule of Reinforcement

Is the reinforcement continuous?

Is the reinforcement intermittent?

What is the rate of reinforcement?

Quality of Reinforcement

Does the individual value the reinforcer?

If you were to place several items in front of the individual, which ones would he/she reach for first?

If you take away the item or stop the activity would the individual try to regain the item or reestablish the activity?

If you take away the item or stop the activity would the individual exhibit interfering behavior to regain the item or reestablish the activity?

Does the individual request the item or activity?

Magnitude of Reinforcement

How much of a given reinforcer is provided?

How long does the individual have access to the reinforcer?

Estimate the intensity of the reinforcer.

Timing of Reinforcement

Is the reinforcer provided immediately after the behavior occurs?

Is there a delay between the occurrence of the interfering behavior and the delivery of the reinforcer? If so, how long is this delay?

CONSEQUENCE VARIABLES ASSESSMENT FORM (CVAF)

Name <u>Robert</u>   Date of Birth <u>11-15-92</u>   Grade <u>10</u>

School/program <u>Oceanview High School</u>   Date form completed <u>11-17-08</u>

Person(s) completing this form <u>Pam Seacraft (School Psychologist)</u>

Interfering behavior <u>Inappropriate verbal behavior</u>

The Consequence Variables Assessment Form (CVAF) is designed to identify variables that reinforce interfering behaviors.

Briefly describe situations in which interfering behavior results in:
- A. Social attention from teachers/staff: <u>teacher verbal reprimands</u>
- B. Social attention from classmates/peers: <u>laughs, argues, stares</u>
- C. The individual obtaining objects: <u>N/A</u>
- D. The individual obtaining activities: <u>N/A</u>

Briefly describe situations in which interfering behavior results in the cessation of, withdrawal from, and/or avoidance of:
- A. Tasks or assignments: <u>N/A</u>
- B. Activities: <u>N/A</u>
- C. Settings: <u>N/A</u>
- D. Social Interactions (Teachers/Staff): <u>N/A</u>
- E. Social Interactions (Classmates/Peers): <u>N/A</u>

Briefly describe those behaviors that appear to result in sensory consequences:
- A. Arousal induction (i.e., increases sensory stimulation): <u>N/A</u>
- B. Arousal reduction (i.e., decreases sensory stimulation): <u>N/A</u>

Briefly describe the following parameters of reinforcement:
- A. Schedule: <u>FR1 to VR3</u>
- B. Quality: <u>highly preferred peers; moderately preferred teacher</u>
- C. Magnitude: <u>brief duration, few comments/reactions</u>
- D. Timing: <u>almost immediate</u>

FIGURE 7.9. Example of a completed CVAF.

Review of the completed forms indicated that only a few relevant antecedent, individual, and consequence variables were identified. Based on the results of these assessments, it was hypothesized that inappropriate verbal behavior typically occurred during unstructured classroom situations, was related to the student's delays in social and self-control skills, and was maintained by social attention from classmates and by the reactions of the classroom teacher. These results suggested that the interfering behaviors were motivated by positive reinforcement (i.e., social attention from classmates and teachers). To further evaluate inappropriate verbal behavior, the school practitioner scheduled direct observations within each of classes and instructed the two teachers in the use of the Functional Behavioral Assessment Observation Form (see Chapter 8).

THE FUNCTIONAL ASSESSMENT INFORMANT RECORD FOR TEACHERS

The FAIR-T (Edwards, 2002) is a teacher-completed record form that is designed for assessing interfering behaviors for the purpose of developing hypotheses about functional relationships between interfering behaviors displayed by students within general education classrooms and environmental events occurring in those settings. The FAIR-T allows educators to gather information about problem behavior, antecedents, maintaining functions, and previously implemented interventions.

The FAIR-T consists of four sections:

- General referral information
- Problem behaviors
- Antecedents
- Consequences

In describing the uses of the FAIR-T, Edwards (2002) stressed that the FAIR-T, by itself, is not intended to generate sufficient information to develop hypotheses about the function of interfering behaviors and stresses that a follow-up interview is the key to the successful use of the FAIR-T. For example, if academic delays are identified, additional assessments (e.g., curriculum-based measures) are indicated. If interfering behavior is identified within the context of specific settings, then follow-up interviews need to explore the specific variables within those settings that trigger interfering behaviors. Edwards (2002) also recommends that hypotheses regarding the function of interfering behaviors generated from the information provided by the FAIR-T could be further evaluated through direct observation. A copy of the FAIR-T is reproduced in Figure 7.10.

(text continues on page 127)

FUNCTIONAL ASSESSMENT INFORMANT RECORD FOR TEACHERS

If information is being provided by both the teacher and the classroom aide, indicate both respondents' names. In addition, in instances where divergent information is provided, note the sources of specific information.

Student _____   Respondent(s) _____

School _____   Age: _____   Sex: M   F   Date: _____

1. Describe the referred student. What is he/she like in the classroom? (Write down what you believe is the most important information about the referred student.)

_____

_____

_____

_____

2. Pick a second student of the same sex who is also difficult to teach. What makes the referred student more difficult than the second student?

_____

_____

_____

_____

3. a. On what grade level is the student reading?   _____
   b. On what grade level is an average student in the class reading?   _____
4. a. On what grade level is the student performing in math?   _____
   b. On what grade level is an average student in the class performing in math?   _____
5. a. What is the student's classwork completion percentage (0–100%)?   _____
   b. What is the student's classwork accuracy percentage (0–100%)?   _____

6. Is the student taking any medications that might affect the student's behavior?
   _____ Yes   _____ No   If yes, briefly explain:

_____

_____

7. Do you have any specific health concerns regarding this student?
   _____ Yes   _____ No   If yes, briefly explain:

_____

_____

8. What procedures have you tried in the past to deal with this student's problem behavior?

_____

_____

(continued)

FIGURE 7.10. Functional Assessment Informant Record for Teachers (FAIR-T). From Edwards (2002). Copyright 2002 by Sopris West, Inc. Reprinted by permission of Rowman and Littlefield.

9. Briefly list below the student's typical daily schedule of activities.

Time	Activity	Time	Activity
___	_____	___	_____
___	_____	___	_____
___	_____	___	_____
___	_____	___	_____
___	_____	___	_____
___	_____	___	_____
___	_____	___	_____
___	_____	___	_____
___	_____	___	_____
___	_____	___	_____
___	_____	___	_____

10. When during the day (two academic *activities* and *times*) does the student's problem behavior(s) typically occur?

Academic Activity #1 _____ Time _____

Academic Activity #2 _____ Time _____

11. Please indicate *good days* and *times* to observe. (At least two observations are needed.)

Observation #1   Observation #2   Observation #3 (Backup)
Date _____   Date _____   Date _____
Time _____   Time _____   Time _____

Problem Behaviors

Please list one to three problem behaviors in order of severity. Do not use a general description such as "disruptive" but give the actual behavior such as "doesn't stay in his/her seat" or "talks out without permission."

1. _____

_____

2. _____

_____

3. _____

_____

1. Rate how *manageable* the behavior is:

   a. Problem Behavior 1
1	2	3	4	5
Unmanageable			Manageable	

   b. Problem Behavior 2
1	2	3	4	5
Unmanageable			Manageable	

   c. Problem Behavior 3
1	2	3	4	5
Unmanageable			Manageable	

2. Rate how *disruptive* the behavior is:

   a. Problem Behavior 1
1	2	3	4	5
Mildly				Very

   b. Problem Behavior 2
1	2	3	4	5
Mildly				Very

   c. Problem Behavior 3
1	2	3	4	5
Mildly				Very

(continued)

124

3. How often does the behavior occur *per day* (please circle)?

   a. Problem Behavior 1   <1–3   4–6   7–9   10–12   ≥13

   b. Problem Behavior 2   <1–3   4–6   7–9   10–12   ≥13

   c. Problem Behavior 3   <1–3   4–6   7–9   10–12   ≥13

4. How many *months* has the behavior been present?

   a. Problem Behavior 1   < 1   2   3   4   entire school year

   b. Problem Behavior 2   < 1   2   3   4   entire school year

   c. Problem Behavior 3   < 1   2   3   4   entire school year

Antecedents: Problem Behavior #_____:_____

	Yes	No
1. Does the behavior occur more often during a certain *type* of task?	_____	_____
2. Does the behavior occur more often during *easy* tasks?	_____	_____
3. Does the behavior occur more often during *difficult* tasks?	_____	_____
4. Does the behavior occur more often during *certain subject areas?*	_____	_____
5. Does the behavior occur more often during *new* subject material?	_____	_____
6. Does the behavior occur more often when a request is made to *stop* an activity?	_____	_____
7. Does the behavior occur more often when a request is made to *begin a new activity?*	_____	_____
8. Does the behavior occur more often during *transition* periods?	_____	_____
9. Does the behavior occur more often when a *disruption* occurs in the student's normal routine?	_____	_____
10. Does the behavior occur more often when the student's *request has been denied?*	_____	_____
11. Does the behavior occur more often when a *specific person is in the room?*	_____	_____
12. Does the behavior occur more often when a *specific person is absent from the room?*	_____	_____
13. Are there any other behaviors that usually *precede* the problem behavior?	_____	_____
14. Is there anything you could do that would *ensure* the occurrence of the behavior?	_____	_____
15. Are there any events occurring in the child's *home* that seem to precede occurrence of the behavior at school?	_____	_____
16. Does the behavior occur more often in *certain settings?* (circle all that apply)	_____	_____

large group   small group   independent work   one-to-one interaction

bathroom   recess   cafeteria   bus

other: _____

(continued)

FUNCTIONAL ASSESSMENT INFORMANT RECORD FOR TEACHERS
(page 4 of 4)

Consequences: Problem Behavior #____:_____

1. Please indicate whether the following consequences occur after the behavior is exhibited.

Consequence	Yes	No
Access to preferred activity	_____	_____
Termination of task	_____	_____
Rewards	_____	_____
Peer attention	_____	_____
Teacher attention	_____	_____
Praise	_____	_____
Ignore	_____	_____
Redirection	_____	_____
Interrupt	_____	_____
Reprimand	_____	_____

2. Is there any task you have stopped presenting to the student as a result of the problem behavior?

    _____ Yes   _____ No   If yes, describe:

    _____

    _____

3. Are there other problem behaviors that often occur after the behavior is exhibited?

    _____ Yes   _____ No   If yes, describe:

    _____

    _____

4. Does the student typically receive praise or any positive consequence when behavior occurs that you would like to see instead of the problem behavior?

    _____ Yes   _____ No

    Comments: _____

SUMMARY

The temptation to rely solely on indirect FBA procedures is alluring. After all, indirect FBA procedures are relatively efficient and cost-effective methods of conducting an FBA. One needs to keep in mind, however, that simply filling out a form that is titled "functional behavioral assessment" does not necessarily constitute an adequate FBA and in many cases is not a best practices assessment approach. A poorly designed indirect FBA form and/or a loosely conducted interview will very likely result in inaccurate assessment results, faulty hypotheses, and ineffective interventions.

In this chapter we described several formal indirect FBA procedures. It has also been our experience that there are some cases in which the results of indirect FBA are in and of themselves sufficient for assessing and understanding behavioral function. In these cases, practitioners could consider first conducting a formal indirect FBA as described in this chapter. If the results of the indirect FBA are consistent and make sense, then additional assessments may not be indicated. The assessment results are then used in designing functional-based interventions. The intervention is implemented and evaluated, and if the intervention proves to be successful, then the assessment process has been validated. More importantly, the intervention has been successful! On a practical level, a *successful* intervention is more important than a *valid* assessment! If, on the other hand, the results of the indirect FBA are suspect or inconsistent across assessment tools, then additional assessments are recommended. The following chapters provide descriptions of direct observation procedures that are used to further assess interfering behaviors.

8

Direct Descriptive Functional Behavioral Assessment

All science is concerned with the relationship of cause and effect. Each scientific discovery increases man's ability to predict the consequences of his actions and thus his ability to control future events.
—Laurence J. Peter

Direct descriptive FBA is one of the most powerful tools in school-based FBAs. It is powerful because each of its procedures is based on direct observations of behavior in the setting and/or situations in which the target behaviors occur. Thus, hypotheses regarding function and triggers are based on systematic observations and not merely on conjecture or solely on indirect information. This chapter contains the actual forms that we use when conducting observations and a description of their use.

Direct descriptive FBA procedures involve the observation and recording of behaviors. The behavior-recording procedures described in Chapter 6 are used when the evaluator is conducting direct descriptive FBAs. It is important to keep in mind that the evaluator is attempting to observe and record behavior within the context of naturally occurring situations when he or she is conducting direct descriptive FBAs. The evaluator needs to be as unobtrusive as possible. Equally important is the selection of the data-recording procedure. The evaluator needs to make sure that the behavior-recording procedure is matched to (1) the dimensions of the behavior and (2) the resources and skills of the observer.

In many cases, observation and recording of behavior are conducted by the evaluator. However, there are situations in which this is impractical. For example, the behavior may be of a very low frequency and consequently the probability of observing the behavior during a scheduled observation is slim to none; or the presence of the observer may cause the target student to change his or her behavior in such a way that the observation session in no way represents typically occurring behavior. In these instances, the observation and recording of behavior by teachers, parents, educational technicians, or others is recommended. In fact, there may be some cases in which self-recording by the referred student is recommended.

We have found that the direct descriptive FBA procedures described in the following sections are applicable within applied settings. With these procedures, teachers and staff typically conduct observations and recordings.

THE TASK DIFFICULTY ANTECEDENT ANALYSIS FORM

This form is particularly useful in those circumstances where other information, from interviews, observations, or one of the assessment forms in the previous chapter, for instance, has indicated that the presentation of difficult tasks may be an antecedent (trigger) for the target behavior. The top portion allows the observer to note the setting in which the analysis occurs, the target behavior, and a description of the task. It is important to describe all relevant features of the task (e.g., in math, if the student is performing calculations or working word problems) so that other variables can be further analyzed if necessary. It is important to mention that this type of analysis may need to be done for each subject (reading, math, science, etc.) or type of task (writing, oral reading in a group, etc.).

Before beginning the observation, you must coordinate with the teacher to identify tasks that are easy (greater than 90% accuracy), medium (70–80% accuracy), or difficult (less than 70% accuracy). You may select tasks that fit each of these categories via examination of work samples and/or curriculum-based measurement (CBM) probes. Once the tasks that fit each category are identified, the teacher should present one of the tasks to the student during the appropriate classroom time. Ideally, one should make repeated observations of the student while counterbalancing the order of presentation of the tasks. Realizing that this is probably unrealistic for most practitioners, one should randomly select which category will be presented and for how long (a minimum is 5 minutes; a maximum might be 10 minutes or so). As soon as the task is presented, begin the 10-second interval recording. If the target behavior occurs, place some type of mark in the box (usually an ? or a ?) that corresponds to the type of task and interval number. If the target behavior does not occur, place a 0 in the corresponding box. Repeat this procedure for each of the three types of tasks. A blank Task Difficulty Antecedent Analysis Form is included in Figure 8.1. An example of a completed Task Difficulty Antecedent Analysis Form is illustrated in Figure 8.2, along with a brief description of the results.

The data in Figure 8.2 indicate that Jason was disruptive during 13% (4/30) of the intervals while reading easy passages, 23% (7/30) of the intervals while reading passages of medium difficulty, and 57% (17/30) of the intervals while reading difficult passages. If time permits, this type of observation should be conducted another time or two on a different day to determine whether these results are consistent. If similar findings emerge from another task difficulty antecedent analysis, then one might reasonably hypothesize that difficult tasks are an antecedent for Jason's disruptive behavior. Intervention, then, would focus on presenting easier tasks while simultaneously remediating reading skills. Presenting relatively easier tasks during reading also allows for the opportunity to reinforce behaviors that are alternative to or incompatible with disruption. As reading skills improve, the difficulty of the tasks might gradually be increased while continuing to reinforce behaviors other than disruption.

TASK DIFFICULTY ANTECEDENT ANALYSIS FORM

Student's name _____ School/grade _____

Setting _____ Date _____

Observer _____ Time _____

Target behavior _____

_____

Task description _____

_____

_____

_____

10-SECOND INTERVALS

	1	2	3	4	5	6	7	8	9	10	11	12	13	14	15	16	17	18	19	20
Easy (90%)																				
Medium (70–80%)																				
Difficult (<70%)																				

	1	2	3	4	5	6	7	8	9	10	11	12	13	14	15	16	17	18	19	20
Easy (90%)																					
Medium (70–80%)																					
Difficult (<70%)																					

FIGURE 8.1. Task Difficulty Antecedent Analysis Form.

TASK DIFFICULTY ANTECEDENT ANALYSIS FORM

Student's name <u>Jason Adams</u>   School/grade <u>Titusville/2nd</u>

Setting <u>Reading Class</u>   Date <u>September 19, 2008</u>

Observer <u>Steuart Watson</u>   Time <u>8:30–9:00</u>

Target behavior <u>During reading class, Jason has been disruptive by calling other students names, running</u>
<u>in the classroom, and refusing to do his work.</u>

Task description <u>Based on CBM probes, easy, medium, and difficult reading passages from his reading</u>
<u>material have been identified. During independent reading time, Jason's teacher will present him with a</u>
<u>medium passage followed by an easy and a difficult passage. Each passage will be presented for 5 minutes.</u>

10-SECOND INTERVALS

	1	2	3	4	5	6	7	8	9	10	11	12	13	14	15	16	17	18	19	20
Easy (90%)	o	o	o	o	o	o	o	x	X	o	o	o	o	o	o	o	x	o	o	o	o
Medium (70–80%)	o	o	o	x	x	o	o	o	O	o	x	o	o	x	x	x	o	o	o	o
Difficult (<70%)	o	x	x	x	o	o	x	o	X	x	o	o	x	x	o	o	x	o	o	x

	1	2	3	4	5	6	7	8	9	10	11	12	13	14	15	16	17	18	19	20
Easy (90%)	o	o	o	o	o	o	x	o	O	o										
Medium (70–80%)	x	o	o	o	x	x	o	o	o	o										
Difficult (<70%)	x	x	x	o	o	o	x	x	x	x										

FIGURE 8.2. Example of a completed Task Difficulty Antecedent Analysis Form.

THE CONDITIONAL PROBABILITY RECORD

The Conditional Probability Record (CPR) is a form that allows the observer to simultaneously observe and record the antecedents and consequences of behavior. The advantage of doing so allows for the analysis of the likelihood (probability) of a behavior given a particular antecedent and the likelihood of a particular consequence following a behavior. Figure 8.3 is a blank CPR. Figure 8.4 presents an example of a completed CPR, along with an explanation of the results.

The 5-minute excerpt in Figure 8.4, taken from the 15-minute observation period, indicates that Mitch was lying and/or rolling on the floor during 60% of the intervals. Further-

CONDITIONAL PROBABILITY RECORD (CPR)

Student _____

Date of observation _____   Observer _____

Setting _____   Time of day _____

Behavior 1 _____   Behavior 2 _____

	Antecedents			Target Behaviors		Consequences		
	Academic	Task	Teacher	Behavior 1	Behavior 2	Teacher	Peers	Academic
0:15								
0:30								
0:45								
1:00								
1:15								
1:30								
1:45								
2:00								
2:15								
2:30								
2:45								
3:00								
3:15								
3:30								
3:45								
4:00								
4:15								
4:30								
4:45								
5:00								

Any of the categories may be coded according to the observer's preferences or the data that currently exist but must remain consistent across observations. Indicate coding scheme here for each of the categories.

Codes:
Academic: Teacher:

Task: Peers:

FIGURE 8.3. Conditional Probability Record (CPR).

CONDITIONAL PROBABILITY RECORD (CPR)

Student <u>Mitch Miles</u>

Date of observation <u>3-17-08</u>   Observer <u>Steuart Watson</u>

Setting <u>Regular Classroom</u>   Time of day <u>1:15–1:30</u>

Behavior 1 <u>Lying and/or rolling on floor</u>   Behavior 2 <u>Not Applicable</u>

	Antecedents			Target Behaviors		Consequences		
	Academic	Task	Teacher	Behavior 1	Behavior 2	Teacher	Peers	Academic
0:15	R	WS	W	—	—	W	Wk	Working
0:30	R	WS	W	—	—	W	Wk	Working
0:45	R	WS	W	—	—	W	Wk	Working
1:00	R	WS	Desk	—	—	Desk	Wk	Working
1:15	R	WS	Desk	√	—	Desk	L	Work stopped
1:30	R	WS	Desk	√	—	Desk	L & R	Work stopped
1:45	R	WS	Desk	√	—	VR	Wk	Work stopped
2:00	R	WS	Desk	√	—	VR	Look	Work stopped
2:15	R	WS	PP	√	—	PG	Wk	Work stopped
2:30	R	WS	PP	√	—	PG	Wk	Work restarted
2:45	R	WS	PP	—	—	PP	Wk	Working
3:00	R	WS	PP	—	—	PP	Wk	Working
3:15	R	WS	W	—	—	W	Wk	Working
3:30	R	WS	W	√	—	W	R	Work stopped
3:45	R	WS	W	√	—	VR	Look	Work stopped
4:00	R	WS	PP	√	—	VR	Wk	Work stopped
4:15	R	WS	PP	√	—	VR	Look	Work stopped
4:30	R	WS	PP	√	—	PG	Wk	Work stopped
4:45	R	WS	PP	√	—	PG	Wk	Work stopped
5:00	R	WS	PP	—	—	PG	Wk	Work restarted

Any of the categories may be coded according to the observer's preferences or the data that currently exist but must remain consistent across observations. Indicate coding scheme here for each of the categories.

Codes:
Academic: R = Reading

Teacher: W = walking around the classroom; PP = physical proximity to target student; VR = verbal reprimand; PG = physical guidance to target student; Desk = sitting at desk

Task: WS = Worksheets

Peers: Wk = working on task; L = laughing at target student; Look = looking at target student; R = reporting behavior of target student to teacher

FIGURE 8.4. Example of a completed CPR.

more, of the intervals in which Mitch was lying/rolling on the floor, 41% of those resulted in a verbal reprimand by the teacher and 33% resulted in the teacher physically guiding Mitch back into his seat. Thus, Mitch's on-floor behavior resulted in some form of teacher attention in 74% of the intervals. Likewise, working on the assigned task resulted in no verbal or physical attention from the teacher. In only 33% of the intervals in which Mitch was working was the teacher in physical proximity to him. Thus, one hypothesis is that Mitch's on-floor behavior is maintained by teacher attention because doing so is at least twice as likely to result in some form of teacher attention than working. There may be some peer influence in the form of looking at Mitch (25% of the intervals) or laughing at him (16%), but these consequences are not as probable as teacher attention. There may also be a negative reinforcement component because Mitch is able to escape the task by lying and rolling on the floor. Given the short duration of the observation and the continuous nature of the task, analysis of the antecedents did not yield particularly helpful information in this case. Or did it? If you carefully examine the CPR, you will notice that the on-floor behavior did not initially begin until the teacher sat down at her desk after walking around the classroom. In addition, the physical proximity of the teacher was an antecedent during 50% of the intervals in which on-floor behavior occurred. Each of the antecedent and consequent possibilities are easily verified through further observation and analysis.

THE FUNCTIONAL BEHAVIORAL ASSESSMENT OBSERVATION FORM

The Functional Behavioral Assessment Observation Form (FBAOF) is an assessment procedure that involves directly observing and recording interfering behavior(s) and associated contextual variables. The FBAOF is typically used to record "behavioral episodes" or "behavioral incidents" involving a single interfering behavior. Each time that an interfering behavior occurs, the observer uses the FBAOF to record the following:

1. Date and time of day.
2. Setting events (i.e., tasks, activities, locations, etc.).
3. Antecedents (i.e., specific environmental, social, instructional, or transitional events that appear to trigger the behavior).
4. Behavior (i.e., the defined interfering behavior).
5. Consequence (i.e., the events that followed the interfering behavior).
6. Effect (i.e., change in rate/intensity of occurrence of the interfering behavior).
7. Staff (i.e., the staff person who recorded the data and/or the staff person working directly with the student).

Note: With the FBAOF the observer typically records and briefly describes the interfering behavior within the column labeled "Behavior." A variation of this method is to record both the behavior and the magnitude of the behavior (e.g., frequency, duration, intensity).

Figure 8.5 is a copy of a blank FBAOF.

FUNCTIONAL BEHAVIOR ASSESSMENT OBSERVATION FORM (FBAOF)

Setting–Antecedent–Behavior–Consequence–Effect

Student's name _____

Date/Time	Setting Events	Antecedent	Behavior	Consequence	Effect	Staff

FIGURE 8.5. Functional Behavioral Assessment Observation Form (FBAOF).

Questions for the Observer to Consider When Using the Functional Behavioral Assessment Observation Form

Date and time: What was the date and time of the incident? How long did the behavior last?

Setting events: Where did the behavior occur? What tasks/activities was the person participating in? Who was interacting with the student?

Antecedents: What were the specific events that occurred immediately prior to the interfering behavior? What were the specific events that triggered the interfering behavior?

Behavior: What did the person do?

Consequence: What happened immediately after the behavior occurred? If relevant, what did peers or staff do after the behavior occurred?

Effect: What impact did the consequence have on the magnitude of the interfering behavior (e.g., frequency, duration, intensity)?

Staff: Who observed the behavior and recorded this information?

When one is using the FBAOF, it is important to differentiate between a "setting event" and an "antecedent." The *setting event* is the general situation in which the behavior occurred. The *antecedent* is the precipitating variable (i.e., the specific event that triggered the behavior).

It is also important to recognize that with some behaviors it may be very difficult to identify the antecedent. In these cases, the trigger may not be an environmental, social, instructional, or transitional event; rather the trigger may be an internally driven (or individual) variable. In these cases, the phrase "not observed" is recorded.

Example of the Use of the Functional Behavioral Assessment Observation Form

Figure 8.6 illustrates the use of the FBAOF to assess the verbal refusal/argumentative behavior of a student with a learning disability over the span of 2 weeks. We first described verbal refusal/argumentative in behavioral terms, then asked staff to use the FBAOF each time that screaming behavior occurred. By recording the behavior and relevant contextual variables, we were able to identify events that appeared to trigger and reinforce the occurrence of verbal refusal/argumentative behaviors. Review of data sheets revealed that verbal refusal/argumentative behavior typically occurred within the contexts of academic tasks (e.g., math worksheets, writing assignments) and when the student was provided with either a task-orientation prompt (e.g., "George, you need to finish your work") or an instructional prompt (i.e., instruction explaining the tasks or to correct an error). Thus, the setting was identified as academic tasks and antecedents were identified as both instructional and task-orientation prompts. When verbal refusal/argumentation occurred, the educational technician who provided prompting responded by walking away. Thus, the consequence following verbal refusal/argumentative behavior was the termination of instructional/task-orientation prompts. This typically resulted in an immediate cessation of verbal refusal/argumentative

FUNCTIONAL BEHAVIOR ASSESSMENT OBSERVATION FORM (FBAOF)

Setting–Antecedent–Behavior–Consequence–Effect

Student's name *George Oppose*

Date/Time	Setting Events	Antecedent	Behavior	Consequence	Effect	Staff
3/29 9:50 AM	Math class independent worksheets	George was asked to complete worksheet	Verbal refusal/ argued	Ignored George and I walked away	George calmed	TH
3/29 10:02 AM	Math class independent worksheets	George was offered instructional support	Verbal refusal/ argued	Ignored George and I walked away	He calmed down	TH
3/30 9:55 AM	Math class small group	I offered to assist George with instructional support	He refused and argued with me	Redirected George back to his desk to finish his work	George swore at me, shouted, and argued	TH
3/30 9:56 AM	Math class small group	Redirected George to complete his work, task-orientation prompt	He swore, argued, and shouted at me	Ignored George and I walked away	He calmed down in about 2 minutes	TH

FIGURE 8.6. Example of a completed FBAOF.

behavior. These findings supported the hypothesis that verbal refusal/argumentative behavior was motivated by negative reinforcement (i.e., verbal refusal/argumentative behavior was "escape motivated" and resulted in the avoidance or cessation of instructional/task-orientation prompting).

THE INTERVAL RECORDING PROCEDURE

The Interval Recording Procedure (IRP) is an FBA procedure involving the direct observation and recording of interfering behavior(s) and associated contextual variables at the conclusion of prespecified intervals (usually 5, 10, or 15 minutes). The IRP is essentially a modified scatterplot assessment that goes beyond documenting the occurrence of interfering behavior within particular times of the day to:

- Identifying specific settings/activities/tasks in which interfering behavior occurs.
- Recording the magnitude of appropriate behaviors.
- Recording the magnitude of interfering behaviors.
- Identifying corelationships among appropriate and interfering behaviors.
- Identifying corelationships among different interfering behaviors.
- Identifying relationships between specific staff and both appropriate and interfering behaviors.

Designing the IRP involves the four steps discussed below.

Step 1: Designing Data-Recording Procedures

Identify interfering and appropriate behaviors.

Describe interfering and appropriate behaviors.

Identify and describe the behavior-recording procedure for each interfering and appropriate behavior (e.g., frequency, duration, intensity, and/or performance-based recording procedures).

Identify intervals (we typically use 15-minute intervals).

Identify the duration of data recording and the number of intervals (e.g., from 8:00 A.M. to 3:00 P.M.; 28 intervals).

Design the data-recording form.

Note 1: We typically include a column that corresponds with each interval in which recorders document the specific tasks/activities in which the student was engaged or in which he or she was expected to participate (i.e., scheduled, planned, or expected tasks/activities) during the interval.

Note 2: We typically include a column that corresponds with each interval in which recorders document the staff/teacher who interacted with the student during the interval.

Step 2: Staff Training

Accurate use of the IRP requires training staff/teachers to implement the procedure with precision. The data derived from implementation of the IRP are only as good as the persons who are collecting the data. If staff/teachers have never used this type of data-recording procedure, we have found the following training model to be very effective:

> Review the labels and descriptions of each target behavior.
> Review the data-recording procedures for each target behavior.
> Role-play scenarios in which staff/teachers practice recording behaviors using the IRP.
> Conduct supervised practice in the use of the IRP with the target student within naturally occurring situations.
> Establish interobserver agreement via simultaneous and independent recording using the IRP by a second observer.
> Monitor staff/teachers in their implementation of the IRP.

Step 3: Implementing the Interval Recording Procedure

Implementing the IRP requires that staff/teachers be committed to using this procedure. It is our experience that staff/teachers consistently use the IRP when they find it to be an *effective* and *efficient* process. The IRP is an effective process when it accurately records the occurrence of behaviors. It is an efficient process when it does not get in the way of providing direct services to students.

Step 4: Analyzing the Data

This is an incredibly important step. Simply collecting but not analyzing the data is comparable to:

- Going to a bookstore, searching for a compelling book, then bringing it home and never reading it.
- Building a sailboat, but never going to sea.
- Training for a marathon, but never running the race.
- Making an elaborate dinner, then not joining your friends and family during the feast. . . .

You get the idea. Obviously, we consider the analysis of data to be a critical and often rewarding part of the process.

Analyzing Antecedents Associated with Behaviors

This involves reviewing the data sheet for one specific recording period and looking for patterns of occurrence of behaviors related to:

Times of day
Specific tasks/activities
Relationships among target behaviors *within* intervals
Relationships among target behaviors *across* intervals
Staff/teachers

Analyzing Trends

This involves graphing the data collected across time (e.g., several days, weeks, or months) and looking for the increase or decrease of behavior across time. Make sure that all raw data are converted to rates (e.g., convert 18 occurrences of self-injury that occurred within 6 hours to three occurrences/hour). Graph the data and identify trends in the graphed data (e.g., increasing, decreasing).

Specific Uses of the Interval Recording Procedure

As part of a problem-solving process, we have found the IRP to be extremely valuable as a data-recording procedure that can be used prior to, during, and after the implementation of an intervention to document the effectiveness of individualized programming:

Prior to intervention—baseline (documentation of behaviors prior to intervention)
During the intervention—objective documentation of behavior change
After the intervention—objective documentation of generalization and maintenance

We also use the IRP as part of our ongoing direct descriptive FBA process. Presently, we are providing psychological consultation services to several programs that have incorporated the IRP within individualized educational programs (IEPs) and individual program plans (IPPs) with persons with disabilities. In these cases, behavioral data are recorded on an ongoing basis. We have found that analyzing previously completed IRP data-recording forms is extremely valuable as part of the FBA process.

In those cases in which one is conducting an FBA and previously recorded data are either not available (i.e., no one has collected any data) or the data collected are not helpful in identifying contextual variables (e.g., frequency data only without any connection to time of day or task/activity), we typically recommend the use of the IRP. After training staff to use the IRP, we recommend the implementation of the procedure for a sufficient amount of time to allow for:

Documentation of current levels of occurrence of behaviors
Identification of contextual variables

Note: The use of the IRP as a form of direct descriptive assessment does not preclude the use of other forms of FBA. We typically use the IRP as just one of our FBA procedures.

Figure 8.7 is a blank IRP data sheet.

INTERVAL RECORDING PROCEDURE DATA SHEET

Time	Target Behaviors																	Staff
	Recording Procedures																	
	Setting and/or Activity																	
Add each column																		
Convert to percent or rate																		

FIGURE 8.7. Interval Recording Procedure Data Sheet.

Example of the Use of the Interval Recording Procedure

The following case illustrates the use of the IRP with a student with Asperger's disorder who received special education services within a middle school program. Figure 8.8 shows the specific behaviors, their definitions, and recording procedures that were developed prior to implementing the IRP.

As you can see, seven behaviors, two appropriate and five interfering, were identified for observation and recording. *Active participation* (AP) behavior was selected as a measure of the student's overall level of engagement throughout the school day. *Initiating social interactions* (ISI) behavior was selected because this historically (i.e., baseline) occurred at very low rates. Both AP and ISI were behaviors that were targeted for improvement within the student's IEP. The remaining five interfering behaviors were identified through indirect FBA interviews and anecdotal observations.

Figure 8.9 depicts a completed IRP data sheet. These data showed that:

- AP varied throughout the school day.
- High AP was associated with low levels of interfering behavior.
- Low AP was associated with high levels of interfering behavior.
- The daily rates/percentages of the target behaviors were as shown in the tabulation.

Behaviors:	AP	Verb. Opp.	Nonverb. Opp.	Prop. Dest.	Verb.Agg.	Phys. Agg.	ISI
Rate or %	66%	4.0/hour	13.2%	1.08/hour	1.70/hour	1 = 0.48/hour 2 = 0.64/hour 3 = 0.16/hour	S = 2.77/hour C = 0.61/hour

- Interfering behaviors occurred most frequently within small group, reading, and spelling.
- Initiation of social interactions was much higher with staff than with classmates.

The IRP is typically used over a span of several days or on an ongoing basis. Reviewing the data collected over a period of time provides very valuable information in identifying contextual variables and the corelationships among variables.

COMPARING AND CONTRASTING THE FUNCTIONAL BEHAVIORAL ASSESSMENT OBSERVATION FORM AND THE INTERVAL RECORDING PROCEDURE

The FBAOF and the IRP are both examples of direct descriptive FBA procedures. There are specific advantages and disadvantages of each:

- The FBAOF is definitely more efficient. The recordings are only made when interfering behavior occurs. In contrast, the IRP is used in an ongoing basis and, as such, requires the observer to record behaviors at the conclusion of each interval.

Active Participation (AP): visual, verbal, motor on-task responding, engaged in the task activity

Recording Procedure: Performance-Based
0 = No AP
1 = 1″ to 2′ 59″ of AP
2 = 3′ to 5′ 59″ of AP
3 = 6′ to 8′ 59″ of AP
4 = 9′ to 11′ 59″ of AP
5 = 12′ to 15′ of AP

Verbal Opposition (Verb. Opp.): one or more of *verbal* refusal to: (a) participate in tasks/activities, (b) follow teacher directions, and (c) follow school rules

Recording Procedure: frequency of occurrence (record as discrete episodes when occurrences of verbal opposition are separated by 15″ of no verbal opposition)

Nonverbal Opposition (Nonverb. Opp.): one or more of laying on the floor, sitting in chair avoiding eye contact, walking away from staff when asked to (a) participate in tasks/activities, (b) follow directions, and (c) follow school rules. Note: a response latency of 30″ is typical, and nonverbal opposition is only recorded *after* 30″ of nonresponding to teacher/staff directions.

Recording Procedure: Duration (record the length of time of the occurrence of Nonverb. Opp.)

Property Destruction (Prop. Dest.): tearing, throwing, and/or damaging own or others' property.

Recording Procedure: Frequency of occurrence (record as discrete episodes when occurrences of property destruction are separated by 15″ of no occurrence of property destruction.)

Verbal Agression (Verb. Agg.): verbal threats (e.g., "I'm going to hit you.")

Recording Procedure: frequency of occurrence (record as discrete events when occurrences of verbal aggression are separated by 15″ of no verbal aggression.)

Physical Aggression (Phys. Agg.): *physical* acts involving hitting, kicking, grabbing of others; spitting on others. These behaviors typically occur as a response set and are recorded as episodes.

Recording Procedure: frequency and intensity of episodes
1 = mild (any single behavior or set of behaviors lasting less than 10 seconds)
2 = moderate (any single behavior or set of behaviors lasting *less* than 1 minute)
3 = severe (any single behavior or set of behaviors lasting *more* than 1 minute)

Initiating Social Interactions (ISI): verbal interactions directed toward teachers or classmates (e.g., initiating "Good morning," requesting help, conversations)

Recording Procedure: frequency and person (i.e., staff or classmate)
S = occurrence of initiating social interaction with teacher/staff
C = occurrence of initiating social interaction with classmate

FIGURE 8.8. Interval Recording Procedure.

INTERVAL RECORDING PROCEDURE DATA SHEET

Time	Setting and/or Activity	AP 0–5	Verbal Opp. frequency	Nonverb. Opp. duration	Prop. Dest. frequency	Verb. Agg. frequency	Phys. Agg. intensity 1, 2, 3	ISI frequency	Staff
8:30–8:45	arrival routine	5	0	0	0	0	0	s,s	MWS
8:45–9:00	breakfast	5	0	0	0	0	0	s,c	MWS
9:00–9:15	breakfast	5	0	0	0	0	0	s	MWS
9:15–9:30	small group—circle	3	III	3'30"	0	0	0	s	MWS
9:30–9:45	small group—circle	2	IIII	4'20"	0	I	0	0	MWS
9:45–10:00	Reading (DTT)*	1	II	30"	I	I	1	0	MWS
10:00–10:15	Reading (DTT)	0	II	14'30"	I	IIII	2	0	MWS
10:15–10:30	Break—snack	5	0	0	0	0	0	s	MWS
10:30–10:45	Break—ind. play	5	0	0	0	0	0	s,c,s	MWS
10:45–11:00	Math—DTT worksheets	3	I	0	I	0	1	0	MWS
11:00–11:15	Math—group	5	0	0	0	0	0	0	MWS
11:15–11:30	Math—group	5	0	0	0	0	0	0	MWS
11:30–11:45	Lunch—prep.	5	0	0	0	0	0	0	MWS
11:45–12:00	Lunch	5	0	0	0	0	0	s,c	TD
12:00–12:15	Brush teeth	5	0	0	0	0	0	s,s	TD
12:15–12:30	Recess	5	0	0	0	0	2	0	TD
12:30–12:45	Music	3	0	0	0	0	0	0	TD
12:45–1:00	Music	2	0	0	0	0	0	0	TD
1:00–1:15	Spelling worksheets	1	III	2'40"	II	III	2	0	TD
1:15–1:30	Spelling worksheets	0	II	12'00"	I	I	1	0	TD
1:30–1:45	Break—ind. play	5	0	0	0	0	0	0	TD
1:45–2:00	small group—coop play	2	II	0	I	I	0	0	TD
2:00–2:15	small group—coop play	1	0	0	0	0	2	s,c	TD
2:15–2:30	Reading (DTT)	3	I	30"	0	0	0	s,s	TD
2:30–2:45	Reading (DTT)	0	III	15'0"	0	0	3	s	TD
2:45–3:00	Prep. go home	5	0	0	0	0	0	s,s,s	TD
	Add each column	86	25	51'30"	7	11			
	Convert to percent or rate	86/130 66%	3.8/hour		1.08/hour	1.70/hour			

Phys. Agg.: #1's = 3, #2's = 4, #3's = 1

ISI: s = 2.77/hour, c = 0.61/hour

*DTT: discrete trial teaching sessions

FIGURE 8.9. Example of a completed Interval Recording Procedure Data Sheet.

- The FBAOF requires some training, but generally folks are able to use this procedure accurately following verbal explanation, written explanation, and modeling. The IRP requires much more extensive training, particularly when observers are using performance-based recording procedures.
- The FBAOF, through the recording of specific antecedents and consequences associated with each occurrence of interfering behavior, provides more specific contextual data than the IRP.
- In contrast to the FBAOF, the IRP provides more information about the magnitude of each behavioral incident, the corelationships among specific variables, the situations in which interfering behavior does not occur, and occurrences and magnitude of appropriate behaviors
- Both the IRP and the FBAOF are useful as an ongoing measure of student behavior.
- The FBAOF is typically used to assess one behavior. A separate form is used for each behavior. The IRP allows for the collection of data for several behaviors on one form. Reviewing the form allows one to get a "snapshot" of the student's performance throughout the school day.

Is one procedure better than another? Which should I use? In many cases we have used both procedures! Blending the results of both assessments tends to yield a rich source of data that enhances our understanding of the variables that influence the display of interfering behavior and the conditions in which we can provide positive behavioral supports.

THE TASK ANALYSIS RECORDING PROCEDURE

The *Task Analysis Recording Procedure* (TARP) is used to teach and record a student's behavior within the context of instructional programming. The TARP is especially effective as a procedure for teaching functional life skills and for progress monitoring (Steege, Mace, Perry, & Longenecker, 2007). Specifically, the TARP is used to:

- Structure instructional procedures.
- Document an individual's level of performance on specific tasks.
- Identify *effective* instructional prompts.
- Identify *ineffective* instructional prompts.
- Document levels of occurrence of interfering behaviors within the context of instructional programming.

This procedure is particularly useful in documenting the increase of appropriate behaviors and simultaneously decreasing the levels of occurrence of interfering behaviors. For example, we used the TARP as a data-recording procedure to measure levels of independence and occurrences of oppositional behavior within functional life skills instruction with a young man with autism who resided in a group home (see pp. 205–210).

Design of the TARP involves the following steps:

Step 1: Designing the Task Analysis

A task analysis involves breaking a complex skill (e.g., making a bed, taking a shower, making a snack, shopping) into its component parts. We recommend a process that includes the following stages:

- Identify the setting and materials in which the skill will be performed.
- Make a list of and sequence the critical behaviors needed to perform the skill.
- Validate the task analysis by having a staff person perform the task following the steps previously identified.

Step 2: Designing the Instructional Procedures

This step involves identification of the procedures that will be used to teach the component behaviors of the task. In most cases, we recommend the use of a procedure referred to as "prescriptive prompting" (Steege, Wacker, & McMahon, 1987). Prescriptive prompting involves (1) an ongoing assessment of instructional prompts used to teach the component behaviors of the task and (2) using the ongoing assessment data to prescribe individually tailored instructional prompting procedures.

We typically recommend the use of the following instructional prompts within the assessment phase and select the effective prompts based on the person's performance:

NSV: Nonspecific verbal (e.g., "What do you do next?")
SV: Specific verbal (e.g., "Pick up the spoon," "Pour the eggs in the bowl")
PS: Picture or symbol (e.g., photo of stimuli for each step of the task analysis)
MD: Model (i.e., demonstrate the specific behavior)
G: Gesture (i.e., point to the materials)
PP: Partial physical (i.e., tactile prompt guiding the person to the materials)
TP: Total physical (i.e., hand-over-hand assistance that leads to completion of the step)

We have used a variety of other instructional prompts, including visual prompts (e.g., photographs or line drawings representing a specific step). We also vary the use of verbal cues, ranging from verbal prompts consistently paired with each presentation of a model, gesture, visual, or tactile prompt to no verbal prompting at all during the instructional phase. Essentially, with the prescriptive prompting method, the instructional program is designed on an individual basis for each person and for each task being taught.

Step 3: Identifying the Interfering Behaviors to Be Recorded

This step involves identifying the specific interfering behaviors (e.g., stereotypy, aggression, self-injury) to be recorded. Interviews of staff/family members and direct observation procedures are usually used to identify and describe interfering behaviors.

Step 4: Designing the TARP Data Recording Form

This step involves developing a data recording form that includes:

- The steps of the task analysis.
- A column for recording correct/independent performance of behaviors.
- A column for recording effective and ineffective instructional prompts.
- A column for recording interfering behaviors.

Data are recorded following the completion of each step of the task analysis. See the example of a TARP Recording Form.

Step 5: Staff Training

Accurate use of the TARP requires training of staff/teachers to implement the procedure with precision. The data derived from implementation of the TARP are only as good as the persons who are collecting the data. If staff/teachers have never used this type of data-recording procedure, we have found the following training model to be very effective:

- Review each step of the task analysis.
- Review each type of instructional prompt.
- Role-play with staff implementation of teaching procedures (i.e., the sequence of steps of the task analysis and various prompting procedures).
- Review the labels and descriptions of each interfering behavior.
- Review the data-recording procedures for interfering behavior.
- Role-play scenarios in which staff/teachers practice using the TARP to record independence, effective prompts, ineffective prompts, and interfering behaviors.
- Early supervised practice of use of the TARP with the target student within naturally occurring situations.
- Establish interobserver agreement via simultaneous and independent recording using the TARP by a second observer.
- Monitor staff/teachers in their implementation of the TARP.

Step 6: Implementing the TARP

Implementing the TARP requires that staff/teachers be committed to using this procedure. It is our experience that staff/teachers consistently use the TARP when they find it to be an *effective* and *efficient* process. The TARP is an effective process when it accurately records the occurrence of behaviors. It is an efficient process when it does not get in the way of providing direct services to students.

Step 7: Analyzing the Data

This is an incredibly important step. Obviously, we consider the analysis of data to be a critical and often rewarding part of the process. Analyzing data involves review of "raw" data sheets and graphs depicting independence and interfering behaviors during baseline and intervention phases. When analyzing TARP data look for relationships among:

- Specific steps and types of *effective* instructional prompts.
- Specific steps and types of *ineffective* instructional prompts.
- Specific steps and interfering behaviors.
- Specific instructional prompts and interfering behaviors.

In the case of interfering behaviors, we have found situations in which problem behavior occurred when a specific type of prompt was used (e.g., verbal prompts) or when the student made an error (i.e., did not complete steps independently and *any* instructional prompt was associated with problem behavior). The key here is to look for patterns of problem behaviors both within and across completed data forms.

Specific Uses of the Task Analysis Recording Procedure

As part of a problem-solving process, we have found the TARP to be extremely valuable as a data-recording procedure that can be used prior to, during, and after the implementation of an intervention to document the effectiveness of individualized programming.

> *Prior to intervention:* baseline (documentation of behaviors prior to intervention)
> *During the intervention:* objective documentation of behavior change
> *After the intervention:* objective documentation of generalization and maintenance

We also use the TARP as part of our ongoing direct descriptive FBA process. Presently, we provide psychological consultation services to several programs that have incorporated the TARP within IEPs and IPPs with persons with disabilities. In these cases, behavioral data are recorded on an ongoing basis. We have found that analyzing previously completed TARP data sheets is extremely valuable as part of the FBA process. An example of the TARP Recording Form can be found in Figure 8.10. Figure 8.11 is an example of a completed TARP Recording Form.

Note: The use of the TARP as a form of direct descriptive assessment does not preclude the use of other forms of FBA. We typically use the TARP as one of our FBA procedures.

TROUBLESHOOTING

If the results of the combination of indirect and direct descriptive FBA procedures are suspect or if the data-based intervention proves to be unsuccessful, then additional assessments may be recommended. But before we go there, let's consider a few factors that may have impacted the validity of the assessment–intervention continuum. At this point, we suggest considering the following questions:

- Did the interview address *all possible* variables (antecedents, individual, and consequences) that might influence the display of interfering behavior?
- Were there any sources of error in the assessment, such as those described in previous chapters, that may have contaminated the results?
- Was a solid conceptual framework based on behavioral principles used as the foundation for understanding behavioral functions?
- Was the intervention based on the results of the FBA?
- Was there consistency across assessment procedures in identifying antecedent, individual, and consequence variables?
- Was a collaborative problem-solving process used in the design of the intervention?
- Was there a systematic plan for evaluating the effectiveness of the intervention?
- Did the folks who were responsible for implementing the intervention:
  - Have any input in the design of the intervention procedures?
  - Have confidence in (i.e., "buy into") the efficacy of the intervention procedures?
  - Implement the intervention with precision?

If there is a resounding "Yes" (from most parts of the country), "Ayyahhh" or "Yup" (from the Mainers), "You betcha" (from the Midwesterners), or any other positive affirmation, then the team may very likely need to consider revisiting the indirect and direct descriptive FBA processes or conducting more formalized assessments. If the latter is the case, then this is where functional behavioral *analysis* procedures are typically recommended.

We want to make it clear that *functional behavioral analysis* methodologies are certainly indicated in some cases. Indeed, in our clinical work there are times when we use functional behavioral analysis procedures after we have conducted indirect and direct descriptive FBAs. For example, the case of Eric Trout (see Chapter 12) includes several FBA procedures, including a functional behavioral analysis. However in this book we have made a conscious decision to emphasize indirect and direct descriptive FBA procedures for the following reasons:

Name _____   Date _____

Target skill _____   Teacher _____

Steps of TA	Independence (+ or –)	Instructional prompts — = Ineffective prompt ( ) = Effective prompt						Interfering behaviors ( ) = Occurrence		
1. Enter bathroom		TP	PP	G	M	SV	NSV	ST	SIB	VOPP
2. Turn on light		TP	PP	G	M	SV	NSV	ST	SIB	VOPP
3. Walk to sink		TP	PP	G	M	SV	NSV	ST	SIB	VOPP
4. Turn on cold water		TP	PP	G	M	SV	NSV	ST	SIB	VOPP
5. Turn on hot water		TP	PP	G	M	SV	NSV	ST	SIB	VOPP
6. Adjust water temperature		TP	PP	G	M	SV	NSV	ST	SIB	VOPP
7. Pick up washcloth		TP	PP	G	M	SV	NSV	ST	SIB	VOPP
8. Wet washcloth		TP	PP	G	M	SV	NSV	ST	SIB	VOPP
9. Wring out wash cloth		TP	PP	G	M	SV	NSV	ST	SIB	VOPP
10. Turn off hot water		TP	PP	G	M	SV	NSV	ST	SIB	VOPP
11. Turn off cold water		TP	PP	G	M	SV	NSV	ST	SIB	VOPP
12. Wash mouth		TP	PP	G	M	SV	NSV	ST	SIB	VOPP
13. Wash chin		TP	PP	G	M	SV	NSV	ST	SIB	VOPP
14. Wash cheek		TP	PP	G	M	SV	NSV	ST	SIB	VOPP
15. Wash other cheek		TP	PP	G	M	SV	NSV	ST	SIB	VOPP
16. Wash forehead		TP	PP	G	M	SV	NSV	ST	SIB	VOPP
17. Open hamper		TP	PP	G	M	SV	NSV	ST	SIB	VOPP
18. Place washcloth in hamper		TP	PP	G	M	SV	NSV	ST	SIB	VOPP
19. Close hamper		TP	PP	G	M	SV	NSV	ST	SIB	VOPP
20. Turn off light		TP	PP	G	M	SV	NSV	ST	SIB	VOPP
Number of steps										
Percentage of steps	% Independence							ST: SIB: VOPP:		

TP: Total physical
PP: Partial physical
G: Gesture
M: Model
SV: Specific verbal
NSV: Nonspecific verbal

ST: Stereotypy
SIB: Self-injurious
VOPP: Verbal opposition

FIGURE 8.10. Task Analysis Recording Procedure (TARP) Recording Form.

From Mark W. Steege and T. Steuart Watson (2009). Copyright by The Guilford Press. Permission to photocopy this figure is granted to purchasers of this book for personal use only (see copyright page for details).

Name _Missy Eater_ Date _9/25/08_

Target skill _Washing face with washcloth_ Teacher _O.C. Dee_

Steps of TA	Independence (+ or −)	Instructional prompts — = Ineffective prompt ( ) = Effective prompt						Interfering behaviors ( ) = Occurrence		
1. Enter bathroom	+	TP	PP	G	M	SV	NSV	ST	SIB	VOPP
2. Turn on light		TP	PP	(G)	~~M~~	~~SV~~	~~NSV~~	(ST)	SIB	VOPP
3. Walk to sink		TP	PP	(G)	M	~~SV~~	~~NSV~~	(ST)	SIB	VOPP
4. Turn on cold water		TP	(PP)	~~G~~	~~M~~	~~SV~~	~~NSV~~	(ST)	SIB	(VOPP)
5. Turn on hot water		(TP)	~~PP~~	~~G~~	~~M~~	~~SV~~	~~NSV~~	ST	(SIB)	(VOPP)
6. Adjust water temperature		(TP)	~~PP~~	~~G~~	~~M~~	~~SV~~	~~NSV~~	ST	(SIB)	(VOPP)
7. Pick up washcloth		TP	PP	G	M	(SV)	~~NSV~~	(ST)	SIB	VOPP
8. Wet washcloth		TP	PP	G	M	(SV)	~~NSV~~	ST	SIB	VOPP
9. Wring out wash cloth	+	TP	PP	G	M	SV	NSV	ST	SIB	VOPP
10. Turn off hot water		TP	PP	G	M	(SV)	~~NSV~~	ST	SIB	VOPP
11. Turn off cold water		TP	PP	G	M	(SV)	~~NSV~~	ST	SIB	VOPP
12. Wash mouth		TP	PP	(G)	~~M~~	~~SV~~	~~NSV~~	ST	SIB	(VOPP)
13. Wash chin		TP	PP	G	(M)	~~SV~~	~~NSV~~	ST	SIB	(VOPP)
14. Wash cheek		TP	PP	(G)	~~M~~	~~SV~~	~~NSV~~	ST	SIB	VOPP
15. Wash other cheek		TP	PP	G	(M)	~~SV~~	~~NSV~~	ST	(SIB)	VOPP
16. Wash forehead		TP	PP	G	M	(SV)	~~NSV~~	ST	SIB	(VOPP)
17. Open hamper	+	TP	PP	G	M	SV	NSV	ST	SIB	VOPP
18. Place washcloth in hamper	+	TP	PP	G	M	SV	NSV	ST	SIB	VOPP
19. Close hamper	+	TP	PP	G	M	SV	NSV	ST	SIB	VOPP
20. Turn off light		TP	PP	G	M	(SV)	~~NSV~~	(ST)	SIB	VOPP
Number of steps	5/20							5	3	6
Percentage of steps	25% Independence							ST: 25% SIB: 15% VOPP: 30%		

TP: Total physical
PP: Partial physical
G: Gesture
M: Model
SV: Specific verbal
NSV: Nonspecific verbal

ST: Stereotypy
SIB: Self-injurious
VOPP: Verbal opposition

FIGURE 8.11. Example of a completed TARP Recording Form.

• The vast majority of referral issues faced by school-based practitioners can be adequately addressed through indirect and direct descriptive FBA procedures.

• The level of description needed to accurately explain all of the complexities, pragmatics, procedural issues, and ethical issues related to conducting functional behavioral analyses is beyond the scope of this book.

• It has been our experience as faculty members who teach graduate-level courses covering FBA procedures that teaching functional behavioral analysis methodologies requires a combination of didactic and clinical instruction that includes (1) assigned readings, (2) lecture/discussion, (3) modeling, (4) role play, and (5) *in vivo* guided practice under the supervision of an experienced behavioral analyst.

In those situations in which functional behavioral analyses are called for and the school-based practitioner is not experienced or competent in conducting this level of assessment, we recommend the following:

• Refer the student to a professional who has training and experience enabling him or her to competently conduct functional behavioral analyses.

• Refer the student to a professional who has training and experience enabling him or her to competently conduct functional behavioral analyses; the school-based practitioner should participate in the evaluation under his or her supervision.

• Use the procedures outlined in Chapter 9 to conduct a brief functional analysis.

SUMMARY

In this chapter we have described several direct descriptive FBA procedures. It has also been our experience that in most cases an assessment process that includes both indirect and direct descriptive FBA procedures is sufficient in assessing and understanding behavioral functions. Moreover, assessments based on this comprehensive blend of procedures usually leads to the development of effective interventions.

Following is a case example in which indirect and direct descriptive FBA procedures were used in the assessment of a student with an emotional disability. The example illustrates and explains the application of several of the assessment procedures that we often use in conducting FBAs. This case example is not intended to be an example of an FBA report (we offer those examples in Chapter 12). Rather, the case of Dawn is offered to show how the integration of indirect and direct descriptive FBA processes result in a thorough understanding of the student's behaviors and their controlling variables. Remember, there may be situations where, after completing the indirect and direct descriptive assessments, definitive functions may not have been identified. In such cases, a brief functional analysis may be indicated. We cover the procedures and methods associated with a brief functional analysis in Chapter 9. Chapter 12 includes a case example where indirect and direct FBA procedures were used in conjunction with brief functional analysis.

CASE EXAMPLE: INDIRECT AND DIRECT DESCRIPTIVE FUNCTIONAL BEHAVIORAL ASSESSMENT

Relevant Background Information

Dawn was a 9-year, 5-month-old third-grade student enrolled in a self-contained program for students with emotional disabilities. In the previous 4 years, psychological evaluations had been conducted on three occasions as part of comprehensive psychoeducational evaluations recommended by the multidisciplinary team. Referral issues included concerns/questions regarding the following: developmental delays, social skills delays, academic skills delays, and interfering behaviors (e.g., screaming and aggressive behaviors). The three psychological evaluations were conducted by three different school psychologists in May 1998, April 2000, and September 2001. These evaluations included the following assessments:

1. Intellectual assessment (e.g., the Wechsler Intelligence Scale for Children, 3rd ed.)
2. Adaptive behavior assessment (e.g., the Scales of Independent Behavior—Revised)
3. Anecdotal observation (e.g., one 15-minute classroom-based observation)
4. Behavior rating scales (e.g., the Achenbach Teacher's Report Form)
5. Projective assessment (e.g., the House–Tree–Person Test, the Thematic Apperception Test, the Tasks of Emotional Development)

Additional assessments (e.g., norm-referenced achievement testing, speech/language evaluations, occupational therapy evaluations) were conducted by other members of the team. Furthermore, psychiatric evaluations/consultations were conducted in June 2000 and September 2001.

Based on these evaluations, the following labels/diagnoses were offered:

1. Pervasive developmental disorder—not otherwise specified
2. Obsessive–compulsive disorder
3. Oppositional–defiant disorder
4. Mixed receptive–expressive language disorder
5. Autistic disorder (autism spectrum disorder)
6. Anxiety disorder

Critique of Previous Assessments

The previous psychological evaluations could be described as "traditional psychological assessments" and, as such, are typical of the school-based psychological evaluations that are routinely conducted by thousands of practitioners each year. These assessments were primarily norm referenced and, while providing valuable information about Dawn's current levels of functioning compared to other children of the same age, provided little useful information for developing interventions to address interfering behaviors. Although the psychological evaluations did a good job of documenting that Dawn had a "disability," confirmed that the interfering behaviors she exhibited were unusual for a child of that age, and determined that these interfering behaviors were disruptive to her acquisition of skills, this information was not particularly useful in designing individually tailored interventions. In fact, review of the psychological reports and Dawn's IEP revealed little if any direct connection between the documents.

Current Disposition

The multidisciplinary team had convened meetings to review Dawn's case on nine occasions over the past 3 school years. Review of minutes of these meetings indicated that on several occasions Dawn's screaming behavior was described as "attention seeking" and as "self-stimulating." The team recommended the use of a "time-out" procedure to address screaming behavior. The team decided that if Dawn exhibited aggressive behavior toward classmates she should be sent home from school. The team also recommended the use of sensory integration techniques as a way of decreasing screaming and aggressive behaviors.

Although the team did not collect data on specific problem behaviors, it did record how many times Dawn had been sent home because of aggressive behaviors and the number of times that time-out had been used. During the first 10 weeks of the 2001–2002 school year, Dawn had been sent home on 12 occasions because of aggressive behavior and had been sent to the time-out area 24 times. The team frequently referred to Dawn's behavior as being "out of control" and reported that problem behaviors had increased in frequency, duration, and intensity.

In mid-November, a team meeting was held to review Dawn's case. During that meeting, Dawn's behaviors were discussed at length. Much of the discussion focused on what to do when Dawn screamed or became aggressive. A variety of interventions were proposed, including sensory diets, token economies, and the continued use of time-out, among others. The team also discussed the option of out-of-district residential placement to "address Dawn's severe behavioral, academic, and social/emotional needs." Dawn's parents objected to placing Dawn in an out-of-district residential placement and asked the school team to develop alternative interventions. At this point, the multidisciplinary team was asking for help: interfering behaviors were escalating, the interventions used by staff were not effective, and sending Dawn to an out-of-district residential placement was not acceptable. Dawn was referred for a comprehensive FBA. Because the school psychologist who regularly provided psychological services to students within the school program did not have training or experience in conducting FBAs, a referral for the evaluation was made to another psychologist within the district who did have a background in conducting FBAs with students with developmental disabilities.

Prior to initiating the FBA, the latter psychologist met with Dawn's family. During the meeting, Dawn's parents made several astute observations and asked some very good questions. For example, "Dawn has been evaluated by school psychologists three times already. She's been diagnosed to death. Do we really need another psych evaluation?" and "What do you plan to do that would be different from what the other folks did?" and "How will your assessments help us to help Dawn?" Read on and see how the school psychologist used the FBA process to address these question and concerns.

The Functional Behavioral Assessment Process with Dawn

Step 1: Indirect Assessment

The initial phase of assessment was conducted through interviews of the special education classroom teacher (Ms. Smith), special education technician (Ms. Jones), and Dawn's parents. The purposes of this interview were to:

1. Specify interfering behaviors that interfere with Dawn's acquisition and/or performance of academic, social, and daily living skills.
2. Describe those behaviors in concrete terms.
3. Identify antecedents or "triggers" of interfering behaviors (e.g., times of day, events, situations in which interfering behaviors typically occur).
4. Identify individual variables that are related to the occurrence of interfering behaviors (e.g., receptive language delays, health problems, academic skills).
5. Identify consequences that occur following interfering behaviors (e.g., social attention from classmates or staff, cessation of tasks, access to activities).
6. Identify reinforcers (e.g., tangibles, preferred activities, or social reinforcers).
7. Describe communication skills (e.g., expressive skills).

The interviews included the use of the following assessment procedures:

- The Functional Behavioral Assessment Screening Form (FBASF)
- The Antecedent Variables Assessment Form (AVAF)
- The Individual Variables Assessment Form (IVAF)
- The Consequence Variables Assessment Form (CVAF)
- The Behavioral Stream Interview (BSI)

RATIONALE

Conducting these interviews served several purposes:

- Information gained during the interviews resulted in the identification and description of each of the interfering behaviors.
- The information gained from conducting the initial interviews was useful in identifying those variables that *might be associated* with the occurrences of interfering behavior.

Note: At this point of the assessment, the information gathered through interviews was considered to be preliminary data and functional relationships (cause–effect relationships) were hypothesized.

- The interview was also very useful in helping interviewees understand that interfering behavior is oftentimes situation-specific. This shifted the focus from the student as being an "interfering child" (suggestive of intrapsychic determinants of behavior) to a model whereby behavior might be viewed as a result of what is oftentimes a complex set of *interacting* environmental and individual variables.

• As in most cases, direct observations of the referred student *followed* the behavioral interviews.

The information gained from the interview was very helpful in determining:

1. Which behaviors to observe and record
2. What type of direct observation procedures to use (e.g., A-B-C, behavioral stream observations)
3. What type of data-recording procedure to use (e.g., frequency, duration, interval, performance-based)
4. The settings in which to conduct the observations (e.g., reading, recess)

ASSESSMENT RESULTS

Identification and Description of Interfering Behaviors. The results of these assessments indicated that the interfering behaviors of concern were screaming and aggression. Screaming was defined as loud yelling of words or emitting screeching sounds (e.g., "EEEEEEE-HHHHH"). Aggression was defined as hitting, kicking, biting, scratching, or gouging of others.

Antecedent Variables. Reported *triggers* of screaming were academic tasks, errors when completing tasks/assignments, physical contact initiated by others, and instructional feedback (particularly corrective feedback). Reported *triggers* of aggression were physical contact initiated by others.

Individual Variables. Reported individual variables associated with interfering behaviors were severe expressive language and social skills delays, sensitivity to touch from others, difficulty in accepting criticism or corrective feedback, and anxiety when in novel situations or when given feedback from teachers.

Consequence Variables. Reported consequence variables of screaming were cessation of instructional tasks and cessation of instructional feedback. Reported consequence variables of aggression were cessation of social interactions, particularly those that included physical contact. During interviews with school staff and Dawn's parents, it was reported that aggressive behavior almost always occurred when others initiated physical contact. Moreover, aggression was typically part of a response chain that included screaming behavior. An example of a response chain is as follows:

Setting event: Dawn was in the self-contained classroom. The expectation was to complete an academic assignment. Dawn was off-task.
Antecedent: The educational technician used gestures and verbal prompts to redirect Dawn to task.

Behavior: Dawn engaged in screaming behavior.

Consequence: The educational technician used gestures and verbal prompts to redirect Dawn to task.

In this example, the consequence (i.e., "The educational technician used gestures and verbal prompts to redirect Dawn to task") for the previous occurrence of screaming also serves as the *antecedent* for subsequent occurrences of screaming.

Antecedent: The educational technician used gestures and verbal prompts to redirect Dawn to task.

Behavior: Dawn engaged in screaming behavior.

Consequence: The educational technician directed Dawn to the time-out area. Time-out was used at this point because it was determined that Dawn's screaming behavior was disruptive to the other students within the classroom. The behavior management plan developed to address screaming behavior specified that time-out be used in these circumstances.

The time-out procedure was initiated with a verbal prompt of "Dawn, your screaming is bothering the other students. You need to go to time-out."

Antecedent: As with the previous consequence, this consequence of time-out also served as the antecedent to more screaming behavior.

Behavior: Dawn engaged in screaming behavior. She did not stand up from her chair to walk to the time-out area.

Consequence: The educational technician initiated the time-out with a verbal prompt of "Dawn, your screaming is bothering the other students. You need to go to time-out" *and* a physical prompt in which the educational technician placed her hand on Dawn's shoulder and attempted to physically guide her to stand.

As with the previous consequence, this consequence served as the antecedent to more interfering behavior.

Antecedent: The educational technician initiated the time-out with a verbal prompt of "Dawn, your screaming is bothering the other students. You need to go to time-out" *and* a physical prompt in which the educational technician placed her hand on Dawn's shoulder and attempted to physically guide her to stand.

Behavior: Dawn engaged in screaming behaviors. She did not stand up from her chair to walk to the time-out area. Dawn also exhibited aggression (i.e., pushed, hit, and kicked the educational technician).

Consequence: The educational technician backed away. Essentially, she withdrew the verbal and physical prompts.

Antecedent: The educational technician withdrew the verbal and physical prompts to time-out.

Behavior: Dawn discontinued screaming and aggression behaviors. She picked up a book and opened it to a section featuring presidents of the United States.

Consequence: The educational technician monitored Dawn but did not interact with her.

In this example, a response chain was in place in which screaming and aggression occurred sequentially. Screaming behavior appears to be motivated by negative reinforcement (i.e., avoidance of instructional demands) and aggression appears to be motivated by negative reinforcement (i.e., avoidance of social/tactile demands). When two behaviors have the same function, they are said to be members of the same response class. The response class is determined by the function, as opposed to the topography, of behavior.

With Dawn, critical questions remained regarding the variables associated with aggression:

- Is physical contact with Dawn a predictor of aggression? In other words, would any physical contact, regardless of related events, result in aggression?

or

- Does aggression only occur when physical contact is provided after an occurrence of screaming behavior?

or

- Does Dawn exhibit aggression when physical contact is provided when she is engaged in preferred activities?

These questions were posed to members of the team. The answer was that aggression never occurred outside of physical contact provided in the context of a behavioral incident in which screaming was occurring. Therefore, it was hypothesized that aggression only occurred during situations in which tactile prompts were provided following an incident of screaming behavior.

Step 2: Direct Descriptive Assessment

Based on interviews with school staff, direct descriptive assessments were conducted to (1) document the occurrences of interfering behavior, (2) document and investigate possible functional relationships, and (3) record the current level of occurrence of interfering behaviors. The following procedures were used:

BEHAVIORAL STREAM OBSERVATION AND RECORDING

The school psychologist, observing Dawn within predetermined settings based on interviews with school staff, conducted this assessment. By discussing with the classroom teacher optimal times for observing Dawn within classroom settings in which interfering behavior typically occurred, the school psychologist was able to increase the probability of observing and recording interfering behaviors.

Behavioral stream observation and recording involved watching and keeping a record of behavioral incidents, as well as keeping track of the sequential flow of antecedents, behaviors, and consequences that constitute such a behavioral incident. Following are examples of descriptions of behavioral incidents using this procedure:

Example 1: Screaming. Dawn was sitting at her desk completing a writing assignment. → The educational technician approached Dawn and offered instructional support (i.e., corrective feedback regarding her writing sample). → Dawn screamed loudly ("EEEEH-HHH!!!"). → The educational technician quickly walked away. → Dawn stopped screaming and returned to the writing task.

Example 2: Screaming. Dawn was completing a reading assignment with teacher assistance. → The teacher corrected her word substitution error. → Dawn screamed ("EEHH!"). → The teacher provided a mild verbal reprimand ("No screaming, please") and pointed to the assignment. → Dawn screamed louder and longer ("EEEEHHHH!!!). → The teacher discontinued instruction and offered to help another student. → Dawn stopped screaming but did not return to task; she opened a book to pages of pictures of Abraham Lincoln (highly preferred activity).

Both of these examples of screaming support the hypothesis that screaming behavior is motivated by escape from academic demands and teacher corrective instruction. In addition, both examples point to another hypothesis, one that was not identified in the interview process, namely, that screaming behavior appears to also be related to access to tangible reinforcers (e.g., a book with pictures of Abraham Lincoln).

Aggressive behavior was not observed during the scheduled observation sessions. Because aggressive behaviors were not observed and to more fully evaluate screaming and aggressive behaviors, additional assessment procedures were implemented.

Note: It is not uncommon for the school psychologist to schedule an observation session and position him- or herself within the classroom to observe and record specific behavior, only to find that the behaviors of concern did not occur at all during the observation session. In these cases, we recommend that the classroom teacher and/or educational technician observe and record the defined target behaviors. The following ongoing FBA procedure is one we have found to be very effective in the evaluation of interfering behaviors:

FUNCTIONAL BEHAVIORAL ASSESSMENT OBSERVATION FORM

This procedure involved the use of the FBAOF in which school staff recorded observed occurrences of aggressive and screaming behaviors on a form that included:

- The time of day
- Setting events (e.g., math, science, recess, small-group reading, staff)
- Antecedents (i.e., environmental triggers)

- Interfering behaviors
- Immediate consequences
- The effect that the consequences had on the frequency, duration, or intensity of the behavior
- The staff person who observed and recorded the behavioral incident

The FBAOF was used for 5 school days. Review of the completed FBAOFs involved analyzing each of the data-recording forms. Analysis involved review of the number of times that interfering behavior occurred and the variables that were associated with each occurrence of interfering behavior. The results of this analysis are as follows:

- Aggressive behaviors occurred 4 times.
- Screaming behaviors occurred 68 times.
- 94% of occurrences of screaming occurred within the context of academic situations.

Note: The FBAOF did not consistently identify specific antecedents associated with screaming behaviors. However, 72% of occurrences of screaming behavior were related to direct instruction that included corrective feedback:

- 6% of occurrences of screaming occurred during nonacademic situations (e.g., lunch, recess, hallway).
- 97% of occurrences were followed by the discontinuation of teacher instructions or academic tasks/demands.
- 100% of occurrences of aggression occurred within the context of academic programming when Dawn was engaging in screaming behavior and when she was physically redirected; also, 100% of these behaviors were followed by the discontinuation of physical contact, teacher instruction, or academic expectations.

Results

Indirect and direct descriptive FBA procedures were used to identify hypotheses about the variables that trigger and maintain interfering behaviors. The results of the FBA were used to generate the following hypotheses:

Hypothesis 1: Screaming behavior appears to be primarily motivated by negative reinforcement (i.e., "escape" from corrective instructional feedback).
Hypothesis 2: Screaming behavior appears to be secondarily motivated by positive reinforcement (i.e., access to preferred tangibles/activities).
Hypothesis 3: Aggressive behavior appears to be motivated by negative reinforcement (i.e., "escape" from physical redirection to a task following occurrences of screaming behavior).

Recommendations

Based on the results of the FBA, the school psychologist recommended the following interventions:

    1. Given Dawn's reaction to physical prompts provided by staff, the use of physical prompting to redirect Dawn to a task is strongly discouraged.

    2. Given that Dawn's screaming behavior typically occurs during academic situations in which she has received corrective instructional supports, the following suggestions are offered:

      a. Teaching Dawn to use self-editing and self-monitoring strategies within academic tasks might well be an effective means of increasing accuracy in completion of assignments, thereby decreasing (and perhaps eliminating) corrective instructional feedback.

      b. Functional communication training strategies might be employed that include teaching and reinforcing Dawn's use of appropriate language as a replacement for screaming behaviors. Because the function of screaming is "escape," teaching her to request a break, to request that the teacher not provide corrective feedback, or another functionally related response could be given consideration.

      c. Differential reinforcement of other behavior (DRO) procedures might be used in which Dawn is reinforced (e.g., by opportunities to read picture books about presidents of the United States for several minutes, with tokens that later could be exchanged for preferred activity/tangible rewards or social reinforcement) for the nonoccurrence of screaming behaviors at prespecified intervals (e.g., 15 minutes, class periods).

    3. The FBAOF might be used to monitor the occurrence of screaming behaviors and to evaluate the effectiveness of such interventions.

    4. Direct behavioral consultation in the design, implementation, and evaluation of the effectiveness of a positive behavioral support plan incorporating the recommended interventions is suggested.

Final Case Disposition

The aforementioned intervention strategies were developed and implemented with Dawn. The interventions were a smashing success. To make a long story short, the implementation of the intervention package resulted in marked reductions in screaming and aggressive behaviors. In fact, within the first week of implementation of the intervention package, aggressive behaviors were eliminated! Screaming behaviors were reduced by 65% during the first week of implementation and occurred at very low rates thereafter. For example, by the end of the school year screaming behavior occurred three and four times during the months of April and May, respectively. Dawn's levels of academic engagement, appropriate social behaviors, work completion, and task accuracy also increased markedly.

9

Brief Functional Analysis
of Behavior

There are in fact two things, science and opinion; the former
begets knowledge, the latter ignorance.
—HIPPOCRATES (460 B.C.–377 B.C.), *Law*

In the first edition of this book, we did not delve into the procedures and practices associated with a functional *analysis* of behavior. Our decision was influenced by several factors, among them:

- Most instances of interfering behavior occurring in the schools do not require an experimental functional analysis.
- Functional analysis may require knowledge, skills, and resources that may not be typically available in the school setting.
- Well-conducted indirect and direct descriptive assessments are valid for most instances of interfering behavior that occur in a school setting.
- There is some question as to the temporal stability of findings generated from functional analysis procedures as behavioral function may change across time, situations, and people.

Since publication of the first edition, readers have undoubtedly gained knowledge, skill, and experience through readings, workshops, and integration of functional behavior assessment into daily practice. We believe that the time is right to introduce a more rigorous procedure into the armamentarium of school practitioners for use when other procedures have failed to clearly identify a function or when circumstances necessitate a more controlled assessment.

FUNCTIONAL ANALYSIS

Functional analysis refers to the process of gathering information to determine relations between variables, particularly functional relations (Shriver, Anderson, & Proctor, 2001).

162

Within the field of applied behavior analysis, a *functional relationship* exists when a cause–effect relationship between variables has been experimentally demonstrated. When we are evaluating the accuracy of FBA procedures, an experimental functional analysis of behavior is considered the most accurate measure of a functional relation and is considered the best "proof" (the gold standard) of the accuracy of hypothesized functional relationships (Shriver et al., 2001). Remember, with indirect FBA and direct descriptive FBA procedures, antecedent and reinforcing consequences are *identified*, but functional relationships are *hypothesized*. That is, there is a high degree of likelihood of cause–effect relationships, but we haven't *proven* these functional relationships. The purpose of functional behavioral analysis is to prove that the hypothesized relationships are in fact causal and not simply "correlational."

Functional (experimental) analysis procedures are used to *confirm* hypotheses regarding the functions of behavior. In contrast to indirect and direct descriptive FBA procedures, functional analysis is the only FBA method that allows practitioners to confirm hypotheses regarding functional relations between interfering behavior and environmental events (Cooper et al., 2007).

A thorough functional analysis includes the following:

- Identification and description of interfering behavior(s)
- Determination of data recording procedure
- Systematic manipulation of antecedents and/or consequences
- Direct recording of interfering behavior
- Graphing and analysis of data to determine functional relations

A functional analysis requires:

- Materials from the natural environment that are associated with occurrences of interfering behavior (e.g., assignments, tasks, toys).
- One or more "therapists" who (1) arrange the environment by manipulating the situation to increase the motivation for interfering behavior and (2) provide prespecified reinforcement contingent on the interfering behavior.
- One or more "evaluators" to record interfering behavior (e.g., using a 6-second partial-interval recording procedure to measure interfering behaviors).

A functional analysis typically involves several assessment conditions: (1) a control condition in which it is expected that interfering behavior will be low and (2) "test" conditions that include a motivating operation (MO) and a reinforcing consequence (e.g., social attention, escape, a tangible). The assessment conditions are essentially structured role-play scenarios (or analogue conditions) that allow for the separate analysis of functional relations. The test conditions are arranged one at a time in an alternating fashion and are repeated several times to determine the extent to which interfering behaviors consistently occur more often in one or more conditions as compared to the others (see Table 9.1).

Basically, after repeating each of the conditions several times, trends emerge. For example:

TABLE 9.1. Functional Analysis Procedures

Condition	Motivating operation	Example of a procedure	Reinforcing consequence delivered	Hypothesized reinforcing consequence
Social attention	Social attention is deprived or withheld, increasing the value of attention as a reinforcer.	Interact with the student, then say "I have some work to do now" and ignore the student.	Social attention is provided only when interfering behaviors occur.	Positive reinforcement: social attention
Escape	Challenging or nonpreferred task is introduced, increasing the value of escape from task as a reinforcer.	"It's time to complete the math worksheets" and present a stack of worksheets.	Brief break (e.g., 10 seconds) from the task is provided only when interfering behaviors occur.	Negative reinforcement: escape from tasks
Tangible	Tangible reinforcer is deprived or withheld, increasing the value of the tangible as a reinforcer.	Permit the student to play with a preferred video game, then remove the game.	Briefly provide the tangible reinforcer only when the interfering behavior occurs.	Positive reinforcement: tangible
Alone	Low levels of environmental stimulation.	Student in a quiet environment without access to toys, materials, or therapist.	Interfering behavior is ignored or neutrally redirected.	Automatic reinforcement: arousal induction
Control	Preferred activities are present, therapist provides response-independent reinforcement, no demands for performance.	Student offered the opportunity to engage in preferred play activity with the therapist providing social reinforcement.	Interfering behavior is ignored or neutrally redirected.	None

Note. Based on Cooper et al. (2007).

- The interfering behavior occurred at high rates in the escape condition but not at all in the other conditions, thus confirming the hypothesis that the behavior is maintained by negative reinforcement.

or

- The interfering behavior occurred at the highest levels during the social attention condition and at much lower levels in all of the other conditions, confirming the hypothesis that interfering behavior is maintained by social attention.

or

- The interfering behavior occurred at the highest levels during the access to tangibles condition and at much lower levels in all of the other conditions, confirming the hypothesis that interfering behavior is maintained by access to tangible items.

or

- The interfering behavior occurred at the highest levels while the student was alone and at much lower levels in all of the other conditions, confirming the hypothesis that interfering behavior is maintained by arousal induction.

or

- There may be situations in which interfering behavior occurs within two or more conditions, suggesting that multiple reinforcing consequences are maintaining interfering behavior.

Functional analysis may involve two general approaches: (1) structural analysis and (2) consequence analysis. Each of these approaches is discussed below.

Structural Analysis

Structural analysis involves arranging and manipulating antecedent conditions and observing and/or recording the occurrence of interfering behavior within that specific context. This type of analysis is typically conducted in order to test hypotheses about variables that trigger the onset of interfering behaviors (O'Neill et al., 1997). Thus, specific consequences are not delivered contingently. The following two cases illustrate how a structural analysis might be conducted.

Example 1: Based on interviews and observations, it was hypothesized that a third-grade student's yelling behavior occurred within the context of difficult tasks (in particular, math worksheets). The school psychologist met with the classroom teacher (Ms. Billie) and arranged for her to present the student with six sets of math worksheets (three easy worksheets and three worksheets that were considered difficult but represented the type of work typically expected of the student). The school psychologist observed and recorded the occurrence of yelling behavior across presentation of the six math worksheets. The results of this analysis showed that yelling behavior occurred at much higher rates during the presentation of the difficult math worksheets and at very low rates to no occurrence of yelling behavior when the student was presented with easier math worksheets. These data were consistent with the results of interviews and observations and confirmed the hypothesis that yelling behavior occurred in the context of difficult tasks. The school psychologist further hypothesized that yelling behavior was reinforced by negative reinforcement (i.e., escape from and/or avoidance of task demands). Subsequent curriculum-based assessments indicated that the math curriculum was "too advanced" for this student. When she was presented with additional instructional supports and modifications in assignments, yelling behavior was eliminated and on-task behavior, task completion, and task accuracy increased markedly.

Example 2: This example illustrates a structural analysis conducted by a school psychologist of a student diagnosed with learning disabilities and auditory processing disorder. Paul was referred by the IEP team for FBA of off-task, hitting, and tantrum behaviors. In addition to measuring the rates of occurrence of interfering behaviors, the school psychologist decided to measure levels of occurrence of appropriate behaviors (i.e., academic engagement). The structural analysis involved observing Paul within *naturally occurring classroom situations* (these situations were selected based on previous direct behavioral observations and interviews with Paul's teachers) and recording occurrences of appropriate and interfering behaviors using a 6-second partial-interval recording procedure. The purposes of this analysis were (1) to determine if his behavior varied under different types of instructional conditions (e.g., visual vs. language), (2) to determine if his interfering behaviors occurred even when no academic tasks/demands were present, and (3) because the teacher noted that his behavior was quite variable, depending upon the type of task he was asked to perform.

Paul was observed within the following situations:

- Free time (no instructional expectations were placed on Paul and no social interactions were provided)
- Visual–motor (VM) instructional tasks
- Language-based (LB) instructional tasks

Within each situation, the following behaviors were recorded:

- Academic engagement (i.e., visual, verbal, and/or motor on-task behavior with IEP objectives)
- Off task
- Hitting
- Tantrum

The results of the structural analysis are shown in the following table (data are presented as percentage of intervals in which the behavior occurred).

Setting	Academic engagement	Off task	Hitting	Tantrum
Free time	12%	0%	4%	0%
Individual VM instructional tasks	68%	2%	12%	0%
Individual LB instructional tasks	22%	24%	66%	12%

During the structural analysis, it was observed that Paul exhibited higher levels of hitting behavior when prompted to participate in language-based instructional tasks (e.g., expressive labeling) and free-time situations. Conversely, he exhibited lower levels of hitting and off-task behavior during visual–motor tasks (e.g., matching tasks, putting together a puzzle, performing a visual discrimination task). Also, off task and hitting behaviors occurred at much higher levels during the language-based instruction.

An additional structural analysis was conducted to further evaluate these findings. This additional assessment involved observing and recording Paul's behavior across naturally occurring classroom situations using a 6-second partial-interval recording procedure. Results are shown in the following table.

Setting	Academic engagement	Off task	Hitting	Tantrum
Language-based tasks	16%	84%	16%	21%
Visually based tasks	89%	11%	0%	0%
Language-based tasks	12%	88%	12%	16%
Visually based tasks	94%	6%	2%	0%

These results confirmed the hypothesis that high levels of off-task and tantrum behaviors were associated with language-based instructional tasks/activities. Conversely, academic engagement was much higher during visually based instructional tasks/activities. These data also revealed another finding, namely, that hitting occurred at higher levels during language-based tasks as compared to visually based instructional situations. During these observations, it was found that hitting also occurred when the teacher or teacher's assistant physically prompted Paul to become academically engaged. Also, tantrum behaviors sometimes occurred following physical prompts to return to a language-based task.

Based on the results of the structural analysis, the following conclusions were offered:

- For whatever reason, language-based tasks are more difficult for Paul which results in interfering behavior.
- There is an inverse relationship between academic engagement and interfering behaviors (i.e., the more engaged Paul is academically, the less likely he is to engage in interfering behaviors).
- Physical prompting to engage in a task will trigger hitting.

A behavior support plan was designed around these conclusions and included several components, among them:

- Providing very brief exposure to language-based tasks and, contingent upon no interfering behavior, access to choose from a menu of reinforcers selected by Paul.
- No longer using physical prompting to engage in an academic task.
- Teaching Paul replacement skills to use when presented with a task that is aversive (e.g., telling the teacher that the task is difficult or asking for help or a break).
- Reinforcing academic engagement throughout the day and not just with visually based tasks.
- Allowing Paul to choose among a variety of similar language-based tasks to work on for brief periods of time.

After implementing these components consistently and accurately for a period of about 8 days, Paul's hitting and tantrumming in all environments decreased, his academic engagement in all tasks increased, and he was able to work for longer periods of time on language-based tasks without exhibiting interfering behavior.

Consequence Analysis

Consequence analysis involves arranging situations and providing specific consequences contingent on the occurrence of specific interfering behaviors. This analysis is typically conducted in order to test hypotheses about variables that *maintain* interfering behaviors (O'Neill et al., 1997). An example follows:

> The fifth-grade classroom teacher had been keeping an anecdotal log of Harley's "angry" behavior. Harley's anger had been defined as pushing desks and chairs, throwing books on the floor, looking mean at the teacher, telling others to shut up, and other similar behaviors. The school psychologist was asked by the principal to consult with the teacher prior to her making a referral to the teacher support team. In examining the anecdotal log, the school psychologist noted that the teacher indicated one of two general things occurred after Harley became angry: she either let him take a 5-minute cool-down period, or she talked with him about the negative effects associated with his behavior. Thus, the school psychologist was unsure if *escape* (i.e., the cool-down period), or if *social attention*, from the teacher talking with him, or *both*, were maintaining the angry behavior. Prior to the next two observations of 30 minutes each, the school psychologist arranged with the teacher for her to systematically provide either attention or escape contingent upon angry behavior to determine which was functionally related to the target behaviors. The data indicated that, although angry behavior occurred when the teacher provided access to a cool-down period, angry behavior occurred three times as much when the teacher interacted with Harley contingent upon his angry behavior. Therefore, it appeared that teacher attention was functionally related to the exhibition of angry behavior by Harley.

BRIEF FUNCTIONAL ANALYSIS

As we mentioned at the beginning of this chapter, not every interfering behavior requires a functional *analysis*. For those behaviors that do, not every one of those will require an extended functional analysis using all of the conditions described above. In such cases, we strongly recommend using a *brief functional analysis* model. The model we advocate for use in schools is similar to the one described by Steege and Northup (1998). The advantages of the brief functional analysis model presented here is that it allows a great deal of flexibility in designing conditions and is very time efficient.

The brief functional analysis model is comprised of four phases:

- Functional behavioral assessment consisting of indirect and direct descriptive methods (these procedures are covered in Chapters 7 and 8).
- Brief standard functional analysis.

- Confirmatory functional analysis.
- Contingency reversal.

The first phase of the brief functional analysis model is actually comprised of the indirect and direct descriptive activities associated with conducting a functional assessment. One can then conduct a brief standard analysis whereby information derived from these procedures (e.g., staff, instructional cues, peer and/or teacher responses to interfering behavior) can be evaluated within the functional *analysis* model. This evaluation is intended to be brief (e.g., approximately 30 minutes). Following the brief analysis, a confirmatory functional analysis is conducted to assess the consistency of the interfering behaviors across specific conditions. Finally, the contingency reversal phase is used to determine if the function identified through the above procedures can be used to increase appropriate behavior. Although this process seems to be quite involved, it is expected that an entire brief functional analysis would only require about 120–150 minutes of total assessment time—much less than is typically required by a more traditional behavioral or psychoeducational assessment. The following case example illustrates the brief functional analysis model in its entirety.

CASE EXAMPLE OF BRIEF FUNCTIONAL ANALYSIS

Velma was an 11-year-old female in the fourth grade. She had been retained in both kindergarten (for social reasons) and in first grade (because of failure to progress academically). At the age of 9, she was diagnosed as emotionally/behaviorally disordered and placed into special education. At the time of referral, she was receiving approximately 1.5 hours of resource room help per day with most of her day spent in a mainstream fourth-grade classroom. The current referral concerns included verbally refusing to do work, swearing, throwing materials, and threatening her teacher and peers.

The first phase of the BFA, indirect and descriptive assessment, consisted of:

- A review of Velma's academic and behavioral records
- Teacher interviews, using a behavioral stream interview format (see pp. 106–110)
- Structured direct behavioral observations

The indirect methods allowed the school psychologist to describe interfering behaviors, identify possible antecedents and consequences, develop hypotheses about function, identify potential reinforcers, and select specific instructional situations where the interfering behavior was and was not likely to occur for purposes of direct observation. This last purpose of indirect methods is of utmost importance for practitioners because it increases the likelihood of actually observing the interfering behavior, more so than merely choosing random observation times. Plus, it is equally important to select times in which the behavior(s) is not likely to occur so that a comparison can be made between the two situations, a comparison that contributes to hypothesis development.

A review of academic records, including the results of both norm-referenced and curriculum-based strategies, indicated that Velma was at instructional level for all of her academic subjects. Interviews with her teacher and teacher assistant indicated that the interfering behaviors were more likely to occur during both math and writing assignments. A review of anecdotal behavior logs and office disciplinary referrals indicated ongoing problems since kindergarten with Velma refusing to do work and using inappropriate language. The most typical outcomes of Velma's interfering behaviors were being sent to the principal's office, being sent home for the day, being sent to the positive action class for a period ranging from 1 day to 5 days, or being sent to an in-room time-out for extended periods of time (e.g., 15–90 minutes). Based on this information alone, one may conclude that the function of Velma's interfering behavior is *escape* from academic task demands—a very reasonable hypothesis given the information at this time. However, her teacher and teacher assistant insisted that *social attention* was the most likely and most consistent consequence for Velma's interfering behaviors. Thus, further interviews with the teacher and assistant were conducted using the behavioral stream format (see pp. 106–110). The behavioral stream interview indicated the following sequence of events that led to interfering behavior:

> Teacher or teacher assistant issues a math or writing task. → Velma either sits with her arms folded or continues with her current task. → Teacher reissues academic task. → Velma says something like, "I don't feel like working on math today" or "I don't know how to do that." → Teacher ignores her verbalizations and moves away to help other students. → After a few minutes have passed, the teacher returns to Velma, sees that she is not working, and tells her that if she does not begin working, a negative consequence will follow. → Velma throws her materials on the floor, yells, and screams profanities at the teacher. → Teacher tells Velma to calm down. → Velma threatens to hit her if she does not move away. → Teacher tells Velma she must go the "quiet chair" in the back of the room to calm down (a procedure that was recommended on her IEP). → Velma goes quietly to the chair where she sits for 10–15 minutes and calms down. → Velma is then asked to return to her seat and another assignment is given.

Although this sequence certainly involved a great deal of social interaction between the teacher and Velma, it does not seem to be the maintaining consequence. Indeed, it appears to us that *escape from the academic task* is the primary function because the consequence of the social interactions result in avoidance of the academic task with the end result being a complete escape and assignment of another task.

To obtain further information on the situations that seem to "set the stage" for interfering behavior, six brief (i.e., 10 minutes) direct behavioral observations (descriptive assessment) were conducted where two nonpreferred tasks (a math task and a writing task) and a preferred academic task (e.g., reading from her social studies book) were given. No consequences were manipulated during this assessment. The school psychologist recorded the occurrence of both appropriate and interfering behaviors during all observations using a 10-second partial interval recording procedure. The results (Figure 9.1) showed that Velma's interfering behaviors were quite predictable when the type of assignment was considered (i.e., preferred vs. nonpreferred assignments).

Now that we had verified that nonpreferred tasks (in this case, writing and math) were the contexts for interfering behavior, we sought to determine the maintaining consequence (i.e., function) for the interfering behavior(s). We did this via three components:

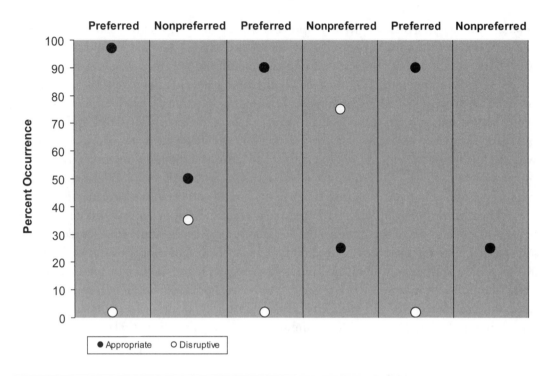

FIGURE 9.1. Rates of appropriate and disruptive behavior for Velma during preferred and non-preferred tasks.

- A standard assessment
- Confirmatory analysis
- Contingency reversal

In the standard assessment, we observed and recorded interfering behavior during one 10-minute session of each of the following conditions:

- A preferred academic task (PAT) where Velma was given a reading assignment from her health book.
- A nonpreferred academic task with brief escape (i.e., 10 seconds) contingent upon interfering behavior (NPAT-E).
- A nonpreferred academic task with social attention contingent upon interfering behavior (NPAT-SA).

The results of the standard assessment indicated that the highest percentages of interfering behavior occurred in the NPAT-E condition. To confirm (and replicate) that nonpreferred tasks with escape produced the most interfering behavior, we conducted a confirmatory analysis that included two sessions of NPAT-E and one session of NPAT-SA. These sessions of the confirmatory analysis were identical to those from the standard assessment. The results of the confirmatory analysis indeed "confirmed" the results of the standard assessment in that escape from nonpreferred academic tasks resulted in a much higher percentage of interfering behavior than nonpreferred academic tasks with social attention. This is a very important finding because, as we mentioned above, the teacher and her assistant were fairly adamant that social attention was maintaining interfering behavior. All of the results thus far strongly indicate that social attention is not functional at all for interfering behavior in the context of nonpreferred academic assignments; rather is is escape from those assignments. Finally, we conducted a contingency reversal phase to determine if we could use escape to reinforce on-task behavior for nonpreferred academic tasks. To do this, we ran two 10-minute sessions where brief escape (i.e., negative reinforcement) from a non-preferred academic task (NR) was provided contingent upon appropriate behavior. We also ran one session, for purposes of comparison, where social attention was provided contingent upon appropriate behavior while working on a nonpreferred academic task (SA). As we expected at this point of the process, the NR conditions resulted in higher percentages of appropriate behavior than the SA condition. Thus, at the conclusion of this brief functional analysis that required only about 145 minutes, we hypothesized and confirmed that escape was the function of interfering behaviors exhibited during work on nonpreferred academic tasks and that escape could be used to reinforce appropriate, work-related behaviors during those same tasks (see Figure 9.2 for a summary of the results). Now that's a lot of bang for the time involved!!

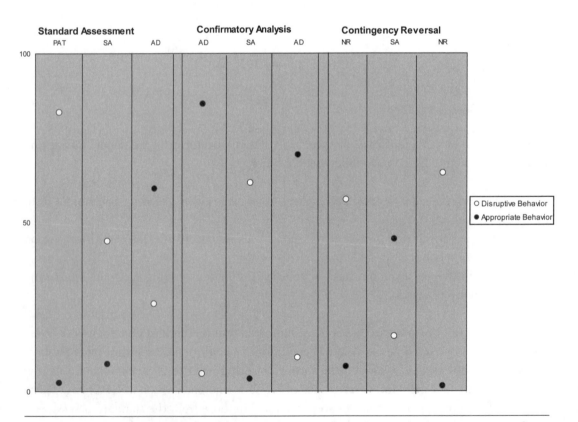

FIGURE 9.2. A comprehensive look at results for Velma from the standard assessment, confirmatory assessment, and contingency reversal.

ISSUES ASSOCIATED
WITH FUNCTIONAL ANALYSIS PROCEDURES

Although functional analysis procedures can be indispensable for assessing certain behaviors in school settings, there are some issues of which you should be aware (see Gresham, Watson, & Skinner, 2001, for a broader discussion). These issues are not sufficiently severe that you should let them bias you against functional analysis. Rather, knowing them allows you to determine when an *analysis* needs to be conducted and the arguments that others might have against conducting such an analysis. We will present four issues that are probably more relevant to your daily practice and offer some advice/opinion on each.

How Consistent Are the Results between the Various Functional Assessment Methodologies (i.e., Functional Assessment, Brief Functional Analysis, and Extended Functional Analysis)? or, Do We Really Need to Do All This Assessment?

Derby, Wacker, Sasso, and Steege (1992) conducted one of the earliest studies in this area and showed that *brief* functional analysis was effective for identifying function and for designing effective intervention. More recent research by Dufrene et al. (2007) has shown a high degree of consistency between the results obtained from direct descriptive procedures and from brief functional analyses. Thus, it may be that well-conducted functional behavioral *assessments* may be sufficient for identifying the function of interfering behaviors in school settings. Of course, brief or even extended functional analysis may be needed in those cases where the FBA did not clearly identify a function or where a PBS developed from the findings of the functional assessment did not result in adequate behavior change. Regardless of whether you use a combination of direct descriptive and indirect procedures or functional analysis, the time required to gather these data are much less than what would be required by the ordinary psychoeducational evaluation.

Are Interventions That Are Based on Function More Effective Than Interventions That Are Based on the Principles of Applied Behavior Modification?

This is actually a very interesting question to us, both practically and empirically. It makes a great deal of logical sense that the most effective interventions would be those that are based on the precise function a behavior serves in a particular environment. In fact, there are literally hundreds of published studies where effective treatment was based on behavioral function. On the other hand, Braden and Kratochwill (1997) asserted that non-FBA interventions can be effective if no empirical link between behavioral function and treatment selection has been demonstrated (e.g., habit reversal for habit disorders). On yet another hand, Lalli et al. (1999) demonstrated that a positive reinforcement intervention was more effective at changing escape-related behavior than a negative reinforcement procedure (because the function of problem behavior was escape, the negative reinforcement procedure should have been more effective, but it wasn't, at least for these five kids). Clearly, more research needs to be conducted in this area to determine under what conditions non-FBA interventions might be sufficient and those conditions under which a functionally derived intervention are necessary.

Are School-Based Teams Able to Accurately and Consistently Conduct Functional Assessments/Analysis and Correctly Determine Function?

A dissertation by Dittmer-McMahon (2001) suggested that teams, when given data from an FBA, often drew incorrect conclusions about function. These same teams had been given intensive and ongoing instruction/supervision in conducting and interpreting FBAs. Perhaps it is not surprising that school-based teams, comprised primarily of educators, would find it difficult to accurately identify function. A study of experienced behavior analysts found that they often disagreed about behavioral function (Hagopian et al., 1997). When presented with data in graph form from a functional analysis, these experienced behavior analysts agreed about 46% of the time! This is a far cry from what we expect of educators working on school-based teams, much less experienced behavior analysts. Although the discussion for why the difficulty in accurately determining function is rather long-winded and probably boring, suffice it to say that *behavior change* is the gold standard when evaluating the effectiveness of teams, their interpretation of FBA data, and their positive behavior support plans.

Are School-Based Teams Really Able to Design Innovative and Effective Positive Behavioral Support Plans?

Without being overly pessimistic, our answer to this is "Without significant assistance from someone with experience in FBA and PBS, the answer, both empirically and from our own experience, is 'Probably not.'" Our opinion is not meant to dissuade teams from attempting to design behavior support plans. Rather, our opinion recognizes that human behavior can be a very complex enterprise. That complexity often proves daunting for team members whose educational training is in education and not psychology or behavior analysis. Even teams that are "well trained" can not learn enough in a few in-service sessions or two-day workshops to acquire in-depth knowledge in behavior change strategies. In the absence of textbook knowledge, teams often turn to behavior change manuals, implementation guides, and the like to guide them in developing behavior support plans. As we have previously noted, these materials are typically not particularly helpful in designing individualized behavior support plans. In other instances, team rely on what they have done before or what they already know how to do without considering other viable alternatives. Given these circumstances, what are teams to do? Our advice is really simple: Make certain that at least one team member has training and experience in the application of behavior change. Doing so will undoubtedly increase the effectiveness and efficiency of team functioning and, most importantly, benefit the student.

SUMMARY

"Where do we go from here . . . ?" Thus far, we have described several procedures that may be used to assess interfering behaviors. Remember, the goals of assessment are to (1) identify and understand the array of variables that contribute to occurrences of interfering behavior, and (2) use this information to design effective behavioral support plans. In the following three chapters, we first discuss an applied model for conceptualizing, understanding, and organizing the myriad variables that impact behavior (Chapter 10). Second, we give you multiple examples of what the outcomes of your FBA should look like (Chapter 11). And third, we provide a model for delivering intervention services in schools that relies on basic teaching principles and information gleaned from this book (Chapter 12).

10

Behavior-Analytic
Problem-Solving Model

Those who fall in love with practice without science are
like a sailor who sails a ship without a helm or a compass,
and can never be certain whither he is going.
—LEONARDO DA VINCI (1452–1519)

One of our mantras is "Interfering behaviors are the result of a complex interaction of motivating, antecedent, individual, and consequence variables." As a result of this acknowledgment and firmly held philosophical position, we developed the behavior-analytic problem-solving model (BAPS) to be used in the identification and description of the contextual variables that contribute to the occurrence of interfering behaviors. Essentially, the purpose of the BAPS is to see "what we're up against." As opposed to a "stand-alone" assessment process, we use the BAPS following the completion of the indirect, direct descriptive, and/ or functional analysis assessments to organize and summarize the findings from our assessments. The BAPS allows us to examine the dynamic relationships among the various variables that support interfering behaviors. We then use this information as the foundation for designing function-based interventions. Following is a list of each of the components of the BAPS, a brief explanation for why we assess this variable (see Chapter 4 for more detailed descriptions), and examples that both illustrate the concept and how we might use this information when designing function-based interventions (*Note: These examples are meant for illustration purposes only and certainly do not represent the vast array of stimuli/ events that occasion, evoke, contribute to, or reinforce interfering behaviors. Moreover, the examples are meant to be person-specific, with intervention tailored to the individual and the contextual variables controlling the behaviors. Finally, in most cases, function-based behavior support plans address several of the components of the BAPS. These examples are only addressing one of the components of what most likely would be a comprehensive intervention package.*)

COMPONENTS OF THE BEHAVIOR-ANALYTIC PROBLEM-SOLVING MODEL

Contextual Variables

Process

Specify the probable contexts in which interfering behavior occurs.

Rationale

Interfering behavior often occurs within different contexts. Each context may have a unique set of controlling variables. Knowing the context of interfering behaviors allows us to anticipate the possibility of interfering behavior and to provide proactive interventions to prevent its occurrence.

Example 1

The interfering behavior typically occurs during math and language arts classes. Within math, the interfering behavior appears to be reinforced by negative reinforcement (i.e., escape from academic demands). Within language arts, the same interfering behavior is reinforced by positive reinforcement (i.e., social attention from classmates). Each context has unique controlling variables and consequently will require a different set of interventions.

Example 2

A student often displays inappropriate social behavior with classmates during unstructured classroom situations. Reducing the number and duration of unstructured situations and/or providing planned activities during these situations reduces the opportunity for the student to engage in interfering behaviors.

Antecedent: Discriminative Stimuli

Process

Specify environmental stimuli or events that signal the availability of reinforcement and then occasion interfering behavior.

Rationale

Some interfering behaviors are "triggered" by stimuli in the environment. By identifying these stimuli, we can then make modifications in the environment to prevent occurrences of interfering behavior.

Example

A parent is grocery shopping with his toddler. While going down the candy aisle, the child screams "Want," points to candy, and immediately starts crying. Sometimes the parent "gives in" and offers the child some of the candy in an effort to "calm him down." In this situation, the candy is a discriminative stimulus (SD) that signals the availability of reinforcement and increases the probability of tantrum behavior. One solution is to avoid walking down the candy aisle (antecedent modification), thereby reducing interfering behaviors.

Antecedent: Unconditioned Motivating Operations

Process

Specify the *unlearned* stimulus condition that evokes interfering behavior.

Rationale

Interfering behaviors are often "triggered" by either the deprivation or presentation of specific stimuli. By identifying these motivational variables, we can modify the antecedent motivating conditions to reduce the probability of interfering behaviors that result in reinforcement.

Example 1

A student has a history of food stealing. Deprivation of food (UMO) increases the value of food as a reinforcer increases and the probability of food stealing behavior increases. When we provide frequent high-quality snacks the hunger pangs (the UMO) are abolished, the motivation to access food is weakened, and the probability of food stealing is reduced.

Example 2

Consider the case of the toddler in the grocery store who engages in tantrum behaviors in order to access candy. The candy served as an SD and being hungry may also have served as an UMO that increased both the value of candy as a reinforcer and the probability of tantrum behavior. Providing a filling snack at the onset of grocery shopping may eliminate the child's hunger pangs and reduce the motivation to access candy.

Example 3

A high school junior has a history of both sleep apnea and chronic migraine headaches. The sleep apnea operates as an UMO (depriving the student of sleep) and the headaches operate as a CMO (presentation of painful stimulus), both of which increase the value of negative reinforcement (avoidance of, escape from) lecture-type instructional sessions and increase the probability of off-task behaviors (e.g., doodling, staring at the floor, laying head on desk, and sleeping in class). In this case, there are two medical issues that relate to interfering behavior. Because of the medical problems, the student would be referred for treatment of a sleep disorder, perhaps weight management (as there is often a high correlation between obesity and sleep apnea), and treatment of the migraines (both operant and medical strategies). In addition, in-school treatment components might include providing prearranged nap times or rest breaks after completing increasingly higher percentages of work, self-monitoring triggers and/or onset of migraine symptoms so that she could engage in palliative activities, and rearranging her schedule such that more demanding academic subjects are completed earlier in the day when she is less fatigued.

Antecedent: Conditioned Motivating Operations

Process

Specify learned stimulus conditions that evoke interfering behavior.

Rationale

Interfering behaviors are often "triggered" by either the deprivation or the presentation of specific stimuli. By identifying these motivational variables, we can modify the antecedent conditions to reduce the probability of interfering behaviors that result in reinforcement.

Example 1

A second-grade student exhibits interfering behavior when directed to read orally. Curriculum-based measurement of reading performance determined that the student's oral reading fluency (ORF) averaged 23.5 words per minute. Error analyses of reading performance revealed numerous omission, substitution, and decoding errors. The direction to read orally operated as a warning stimulus (CMO-R), increased the value of negative reinforcement (avoidance/escape), and increased the probability of interfering behaviors that resulted in avoidance/escape of oral reading. Modifying the reading curriculum for the student from the previous "frustrational level" to an instructional level not only decreased interfering behavior during instructional sessions (which gave her teachers the opportunity to reinforce reading-compliant behaviors), but also increased oral reading behavior and, ultimately, reading fluency.

Example 2

Erin, a middle school student with mild developmental disabilities who lives on a horse farm with her family, has a strong preference for looking at pictures of horses, reading books about horses (especially if these have lots of pictures), and flipping through equine catalogs. During past school years, her teachers have given Erin access to these materials during her break times . . . often jokingly saying that "Erin is just *horsing around*." Without conducting a preference assessment or a discussion with Erin about her behavior, the IEP team decided to design interventions to increase Erin's reciprocal social interaction skills (e.g., conversational skills) with classmates, small-group recreation-leisure skills with class-mates (e.g., card games, board games), and independent leisure skills (e.g., knitting) during her break times. The overall goal was to increase social-recreation skills and to decrease stereotypic "horsing around" behaviors. Erin's classroom teachers then removed all horse-related materials from the student break area and started to provide direct instruction in social-recreation leisure skills. Following two weeks of instruction, the teachers reported Erin was exhibiting a high rate of verbal opposition, property destruction, and aggression directed toward teachers. On a few occasions, staff had offered her books/magazines/cata-logs as a way to "calm her down." In this example, deprivation of horse-related materials served as a CMO and (1) increased the values of access to these materials and (2) increased the probability of interfering behaviors. The team next modified the instructional format by (1) providing a visual schedule depicting the sequences of instructional sessions and brief breaks, and (2) access to the books/magazines/catalogs contingent on no occurrences of interfering behavior during the previous instructional session. This resulted in an imme-diate reduction of interfering behaviors and, over time, an increase in Erin's acquisition of appropriate social-recreation skills.

INDIVIDUAL VARIABLES

Individual variables are a specific individual's sensitivities or internal states that contribute to the occurrences of interfering behavior. (Note: it is important to recognize that these vari-ables *do not cause interfering behavior*. Rather, these are variables that interact with environ-mental stimuli/events to produce interfering behaviors.) These sensitivities and internal states are usually directly related to specific UMOs and CMOs. Identifying these sensitivities and the specific corresponding antecedents provides the team with information to design person-centered interventions.

Individual Mediating Variables

Process

Specify individual sensitivities or internal states that contribute to interfering behavior.

Rationale

There are some situations in which a student may be particularly sensitive to environmental variables (e.g., sudden loud noises, large crowds, the behavior of classmates) or experience internal states (e.g., anxiety, depression, thought disorders) that following interactions with the environment trigger the occurrences of interfering behavior.

Example 1

Harold is a high school student diagnosed with Asperger's disorder who is very sensitive to loud noises (e.g., school bell, screaming behavior exhibited by classmates, chair scraping across the floor) and laughing behavior of others (i.e., when other people laugh loudly). These stimuli/events are antecedents to interfering behavior (e.g., repeatedly yelling "Stop!"). Antecedent modification is a strategy for reducing interfering behavior by altering or eliminating the stimuli/events that occasion and evoke behavior. In this case, it is not practical to eliminate or alter the school bell. The other antecedents are not predictable or controllable. The IEP team decided to teach Harold coping skills (e.g., self-monitoring, self-control, and self-reinforcement) as a replacement for interfering behaviors. Harold was provided with a wrist watch timer that beeped 1 minute before the bell rang so that he could predict the ringing of the bell. He then used his coping skills immediately prior to the bell ringing. This resulted in an immediate and marked reduction in interfering behaviors. Harold also participated in daily role-play sessions in which he practiced using his new coping skills in response to antecedent stimuli/events (e.g., the school psychologist and social worker taking turns role-playing the screaming behavior of a classmate, the scooting of a chair, and the laughing behavior of others and taking turns prompting, modeling, and reinforcing Harold's use of coping skills). Harold was provided with a written script of the coping skills routine, a data collection form, and a self-reinforcement plan. This intervention package resulted first in a reduction and then in total elimination of Harold's interfering behaviors.

Example 2

Jenny is a 13-year-old high-achieving student in the ninth grade. Both of her parents are college professors and have lofty expectations regarding her academic progress. In fact, they lobbied to place her in the advanced precalculus class at her high school. Her teacher has noted that Jenny has been underperforming (i.e., making C's or lower) on all of her quizzes and exams. In fact, the teacher has observed on multiple occasions that Jenny evidences unusual behaviors (e.g., sighing loudly, rapidly turning her head and looking around the room, sweating, asking to use the restroom multiple times, complaining of nausea, and running her hands through her long hair) at the onset and throughout quizzes and exams. Further assessment indicated that Jenny did indeed have the requisite knowledge to pass the test with an A, but that she became "nervous" when asked to complete the problems within a specified period of time. Yes, it looked as though Jenny was experiencing some moderate to significant anxiety that interfered with her performance on timed math tests. Thus, these quizzes and exams had become conditioned motivating operations for cueing anxious behaviors and real physiological symptoms and making avoidance behaviors much more reinforcing. To treat her anxiety and improve her performance on timed math tests, the team implemented a number of strategies simultaneously: (1) Jenny was given awareness training to teach her to detect the early signs of anxiety, (2) Jenny was taught anxiety management strategies like controlled breathing and progressive muscle relaxation to use when she detected any signs of anxiety, (3) Jenny's math quizzes and exams were modified such that the first four to five items were ones that she had already practiced and shown to be 100% correct, and (4) Jenny was told to take as much time as she needed to complete the exam/quiz. This last recommendation may bother some educators, but in actuality Jenny never used more time than the teacher would have allotted. It was the conspicuous timing aspect that seemed to be one of the triggers for anxious behavior. These strategies resulted not only in a decrease in anxiety, but in an increase in math performance as well as self-reported usage of anxiety management strategies in other situations.

Individual Behavior Deficits

Process

Specify behavior deficits (e.g., communication, academic, and/or social) that contribute to the interfering behavior.

Rationale

In our experience, when conducting an FBA, the vast majority of interfering behaviors are directly related to behavioral deficits. In fact, in almost all cases, we are able to reframe interfering behavior as a behavioral deficit. For example, behavior reinforced by negative reinforcement (escape from tasks) may be reframed as a deficit in appropriate communication skills (e.g., requesting a break). Or aggressive behavior between classmates may be reframed as deficits in conflict resolution skills. Or stereotypy reinforced by automatic reinforcement (arousal induction) may be reframed as a deficit in independent recreation-leisure skills. Each behavior deficit, then, is a skill that could be taught and reinforced as a replacement for interfering behavior. Generally, we advocate for a "FAIR-PAIR" model of intervention—that is, it is only "fair" to "pair" a behavior to increase with each interfering behavior we plan to reduce/eliminate.

RESPONSE COVARIATION

Response covariation is observed to occur when an intervention addressing behavior A results in a change in behavior B. Most of our interventions addressing problem behavior focuses on *increasing* participation within assigned tasks and activities. These interventions either involve reinforcing behaviors that are within the person's repertoire or developing skills to increase the individual's range of behavioral assets. When target behaviors are incompatible with the interfering behaviors, the increase in the former is typically paired with a decrease in the latter. When two behaviors are so related, we refer to this as an *inverse relationship* (i.e., as one behavior increases the other behavior decreases). The model of response covariation is one of the foundations of a function-based behavior support plan.

Example 1

Robyn is a student with cerebral palsy who exhibits hand biting behavior. This behavior typically occurs when she is not engaged in tasks/activities (e.g., during transitions from either one room to another, between instructional sessions, during "break time"). The FBA indicated that hand biting is reinforced by automatic reinforcement (arousal induction). Stimulus preference assessments indicated that Robyn preferred a specific genre of music (hard rock). The IEP team developed an intervention in which Robyn was provided a microswitch, a tape recorder with tapes of hard rock music, and headphones during transitions and breaks. When she pressed the microswitch, it activated the tape recorder. Pressing the microswitch was incompatible with hand biting. This resulted in an increase in switch-pressing behavior and an elimination of hand biting.

Example 2

Russ is a third-grade student with a specific learning disability in reading. When he reads grade level materials orally, he intermittently uses a closed fist to hit his leg or chin. The FBA included an assessment and analysis of Russ's reading skills. The school psychologist also recorded occurrences of self-hitting behavior (SHB) during oral reading. The results of reading assessment showed the following:

	First-grade passage	Second-grade passage	Third-grade passage
Oral reading fluency (ORF)	45 wpm	35 wpm	25 wpm
Decoding errors	1	7	12
Substitution errors	0	2	1
Omission errors	0	0	3
SHB	1	5	10

The data also showed a very high (80%) correspondence between decoding errors and SHB. Based on the results of assessment, the IEP team modified the reading program in the following ways (1) direct explicit instruction in phonics (word attack skills) for three 20-minute sessions per week, (2) controlled reading materials, and (3) prereading and repeated reading strategies with grade-level materials. Within a few weeks, this intervention resulted in (1) a marked increase in reading fluency, (2) a significant reduction in reading errors, and (3) an elimination of self-hitting behaviors.

Behavior

Process

Identify and operationally define the interfering behavior. Consider response effort.

Rationale

Be sure to be specific about identifying and describing the interfering behavior. The behavior may be part of a larger response set (e.g., aggression, self-injury, opposition, tantrum) so that there are many situations in which we may need to analyze each of the behaviors separately. For example, the response set may be aggression which may include hitting, kicking, hairpulling, and biting. Each of these behaviors may be controlled by a different set of antecedents and consequences and/or be related to different individual mediating and behavior deficits. Being specific about the behavior allows for more precise analysis.

RESPONSE EFFORT

Response effort is one of the variables we consider when applying the *matching law* (see Chapter 4). *Response effort* refers to the level of difficulty involved in engaging in the behavior: the amount of energy needed to exhibit the behavior. It is very difficult to accurately *measure* response effort. However, it is important to consider response effort because it relates to the likelihood of the occurrence of behavior, whether it is interfering or appropriate behavior. All else being equal, we typically engage in behaviors that require the least amount of effort. If the interfering behavior requires little effort and the potential replacement behavior is extremely effortful, the intervention may be ineffective because of the difference in effort required by each of the responses. One strategy is to modify the replacement behavior by increasing its efficiency or by reducing its level of effort. Other strategies involve increasing the reinforcement available for the replacement behavior (see sections on parameters of reinforcement).

Example 1

Steve is a middle school student who exhibits inappropriate verbal behaviors (e.g., swearing at teachers, swearing at students). Analyzing "inappropriate behaviors" is too global. In this case, using the BAPS to analyze each of the specific behaviors was recommended. The result was that swearing at teachers was reinforced by negative reinforcement (avoidance of and escape from tasks) while swearing at classmates was reinforced by positive reinforcement (social attention/reactions). Moreover, further analysis revealed a completely different set of MOs, CMOs, and individual variables (both mediating and deficit). Thus, "swearing at teachers" and "swearing at classmates" required very different function-based support plans.

Example 2

Consider again the case of Russ. He exhibits visual off-task behaviors (e.g., looking out the window, looking around the classroom) when presented with grade-level reading materials during sustained silent reading sessions. Based on the results of the FBA, it was clear that the amount of effort required for Russ to read third-grade passages is high. Conversely, the amount of effort to engage in off-task behavior is low. Modifying the task demands (i.e., switching from a frustrational level to an instructional level of reading materials) would be one solution for increasing Russ's on-task reading behavior and for reducing visual off-task behaviors.

Reinforcing Consequence(s)

Process

Identify the consequences that reinforce interfering behavior.

Rationale

Differentiating the specific consequences that reinforce and maintain interfering behaviors is critical to understanding of *why* these behaviors occur. Knowing the reinforcing consequences is beneficial for two reasons:

- We know what not to do (i.e., don't provide the reinforcing consequence).
- We have identified a reinforcer that may be used to strengthen alternative and appropriate behaviors.

Knowing What Not to Do: Extinction

One of the most powerful intervention strategies available for use is *extinction*. Extinction is defined as no longer reinforcing a previously reinforced behavior. The primary effect is a decrease in the frequency of the behavior until it reaches an acceptable level or ultimately ceases to occur completely. Essentially, extinction involves withholding the reinforcing consequence. So for a behavior reinforced by positive reinforcement, one no longer provides the specific positive reinforcer when the behavior occurs. Likewise, for a behavior reinforced by a negative reinforcer, one no longer follows the behavior with avoidance or escape. It is important to remember that extinction is not necessarily the same as ignoring (see the box below for an explanation).

EXTINCTION ≠ IGNORING

Many folks think that extinction is the same as ignoring. Ignoring is a strategy whereby *attention* is withheld when a behavior occurs. *If* attention is the function of the interfering behavior, then extinction is ignoring. However, if attention is not the function of the interfering behavior, it is not extinction because extinction means withholding whatever is reinforcing the interfering behavior, whether it is attention or not. Many folks also *assume* that attention is reinforcing a behavior when in fact it is not. In those cases, ignoring will likely have no effect on the behavior. So one must be extremely careful when using ignoring because the behavior may worsen, in part, due to the person accessing other reinforcers (such as candy, cookies, or playing in the street) or possibly resulting in extremely negative consequences for the child. Imagine telling your 6-year-old that you are going to ignore his or her playing-in-the-street behavior!

EXTINCTION . . . *TAKE TWO*

Caution: One may experience an *extinction burst* or a *response burst* (i.e., a sudden and dramatic increase in the occurrence of the interfering behavior) when withholding reinforcement.

In the late 1970s I (Steege) was a houseparent in a group home serving children with developmental disabilities. Kent, age 17, had very limited communication and independent

(continued)

(box continues)

leisure skills. He also engaged in inappropriate kissing behavior (e.g., sneaking up on someone, even folks he did not know, and planting a sloppy kiss on the face) that we hypothesized to be reinforced by positive reinforcement (social attention, reactions of others). After attending a one-day workshop on "behavior management" in which planned ignoring was enthusiastically discussed, my wife, Lisa, and I decided to ignore Kent each time he displayed this kissing behavior. One evening we were hanging in the family room watching a movie on TV. Kent snuck up from behind and kissed me on the cheek. I stoically offered no response. I was a rock. I froze all facial features and held my body rigid for 30 seconds. A few minutes later, Kent kissed me again. And I then used my "I am a statue" planned ignoring strategy. This pattern repeated itself several more times over the next 5 minutes and then Kent unleashed a full-fledged "shock and awe" wave of unrelenting kissing. The kisses were steadily increasing in duration and intensity. Moreover, the time between kisses (a more fancy term would be "interresponse time") was diminishing to only a few seconds. I did not know what to do. Now at this point I need to admit that I am a counter. Yes, I like to count things . . . I've got this thing for data . . . and when the kissing behavior had reached a frequency of 85 that evening, I was starting to get a bit frustrated. After another barrage of kissing, I looked at Lisa and pleaded for help. With an expression of heartfelt sympathy and compassion she leaned over and empathically whispered "You're screwed." So, when the kissing behavior surpassed 104, I jumped up from the couch, looked Kent square in the eyes, and yelled "Stop! That's it! No more kissing." With a mocking smile and a definite air of victory, Kent sat on the couch and relaxed into a state of triumphant victory.

Now, That's a Response Burst!

So what went wrong? Several things, of course. My behavior of watching TV lead to a temporary deprivation of social interaction with Kent (a CMO increasing the value of attention and the probability of kissing behavior as a way to obtain attention/reactions). Kent's deficits in independent leisure and communication skills meant that (1) he was bored and (2) he did not have in his repertoire more appropriate ways of initiating or maintaining social interactions. I made the mistake of *ignoring Kent, not just Kent's kissing behavior.* This is a subtle but critical point. By ignoring Kent, I increased his motivation for obtaining attention (and it usually doesn't matter whether the attention is positive or negative in nature).

So what should I have done? Several things, of course. I should have recognized that Kent was bored and engaged him in a functional task or preferred activity and reinforced his participation. I should have conducted an assessment of reinforcer preferences to identify effective and powerful reinforcers to use with Kent that might compete with the social attention he received following kissing behavior. I should also have provided noncontingent reinforcement (response-independent reinforcement) by offering social feedback intermittently throughout the tasks/activity. If kissing occurred, I should have briefly ignored this behavior and then immediately redirected Kent to the task/activity and provided social reinforcement contingent on appropriate behavior. I should have used functional communication training (FCT) strategies to teach appropriate communication behavior as a replacement for inappropriate kissing. I'm sure there's more I could have done, but this is a good start and gives you a really clear idea of why a powerful behavior change strategy worked against me.

Therefore, before proceeding with extinction procedures, make sure that you (1) can withstand and tolerate a response burst and (2) have manipulated relevant SDs, UMOs, CMOs, replacement behaviors, and reinforcing consequences to reduce the probability of the burst in behaviors and to increase more appropriate responses.

Using Reinforcing Consequences to Strengthen Alternative and Appropriate Behaviors

EXAMPLE 1

Kim is a fifth-grade elementary student who engages in swearing behaviors with teachers. The FBA identified positive reinforcement (reactions of teachers) as the primary reinforcement for these behaviors. Extinction would involve withholding the positive reinforcement (planned ignoring) each time swearing occurs. To combat a potential response burst and as a way of increasing an alternative and more appropriate behavior, the IEP team decided to teach and reinforce appropriate social interaction skills as a replacement for swearing behaviors. The reinforcing consequence (i.e., attention) that maintained swearing behavior was used to reinforce appropriate social interaction skills.

EXAMPLE 2

Hal is a student with severe developmental disabilities who engages in self-injurious lip- and cheek-biting behaviors. The FBA showed that SIB was reinforced by negative reinforcement (i.e., escape from demands). The IEP team implemented a strategy in which Hal was taught to sign "break" during instructional programming. In this case, the same negative reinforcement that was maintaining SIB (i.e., a break from tasks) was used to increase a functional communication behavior (see Steege et al., 1990).

Parameters of Reinforcement

Process

Identify or estimate the following:

- Schedule of reinforcement
- Quality of reinforcement
- Magnitude of reinforcement
- Timing of reinforcement

Rationale

To compete with the reinforcing consequence that is maintaining interfering behaviors, we need to understand what we are up against. Knowing the schedule, quality, magnitude, and timing of reinforcement provides the necessary information we need to determine how *robust* the reinforcing consequence is—that is, the strength of the behavior consequence relationship. We can then use this information to design a more powerful reinforcing consequence to effectively compete with the reinforcement that follows interfering behavior.

Example

Terry is a preschool student who displays tantrum behaviors (e.g., a response set including crying, property destruction, pinching staff, and biting her hands) when she is prompted to participate in instructional sessions. The results of the FBA showed that tantrums predictably resulted in an immediate cessation of instruction (negative reinforcement) and an opportunity for the student to engage in brief stereotypy (automatic reinforcement). Systematic observations and recording of on-task, tantrum, and stereotypy revealed that Terry was engaged in much higher rates of interfering behaviors than on-task/appropriate behaviors. The schedule of reinforcement was continuous (i.e., positive and negative reinforcement occurred each time the behavior occurred), the quality of reinforcement was high (escape from instruction and opportunity for preferred self-stimulatory stereotypy), the magnitude of reinforcement was high (i.e., typically several minutes of sustained escape and stereotypy), and the timing was immediate (escape and subsequent stereotypy occurred immediately after tantrum behaviors).

The IEP team conducted an assessment of reinforcer preferences and determined that specific edibles (Goldfish crackers, chocolate chips, and dill pickles) were highly reinforcing to Terry. The team designed a strategy to address the schedule, quality, magnitude, and timing of reinforcement that included the following components:

- Providing small pieces of edible reinforcement contingent on appropriate behaviors and the nonoccurrence of interfering behaviors on a dense and variable schedule of reinforcement (i.e., on average every 15 seconds).
- Teaching Terry to use a visual communication strategy to signal "I want a break" and then immediately providing a brief break from the task and allowing Terry to engage in brief periods of stereotypy (see Charlop, Kurtz, & Casey, 1990; Charlop & Haymes, 1996).

This immediately resulted in a marked decrease in tantrum behaviors, a slight decrease in stereotypy, and a moderate increase in appropriate behaviors. Gradually, the team modified the plan by requiring Terry to engage in longer durations of appropriate behavior before she could earn a break. Within 2 months, Terry was, on average, participating in instructional sessions for up to 45 minutes with 88% on-task behavior, 10% stereotypy, and 15–25 seconds of tantrum behavior.

DESPERATELY SEEKING THE SCHEDULE OF REINFORCEMENT . . . AN ELUSIVE ENDEAVOR

In applied settings, determining the exact schedule of reinforcement is often difficult. Why, you may ask? Reinforcement seems like a pretty straightforward process. Although there are many reasons, perhaps the most likely culprits are (1) intermittent schedules, in particular, are sometimes very hard to detect; (2) you may be uncertain about which stimulus is actually the reinforcer when there are several stimuli that occur after the interfering behavior and that occur almost simultaneously; (3) the reinforcement schedule may change simply because you are observing; and (4) reinforcement schedules in the real world are often "mixed"; that is, reinforcers occur sometimes after every incident of the interfering behavior, sometimes after 5 minutes of the behavior, and sometimes after the person has exhibited the behavior 50

(continued)

(box continues)

times. All of these make pinpointing the exact schedule of reinforcement that is in effect, and *functional*, for an interfering behavior very difficult.

Knowing this, what are you to do? Well . . . as we see it, you have several options. The first is to collect all the data you can and see in which direction it is pointing. You don't have to be 100% certain about the reinforcement schedule to design an effective intervention. The second option is to bring the interfering behavior under control of a reinforcement schedule that you specify. A third option is to hedge your bets and design the thickest reinforcement schedule possible for the replacement behavior so that there is little risk of the interfering behavior being more reinforcing than the replacement behavior.

BEHAVIOR-ANALYTIC PROBLEM-SOLVING FORMS

A blank Behavior-Analytic Problem-Solving (BAPS) Recording Form is shown in Figure 10.1. As opposed to a "stand-alone" assessment process, we use the BAPS following the completion of the indirect, direct descriptive, and/or functional analysis assessments to organize and summarize the findings from our various assessments. The first thing we do when completing the BAPS is to identify the interfering behavior, which is located at the center of the BAPS Recording Form. Next, we identify the surrounding variables that are relevant to that specific interfering behavior. This allows us to examine the ebb and flow of the complex array of variables that impact the interfering behavior.

The BAPS also allows us to examine the dynamic relationships among the various variables that support interfering behaviors. We then use this information as the foundation for designing function-based interventions. Each of the "boxes" in the BAPS model provides us with potential areas for intervention. Examples of completed BAPS Recording Forms for a variety of interfering behaviors are seen in Figures 10.2, 10.3, and 10.4. See Figure 10.5 for a sample BAPS Functional Behavioral Assessment Form.

Note: To see how the information from the BAPS is communicated via a report and how it is translated into function-based interventions, see Hal's FBA report in Chapter 12.

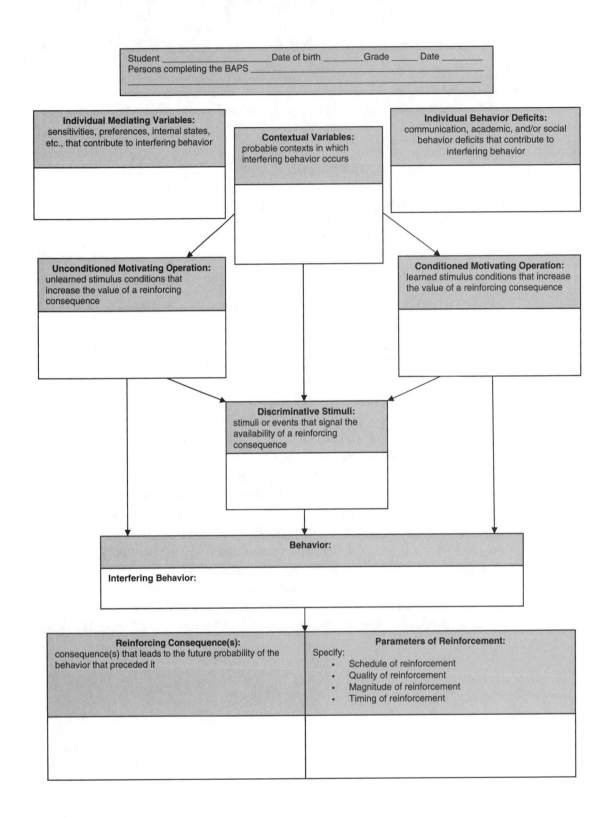

FIGURE 10.1. Behavior-Analytic Problem-Solving (BAPS) Recording Form.

Reprinted with permission from John F. Murphy Homes, Inc. From Mark W. Steege and T. Steuart Watson (2009). Copyright by The Guilford Press. Premission to photocopy this figure is granted to purchasers of this book for personal use only (see copyright page for details).

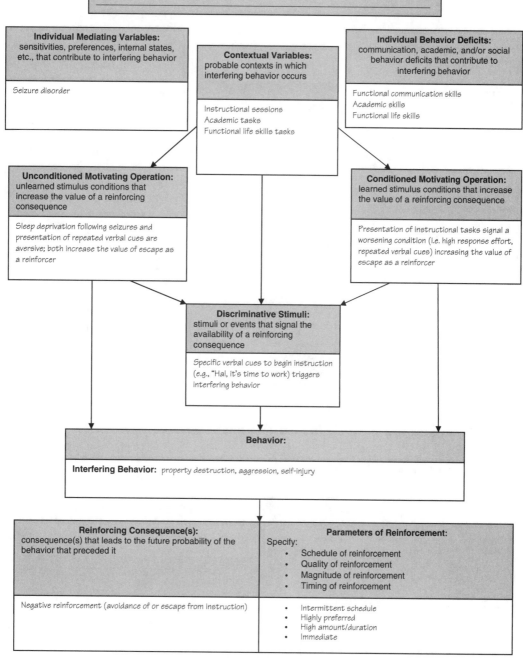

FIGURE 10.2. Example of a completed BAPS Recording Form.

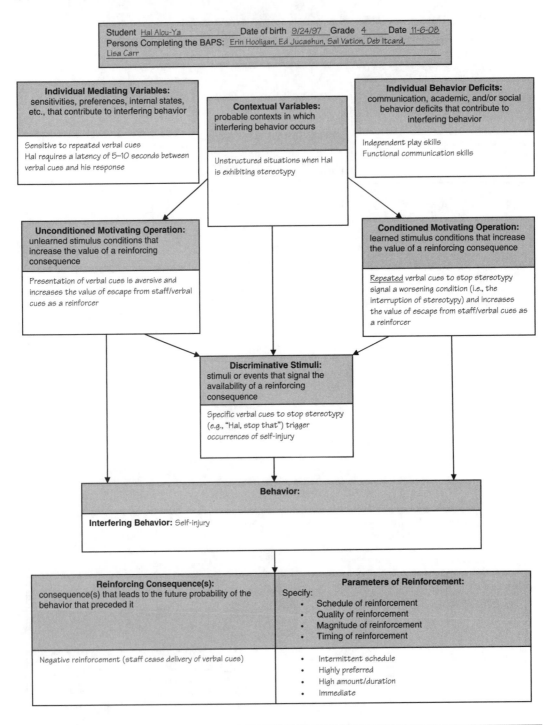

FIGURE 10.3. Example of a completed BAPS Recording Form.

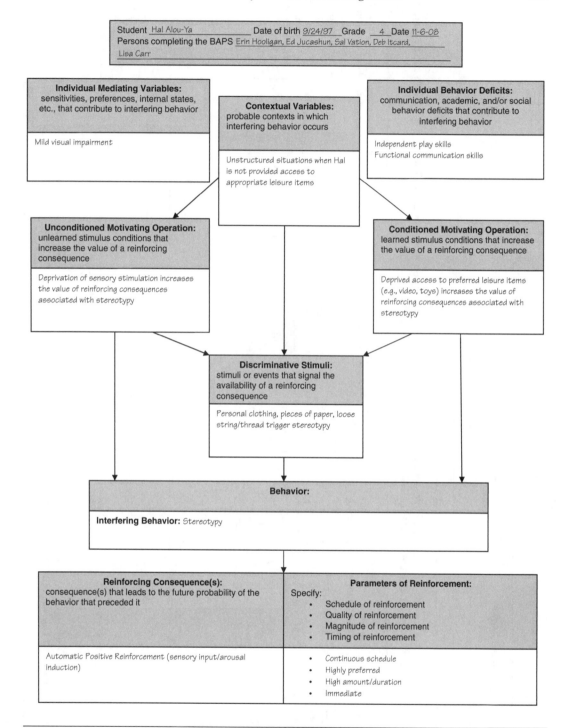

Student _Hal Alou-Ya_   Date of birth _9/24/97_ Grade ___4_ Date _11-6-08_
Persons completing the BAPS _Erin Hooligan, Ed Jucashun, Sal Vation, Deb Itcard,_
Lisa Carr

Individual Mediating Variables: sensitivities, preferences, internal states, etc., that contribute to interfering behavior

Mild visual impairment

Contextual Variables: probable contexts in which interfering behavior occurs

Unstructured situations when Hal is not provided access to appropriate leisure items

Individual Behavior Deficits: communication, academic, and/or social behavior deficits that contribute to interfering behavior

Independent play skills
Functional communication skills

Unconditioned Motivating Operation: unlearned stimulus conditions that increase the value of a reinforcing consequence

Deprivation of sensory stimulation increases the value of reinforcing consequences associated with stereotypy

Conditioned Motivating Operation: learned stimulus conditions that increase the value of a reinforcing consequence

Deprived access to preferred leisure items (e.g., video, toys) increases the value of reinforcing consequences associated with stereotypy

Discriminative Stimuli: stimuli or events that signal the availability of a reinforcing consequence

Personal clothing, pieces of paper, loose string/thread trigger stereotypy

Behavior:

Interfering Behavior: Stereotypy

Reinforcing Consequence(s): consequence(s) that leads to the future probability of the behavior that preceded it

Parameters of Reinforcement:
Specify:
- Schedule of reinforcement
- Quality of reinforcement
- Magnitude of reinforcement
- Timing of reinforcement

Automatic Positive Reinforcement (sensory input/arousal induction)

- Continuous schedule
- Highly preferred
- High amount/duration
- Immediate

FIGURE 10.4. Example of a completed BAPS Recording Form.

Student _____ Person(s) completing form _____

Date of birth _____ Grade _____ Date(s) form completed _____

School _____ School district _____

Operationally Defined Interfering Behavior(s):

1. _____

2. _____

3. _____

Interactionism: Interfering behaviors are the result of a complex interaction of antecedent, individual, and consequence variables. This form is designed to be used in the identification and description of the contextual variables that contribute to the occurrence of interfering behaviors.

Contextual Variables Specify probable contexts in which interfering behavior occurs	Antecedent: Discriminative Stimuli Specify stimuli or events that occasion interfering behavior	Antecedent: Unconditioned Motivating Operation Specify the unlearned stimulus condition that evokes interfering behavior (see Figure 5.1)	Individual Mediating Variables Specify individual sensitivities, preferences, internal states, etc. that contribute to interfering behavior	Antecedent: Conditioned Motivating Operation Specify learned stimulus condition that evokes interfering behavior (see Figure 5.1)	Individual Behavior Deficits Specify behavior deficits (e.g., communication, academic, and/ or social) that contribute to the interfering behavior	Behavior Specify interfering behavior and response effort	Reinforcing Consequence Specify reinforcing consequence (see Figure 5.2)	Parameters of Reinforcement Specify: • Schedule of reinforcement • Quality of reinforcement • Magnitude of reinforcement • Timing of reinforcement

(continued)

FIGURE 10.5. Behavior-Analytic Problem-Solving Model: Functional Behavioral Assessment Form.

Behavior-Analytic Problem-Solving Model: Functional Behavioral Assessment Form *(page 2 of 2)*

Contextual Variables	Antecedent: Discriminative Stimuli	Antecedent: Unconditioned Motivating Operation	Individual Mediating Variables	Antecedent: Conditioned Motivating Operation	Individual Behavior Deficits	Behavior	Reinforcing Consequence	Parameters of Reinforcement

11

Function-Based Interventions

Years ago, Dan Reschly made a statement that went something like this: "The only good assessment is the one that results in effective intervention." That premise has been a driving force throughout our entire professional careers. From our perspective, assessments that result only in the identification of a diagnosis or special education placement are inadequate (see Chapter 1 for more discussion on this matter). FBAs are conducted for the primary purpose of identifying the variables that contribute to interfering behaviors, with the results used to design individually tailored interventions (have we said this enough times by now?). Hence, a properly conducted FBA should have high treatment utility.

FBAs have treatment utility when they result not only in the design and implementation of interventions but in those interventions that lead to *socially significant behavioral outcomes*. Sounds great, huh? Well, in theory this makes perfect sense and when done correctly this process is incredibly effective. However, linking interventions to assessment results is not a straightforward process. Just as FBA is the science of human behavior, the design of interventions is a creative endeavor that includes the consideration of a myriad of potential proactive and reactive strategies. Consequently, we cannot begin to provide an adequate description of all the interventions that could be used to address the array of interfering behaviors that occur within school settings in this chapter.

"But wait a minute!" you exclaim and ask, "I thought that the FBA would tell me which behavioral interventions to use to address interfering behavior?" Well, on one level it does. On another level it does not. Let's consider both of these levels. At the most basic level, the results of the FBA often tell us more about *what not to do* than *what to do*. Consider the case of Tara, where the FBA pinpointed that oppositional behavior (e.g., arguing with teachers, refusing to complete tasks) occurred when she was asked to complete academic assignments. The team decided that the consequence to oppositional behavior would include verbal redirection to tasks. If redirection did not result in compliance and the behavior became "too disruptive," a time-out procedure was recommended. This intervention package was implemented for 3 weeks and resulted in a marked increase in oppositional behaviors. Based on the results of the FBA, the school psychologist offered the hypothesis that oppositional behavior appeared to be motivated by negative reinforcement (i.e., escape and/or avoidance of academic demands). She explained that the results of the FBA indicated that time-out, although designed and intended to reduce oppositional behavior, actually strengthened (i.e., increased the frequency of) Tara's oppositional behavior. In this example, the results of the FBA clearly showed that time-out was contraindicated. In short, the FBA tells us what not to do but does not necessarily tell us what to do.

Historically, interventions addressing problem behaviors have been reactive. Reactive interventions include strategies that are implemented *after* problem behavior occurs. Reactive interventions answer the following questions: "What should we do when problem behavior _____ occurs?" or "What do we do when she does _____?" In one sense reactive behavioral interventions are based on "an-eye-for-an-eye" philosophy and emphasize the *reduction* of problem behaviors. However, from our perspective, the reduction or elimination of problem behavior is necessary but hardly sufficient. We need to design not only interventions that eliminate problem behaviors but also interventions that result in the *acquisition* of socially meaningful behaviors. Positive behavior support (PBS) methodologies are designed to do just that. So, what do we mean by PBS?

FUNCTION-BASED BEHAVIOR SUPPORTS

Historically, when teams designed interventions to address interfering behavior they focused on:

1. What to do *after* the interfering behavior occurred (reactive interventions) and
2. *Reducing* interfering behaviors

FBA transformed how we understand behavior. PBS guided our use of the results of the FBA by emphasizing the use of *positive* intervention strategies

1. What to do *before* interfering occurs (proactive interventions)
2. *Increasing* appropriate behaviors

A shortcoming of interventions that include only these positive types of strategies is that team members are not informed of what to do if and when interfering behavior occurs.

We prefer the term "function-based behavior supports" and advocate for a model in which we address each of the variables that contribute to interfering behavior and a set of strategies to implement when "the _____ hits the fan." When dealing with serious and potentially dangerous interfering behaviors, team members need to know how to respond in those situations in which interfering behavior occurs.

You will see in our case examples that we include reactive procedures within our function-based behavior support plans. We will also see that our plans are context-driven. Context-driven plans address the specific controlling variables that are unique to the particular situation. These plans also emphasize the importance of:

(continued)

(box continues)

- *Anticipating* interfering behavior.
- Modifying antecedents to reduce the probability of interfering behavior.
- Cueing, teaching, and/or reinforcing appropriate behavior.
- Reacting in a way to eliminate reinforcement of interfering behavior (extinction) or reducing the amount of reinforcement.
- Reacting in a way that directs the student to appropriate behavior (e.g., response interruption, redirection).
- Reacting in a way that is safe for the individual and others in his or her environment.

POSITIVE BEHAVIOR SUPPORTS

Koegel, Koegel, and Dunlap (1996, p. xiii) described PBS interventions thus:

Positive behavioral support refers to the broad enterprise of helping people develop and engage in adaptive, socially desirable behaviors and overcome patterns of destructive and stigmatizing responding. The term typically refers to assistance that is provided for people with developmental, cognitive, or emotional/behavioral disabilities; however, the principles and approaches have much greater generality. Positive behavioral support incorporates a comprehensive set of procedures and support strategies that are selectively employed based of an individual's needs, characteristics, and preferences. These procedures are drawn from the literatures in operant psychology and applied behavior analysis as well as other disciplines and orientations that offer demonstrable improvements in a person's behavior and manner of living.

Also, PBS refers to interventions:

- That consider and modify the contexts within which interfering behaviors occur.
- That address the functionality of the interfering behaviors.
- That can be justified by their outcomes (i.e., outcomes that are acceptable to the individual, the family, and the supportive community).

Components of Positive Behavior Support Plans

At a minimum, a PBS plan should include the following:

- Identifying information
- Goals of the plan
- Identification and description of interfering behaviors
- Hypothesized function of interfering behaviors
- Identification and description of intervention components
- Antecedent modification
- Replacement behavior

- Procedures for teaching replacement behavior
- Procedures for reinforcing replacement behaviors
- Reactive procedures (if applicable)
- Description of data-recording procedures

The PBS plan might also include the following:

- *Supports for teachers/staff:* identify the resources that will be available as support for team members who will be implementing the PBS plan.
- *Training procedures:* identify the types of training procedures that will be used to make sure that team members implement the interventions with precision.
- *Treatment integrity:* identify procedures used to make sure that the intervention is implemented with precision over time, across staff, across settings, and so on.
- *Evaluation of interventions:* identify the procedures that will be used to evaluate the effectiveness of the intervention.
- *Programming for maintenance and generalization:* identify the procedures that will be used to promote ongoing maintenance and generalization of intervention effects.

Selecting Interventions

Again, the results of the FBA do not actually prescribe specific interventions. Rather, the FBA points you in the right direction. Now you're faced with an overwhelming menu of behavioral interventions from which to choose (like the list generated above for Tara). You've been there before—so many choices, so little time! So what do we recommend? First, consider *all* of the variables that influenced the occurrence of the interfering behavior (*Tip*: Let the BAPS model help you). And, for each variable that contributes to the occurrence of the interfering behavior, a specific intervention needs to be developed. In the following subsection, we provide examples that illustrate how the results of the FBA can be used to guide the identification of intervention strategies. Given the complexities of human behavior and the vast array of evidence-based interventions, the following examples are offered as a sampling of possible interventions.

A WORD OR TWO ABOUT TIME-OUT

Or, Time to Set the Time-Out Record Straight

Time-out is one of the most overused and misunderstood reactive procedures to address problem behavior. Technically speaking, the term is "time-out from reinforcement." Time-out from reinforcement is a Type II punishment technique and is designed to weaken (or reduce) behavior. When used correctly, time-out from reinforcement typically involves removing the person from a reinforcing environment and placing the person in a neutral setting (i.e., an environment that is devoid of reinforcement) contingent on the occurrence of a prespecified problem behavior. When implemented consistently, the problem behavior is eventually eliminated.

(continued)

(box continues)

However, in cases where the interfering behavior is motivated by negative reinforcement (i.e., escape from or avoidance of nonpreferred stimuli/situations/tasks/persons), the use of time-out actually strengthens as opposed to weakening the problem behavior.

You may ask, "How can that be? Time-out is a form of punishment. How can punishment reinforce behavior?" In behavior analysis there's an old saying that goes something like this: "Time-out from reinforcement is effective to the degree that the time-in environment is reinforcing." In cases in which the time-in environment is not reinforcing and perhaps aversive (e.g., oral reading for a student with a reading fluency disorder), using time-out when problem behavior occurs results in the removal of the individual from the nonpreferred situation. In such a case, the use of time-out designed to reduce behavior actually results in the strengthening of the behavior. When we discover situations like that we generally use another old saying found in the behavior analysis archives that goes something like this: *"Stop using time-out!"*

Antecedent Variables

When antecedent variables are identified as contributing to the occurrence of problem behavior, consider the following strategies:

Antecedent Modification

Antecedent modification involves modifying the antecedent to reduce the probability of problem behavior.

EXAMPLE 1

Aggressive behavior occurred when staff physically intervened to stop a student's self-injurious behavior. Aggression was determined to be motivated by negative reinforcement. Self-injury occurred during unstructured situations and was determined to be motivated by automatic positive reinforcement. Antecedent modification included (1) reducing unstructured situations by teaching independent and small-group leisure skills and (2) discontinuing the use of physical blocking when self-injury occurred. These modifications resulted in a marked decrease in self-injury and an elimination of aggressive behavior.

EXAMPLE 2

Aggression and property destruction behaviors were determined to be reinforced by negative reinforcement (i.e., avoidance of and escape from discrete trial teaching sessions). The FBA showed that task materials (clipboard with data sheet, flashcards, objects, etc.) operated as a CMO (warning stimulus) and therefore increased the value of negative reinforcement and evoked interfering behaviors. The IEP team altered the instructional format by teaching the same objectives using an incidental teaching format. This resulted in a acquisition of skills without occurrences of interfering behaviors.

EXAMPLE 3

Disruptive behavior occurred when a student was given a worksheet full of math problems to complete independently at his seat. A comprehensive FBA indicated increased compliance with academic requests when the teacher reduced the length of the math assignment and when she helped the student with the first problem or two on the worksheet. Thus, the intervention consisted of decreasing the length of the work assignment by at least half and assisting the student with the first problem on the worksheet. These very simple academic adjustments resulted in elimination of this student's rather severe disruptive behavior. As the student's compliance increased and continued, the length of the worksheets was very gradually lengthened until he was completing an entire worksheet without disruption.

EXAMPLE 4

Jacque, a junior in high school, engaged in disruptive behavior (verbal opposition, refusal to participate, arguing with teachers, etc.) on what appeared to be an unpredictable schedule. Staff often stated that the behavior appeared to "come out of the blue" or "for no rhyme or reason." Several times she was sent to in-school suspension where it was reported that she often snoozed. The results of the FBA showed that disruptive behaviors occurred much more frequently on school days that were preceded by nights when Jacque worked the late shift at a local fast food restaurant. The student typically worked until 11:00 P.M. and arrived home at 11:30. The student reported that she was typically "really wound up" after work, often staying up until 1:00 or 2:00 A.M. and falling asleep watching TV. She then needed to be up by 6:00 A.M. to get to school on time. Thus, she was often sleep-deprived and on those school days she said she felt moody, irritable, and generally "just kind of pissed off." Sleep deprivation is a UMO that increases the value of behaviors that lead to sleep as a reinforcer. Sleep deprivation was also the root cause of an altered state (moodiness, irritability) that increased (1) the value of escape from both interactions with teachers, lectures, and assignments and (2) the probability of disruptive behavior. Conjoint behavioral consultation (parent, school staff, and Jacque) resulted in a treatment package that included a modification of the work schedule to allow Jacque to be home by 10:00 P.M. and setting a timer on the TV so that it would turn off by 11:30 P.M. This resulted in increased duration of sleep and a reduction of school-based disruptive behaviors.

EXAMPLE 5

LaKendra was a normal functioning kindergartener in every regard except in her behavior. On a daily basis, she engaged in a multitude of disruptive behaviors including rolling around on the floor, dropping from her chair to the floor, yelling and screaming, refusing to do work, refusing to follow directions, and more. About every 2 weeks, LaKendra had what her teacher and principal described as a "meltdown." Her meltdowns included some of the daily behaviors noted above, but then escalated into running around the classroom damaging property, removing her clothes, blowing snot and spit into her hands and rubbing the mixture all over her body, and running out of the classroom. Quite obviously, this caused quite a stir at the elementary school. Our interviews indicated that LaKendra lived in a foster home across the street from the school with eight other children, including two infants. The results of our FBA were quite clear: the reinforcing consequence of Lakendra's behaviors was social attention. Further, we hypothesized that lack of adult attention in the home environment was a CMO that made attention from teachers much more reinforcing. Our treatment package was rather simple: when LaKendra arrived at school in the morning, she spent 20 minutes one-on-one with a preferred teacher while eating her breakfast,[1] her classroom teacher was instructed to provide her with noncontingent social attention every 3 minutes, and disruptive behaviors were ignored. After only 5 days, the daily misbehaviors were almost completely eliminated and there was never another meltdown!

Teaching Coping Skills

There are some situations in which one simply cannot rearrange the environment or modify the environmental triggers. In these cases we have found that teaching the student to cope with or tolerate the environmental triggers is an effective strategy.

EXAMPLE

A student with a diagnosis of anxiety disorder reported that she became extremely tense, irritable, and antisocial (e.g., screaming at peers, yelling obscenities) when passing in the hallways of her high school between classes. Although one alternative could be to allow her to walk from class to class either immediately prior to or after the scheduled passing time, this meant that she would miss instructional times and had the potential of being stigmatizing. The school psychologist implemented a relaxation training intervention with the student that resulted in significant decreases in her anxiety and her subsequent antisocial behaviors during passing times.

Social Skills Deficits

EXAMPLE

A student's disruptive behaviors (e.g., irrelevant comments during class discussion, laughing loudly, throwing spit balls at classmates) were determined to be motivated by positive reinforcement (i.e., social attention from peers). An individual variable that was contributing to this student's disruptive behavior was his social skills deficits. Additional assessments (i.e., social skills assessments) were conducted and, based on those results, specific skills were

---

[1] Our rationale for including the 20 minutes of undivided morning attention went something like this: *When LaKendra comes to school every day, her "attention tank" is empty. Her job is to fill up that tank in the most effective and efficient way that she knows how. Unfortunately for us, she has learned that the best way to fill her tank is through these behaviors. Instead of her filling her tank this way, let's fill it for her every morning by giving her this huge dose of attention. As she goes through her day, we are going to "top off her tank" with frequent attention from the teacher, no matter what she is doing at the time.* This rationale seemed to make sense for the teachers and we even noticed that they began to use this terminology for other children.

targeted for training. Teaching of age-appropriate social skills that resulted in an increase in prosocial interactions with classmates resulted in a decrease in the student's disruptive behaviors.

Academic Skills Deficits

EXAMPLE

A student's oppositional behaviors (e.g., refusal to read aloud, throwing materials, hitting classmates) occurred during small-group oral reading instruction. This oppositional behavior was determined to be motivated by negative reinforcement (i.e., escape or avoidance of difficult tasks). Additional assessments (i.e., curriculum-based assessments) indicated that, although he was in the fourth grade, his reading skills were barely at the second-grade level. Based on these assessments, direct instruction in basic reading skills including phonics and sight words resulted in his increased reading accuracy and comprehension. As the student's reading skills improved, his oppositional behaviors decreased.

FUNCTIONAL COMMUNICATION TRAINING

With many individuals, expressive communication skills are often associated with occurrences of interfering behaviors. In these cases, teaching communication skills as a replacement for interfering behaviors has been shown to be very effective. This type of procedure is referred to as "functional communication training" (FCT). Teaching communication skills that are functionally equivalent with the interfering behavior is typically more effective than just teaching expressive language skills in general. For example, with a student diagnosed with an expressive language disorder whose disruptive behavior is motivated by social attention, teaching the student to request attention using an FCT strategy (e.g., sign language, picture/symbol exchange) leads to the same functional outcomes (i.e., attention) as self-injury. Over time, the student will display increased use of appropriate means of requesting attention and a significant reduction of attention-seeking self-injury.

Consequences

Relative to designing interventions, the identification of the variables that reinforce interfering behaviors is important in two ways: First, as discussed previously, this information tells us *what not to do*. Knowing what not to do then becomes a critical component of the intervention. Knowing what not to do usually involves using an extinction procedure. Extinction is a procedure in which the team makes a determined effort to avoid providing the reinforcing consequence contingent on the occurrence of the interfering behavior. To be really precise, if reinforcing attention is withheld contingent upon an interfering behavior, we are using *attention extinction*. If we are withholding a reinforcing tangible contingent upon the occurrence of an interfering behavior, we are using *tangible extinction*. If we are preventing escape or avoidance contingent upon interfering behavior, then we are using *escape extinction* or *avoidance extinction*. This level of terminological precision is sometimes necessary to remind everyone on the team about the exact nature of the intervention. In short, when we are using any type of *extinction*, we do not provide the reinforcing consequence anymore. That is easier said than done, however. One of our general rules when using extinction is to ask this question: "Can we still withhold _____ if the behavior becomes five or ten times worse than it is now?" If the answer is no, we tend not to use extinction.

The second way in which the identification of the variables that reinforce interfering behavior is important is that we have identified a reinforcing consequence that may be applied to other types of behavior. This is of critical significance. We often hear comments such as "We can't find anything with which to reinforce Steven" and "Nothing seems to motivate him." Really?!? Remember, all behavior is reinforced by something in some way or other. The variables that are reinforcing consequences of *interfering behavior* can also be used to reinforce *appropriate behavior*. Consider the following examples.

Positive Reinforcement

Positive reinforcement may be used to increase appropriate behavior, thereby decreasing interfering behavior.

EXAMPLE

Maggie's inappropriate behavior in the grocery store was determined to be reinforced by eventual access to candy. When she went to the grocery store with her father, she often whined, cried, and shouted, "Candy . . . candy, I want candy, I neeeeed candy." Her father, in an attempt to be stern, consistently said "No candy" during the initial phases of grocery shopping. However, after a few minutes of Maggie's constant verbal bombardment, he usually broke down and provided Maggie with an edible treat (tangible reinforcement). Of course, at his point she stopped whining and fussing. In this example, Maggie's whining/fussing behaviors are motivated by positive reinforcement in the form of *access to a tangible*. Perhaps just as important for understanding this interaction is that Maggie's father's strategy of providing a treat was negatively reinforced (i.e., when he gave her the treat her disruptive behavior stopped). Thus, we can see why Maggie's annoying behavior persisted when in the grocery store and why her father gave in. The solution to this "double-whammy" reinforcing situation was easy. Because Maggie's behavior was motivated by tangible reinforcement (candy), her father simply provided her with a treat as soon as they entered the grocery store. The treat was a small box of animal crackers (cookies). While not candy, this was still a form of edible reinforcement and a treat for Maggie. Eventually, this procedure was modified to include brief shopping and prompting Maggie to use appropriate verbal skills: "Dad, cookies please." Guess what? . . . No more whining and fussing while shopping.

Negative Reinforcement

Negative reinforcement may be used to increase appropriate behavior, thereby decreasing interfering behavior. Steege and Northup (1998) and Steege et al. (1990) described interventions addressing escape-motivated interfering behavior in which negative reinforcement (i.e., brief escape from task contingent on appropriate behavior) was used to both increase appropriate behavior (e.g., math tasks and communication skills, respectively) and to decrease interfering behaviors (e.g., oppositional and self-injurious behaviors, respectively).

EXAMPLE

Sara's disruptive behavior in the classroom was determined to be motivated by negative reinforcement (i.e., escape from and avoidance of math worksheets). The team developed a procedure that included providing Sara with brief breaks following the accurate completion of small sets of math problems (see Steege & Northup [1998] for a detailed explanation of this procedure). This resulted in more frequent breaks (i.e., reinforcement), an increase in task completion and accuracy, and a significant reduction in disruptive behavior. In this example, negative reinforcement was used to increase appropriate behavior.

CASE EXAMPLE OF FUNCTIONAL BEHAVIORAL ASSESSMENT AND FUNCTION-BASED INTERVENTION

As we have stated previously in this book, one of the limitations of FBA methods, particularly functional analysis procedures, is the difficulty of assessing both dangerous and low-rate behaviors. Jerry, a 21-year-old man diagnosed with autism had recently moved from an out-of-state residential school placement back to his home community in Maine. Jerry had a long history of severe aggressive behaviors that often resulted in injuries to staff. As a result, staff had very low expectations for Jerry. Consequently, Jerry participated in very few functional activities throughout the day. When staff did prompt Jerry to participate in tasks or activities, he often engaged in a pattern of behaviors that included verbal opposition ("Not much"), agitation (e.g., slapping his leg), mild aggression (e.g., pushing staff), and occasionally severe aggression (e.g., biting, pulling hair). This presented a real dilemma for the clinical team. A central question was "How do we engage Jerry in instructional programming without provoking severe aggressive behaviors?" The following illustrates how we addressed this question. Read on . . .

In Jerry's case, we assessed low-rate and high-intensity target behaviors by conducting a functional analysis of identified precursor behaviors. Additional assessments to identify effective reinforcers and instructional methodologies were also conducted. Following assessment, function-based interventions were implemented and resulted in (1) marked reductions in precursor behaviors, (2) elimination of high-intensity interfering behaviors, and (3) acquisition and maintenance of functional life skills. The intervention package was then extended to 12 additional skill programs with comparable results.

Functional Behavioral Assessment Procedures

Due to the low rate (i.e., several occurrences per month), unpredictability (i.e., across times of days, activities, staff, and locations), and intensity of aggressive behaviors, direct experimental analyses were deemed inappropriate for this situation. Instead, aggressive behavior was assessed indirectly by conducting a functional analysis of *precursor behaviors*. A precursor behavior was identified to be a response that predictably occurred prior to the occurrence of interfering behavior. Additionally, a precursor behavior was identified to be a member of the same response class as the target behavior when the following two conditions were met: (1) when the response was not reinforced, the aggressive behavior occurred and (2) when the response was reinforced, the aggressive behavior did not occur. When all of these conditions were met, we determined that the precursor behavior and the aggressive behavior belonged to the same response class. Based on descriptive observations and recordings of incidents of aggressive behaviors, oppositional behaviors were identified to be precursors to aggression. It was hypothesized that interventions designed to address this precursor behavior would reduce occurrences of both aggressive and precursor behaviors.

A three-phase assessment process was used to identify reinforcers, to evaluate interfering behaviors, and to determine the most effective and efficient way of teaching Jerry functional life skills.

Phase 1: Assessment of Reinforcer Preferences

Informal assessment of reinforcer preferences was conducted by observing Jerry within the context of several natural situations and recording his selection of items. During free time, Jerry consistently picked up a magazine or book and said "Read." During snack time, Jerry picked up and ate specific snack food items.

Phase 2: Functional Analysis of Precursor Behavior and Appropriate Behavior

A functional analysis of precursor behavior and appropriate behavior was conducted by observing and recording Jerry's oppositional behavior and participation in a functional task within 15 analogue conditions (see Figure 11.1 and 11.2). A 6-second partial-interval recording procedure was used to record both behaviors. Analogue antecedent conditions

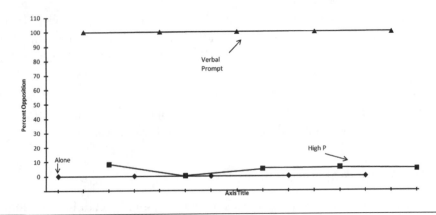

FIGURE 11.1. Functional analysis of precursor behaviors.

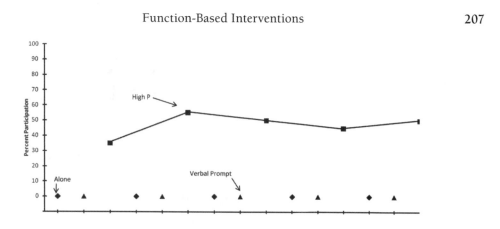

FIGURE 11.2. Functional analysis of appropriate behaviors.

were conducted within the living room of the group home. Two separate conditions were presented. Condition 1 included a verbal prompt cueing Jerry to a task (e.g., "Jerry, it's time to unload the dishwasher"). Condition 2 involved first engaging Jerry in a series of high-probability behaviors within the context of a preferred activity (e.g., turning the pages of a book, pointing to pictures in a magazine) and next immediately delivering the verbal prompt to initiate the task (e.g., "Jerry, it's time to unload the dishwasher"). An alone condition in which Jerry was observed within the same setting but with no demands was conducted as a control condition. The results of functional analysis indicated that oppositional behavior occurred at the highest rates and participation occurred at the lowest levels during instructional sessions that were preceded by verbal prompts only (e.g., "Jerry, it's time to . . ."). In contrast, low rates of opposition and high rates of participation were recorded when verbal prompts were preceded by a high-probability response sequence procedure. Neither opposition nor appropriate behaviors occurred during the alone condition.

Phase 3: Assessment of the Effectiveness, Efficiency, and Evocative Effects of Instructional Procedures

Prior to assessment, staff within the group home had relied upon a least-to-most prompting strategy to teach functional life skills (i.e., moving from the least intrusive prompt to the most intrusive prompt). Anecdotal observations indicated that both oppositional and aggressive behaviors occurred during these instructional sessions. An assessment was conducted to evaluate the effectiveness, efficiency, and interfering behavior-evoking effects of two instructional prompting strategies: (a) least-to-most and (b) prescriptive (Steege et al., 1987). The assessment involved 10 instructional sessions teaching Jerry a novel functional skill during which instructional methods were randomly counterbalanced. Dependent measures included (1) percentage of steps of the task analysis completed independently, (2) cumulative duration of training time, (3) cumulative wasted prompts, and (4) percent occurrence of oppositional behavior (see Figure 11.3). The results of assessment demonstrated that compared to the least-to-most strategy, the prescriptive method of instruction was more effective (i.e., resulted in more steps completed independently), more efficient (i.e., required

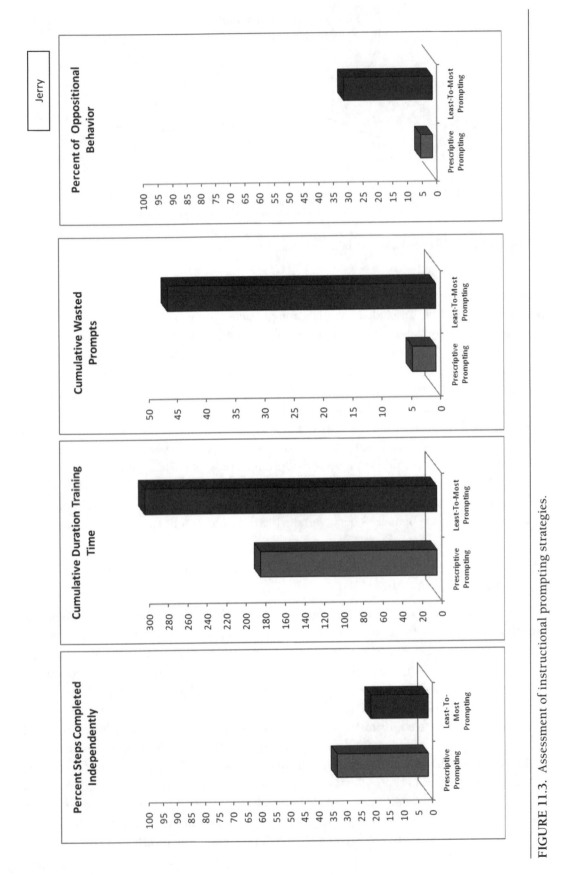

FIGURE 11.3. Assessment of instructional prompting strategies.

208

less instructional time and fewer instructional prompts), and evoked much lower rates of oppositional behavior.

Function-Based Intervention

Based on the results of assessments, an intervention package was designed to teach Jerry functional life skills and to decrease/eliminate both precursor oppositional and aggressive behaviors. The intervention package included the following components: (1) high-probability response sequence procedure to establish behavioral momentum, (2) task analysis of each functional life skill, (3) prescriptive prompting instructional procedure, and (4) edible reinforcement. During the intervention phase dependent variables were (1) opposition, (2) aggression, and (3) percentage of steps completed independently. Data were recorded at the completion of each step of the task analysis using the Task Analysis Recording Procedure (see Chapter 8).

Data showed that prior to intervention, Jerry engaged in high rates of oppositional behaviors and displayed skill deficits on targeted functional skills. The intervention package was implemented for 20 weeks. Results indicated a marked reduction of precursor behaviors and an increase in functional skills when the intervention was implemented. Further, there were no occurrences of aggressive behaviors during implementation of the intervention. A withdrawal of the intervention resulted in an immediate reversal of treatment gains. A return to the intervention package resulted in high levels of independent task completion and very low to no occurrence of opposition behavior (see Figure 11.4).

Effects

Progress monitoring showed that intervention gains were maintained for over 3 years. Furthermore, when the intervention package was applied to 12 additional functional life skill programs, it resulted in comparable low rates of opposition, high levels of independent task completion, and no occurrences of aggression.

The results of this case demonstrated that severe interfering behaviors could be successfully assessed and treated by focusing on precursor behaviors. This study also demonstrated the utility of combining several assessment procedures to identify (1) the variables that contribute to the occurrence of opposition and aggression, (2) a method for increasing initial compliance to instructional demands for behaviors determined to be maintained by negative reinforcement, (3) effective and efficient instructional procedures, and (4) effective reinforcers. Finally, this case illustrated a "nip it in the bud" model of behavior analysis that has implications for both low-rate and/or high-intensity behaviors that often occur within schools and other applied settings and have heretofore been difficult for practitioners to assess and intervene.

A special note of appreciation is extended to Tiffany Haskell Liegh who was instrumental in all phases of Jerry's assessment and treatment. Also, thanks to Erin Sullivan for editorial and technical supports.

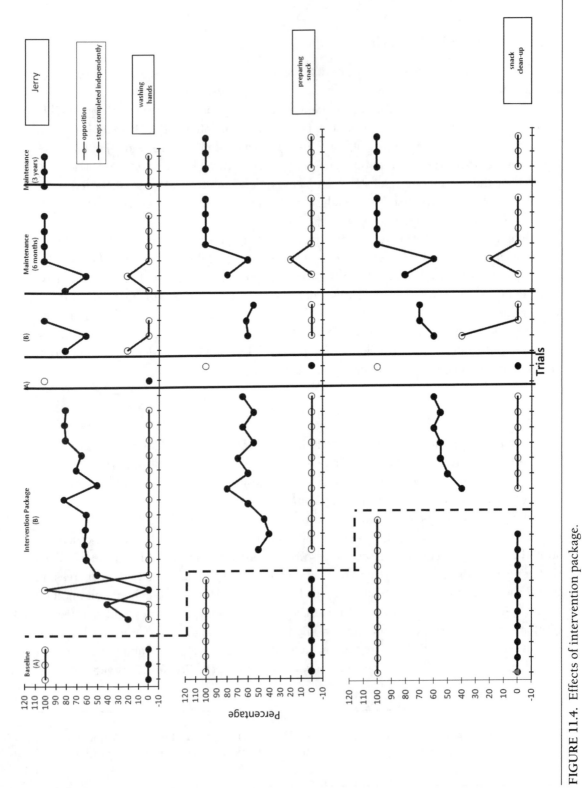

FIGURE 11.4. Effects of intervention package.

210

SUMMARY

We did not attempt to describe in excruciating detail the components of every type of intervention that is available for several reasons. First, doing so would have been akin to providing a cookbook of interventions, which is of little value to most practitioners and goes directly against our philosophical grain. Second, there are some excellent practice-oriented books that describe various types of interventions, particularly those that are grounded in applied behavior analysis (ABA). Third, the size of this chapter would have been quadrupled had we gone into minute detail regarding the selected interventions. Fourth, we wanted you to understand the rationale for choosing or designing interventions so that you could produce your own interventions rather than merely pulling one from this book. If you understand the rationale and basic principles of linking a particular intervention to the results of your FBA, that is winning the battle that will ultimately win the war against interfering behavior.

12

Sample Functional Behavioral Assessment Reports

Two of the most frequently asked questions about the FBA process are "What type of documentation is needed?" and "How much documentation do I need?" In actual practice, the answer to both questions is that the type and extent of documentation that is needed depends upon the following factors:

- The complexity of the case.
- The procedures used.
- The likelihood of legal proceedings arising out of the FBA.
- School district policies and procedures.
- State department of education requirements.
- What is generally considered to be best practice in the field.

It is far beyond the scope of this book to review and critique typical school district policies and procedures that relate to FBAs and individual state departments of education requirements. Instead, it is our hope that after reading this book the practitioner will be able to judge for him- or herself the adequacy of the procedures his or her particular district has in place. We offer four examples of reports that capture the components that we have discussed throughout the book. We have provided these different formats so that you have a variety to select from as you seek to document and convey information from your FBAs and PBS plans.

COMPONENTS OF
A FUNCTIONAL BEHAVIORAL ASSESSMENT REPORT

At a minimum, the FBA report should include the following:

- Identifying information (e.g., name, age, school/agency, date of report).
- Reason for referral.
- Assessment procedures.
- Description of assessment procedures.
- Assessment results.
- Identification of interfering behaviors.
- Description of interfering behaviors.
- Current level of occurrence of interfering behaviors.
- Identification of antecedent variables (SD, UMO, and/or CMO).
- Identification of individual variables.
- Identification of consequence variables.
- Parameters of reinforcement.
- Hypothesized function(s) of interfering behaviors.
- Examples that illustrate how antecedent, individual, and consequence variables influence the occurrence of interfering behaviors.
- Evidence- and function-based interventions.

The FBA report might also include the following:

- *Survey of reinforcers:* identification of variables that serve to reinforce behaviors
- *Behavioral deficits:* identification of behaviors or skills that the student needs to learn or needs to perform consistently
- *Implementation and evaluation of recommended intervention(s):* description, implementation, and evaluation of interventions that are based on the FBA results

FUNCTIONAL BEHAVIORAL ASSESSMENT DOCUMENTATION FORM

One basic requirement for *all* FBAs is that there must be in place one form that captures important details such as the date on which the FBA was initiated, the procedures utilized, the date on which the FBA was completed, and the outcome of the FBA. In essence, this form should serve as a cover sheet for a student's FBA file. It is not meant to replace a written FBA report; rather, it is a means by which to summarize and provide easy access to the most salient information for a particular student. We have included an example in Figure 12.1 to serve as a sample documentation form that we use. This is not meant to be a perfect example of an FBA documentation form. Instead, it is offered as a model for those wishing to construct their own form.

SAMPLE FUNCTIONAL BEHAVIORAL ASSESSMENT REPORTS

The length of an FBA report depends upon at least two primary factors: (1) the complexity of the case, and hence the various procedures actually used in the FBA; and (2) the likeli-

Student name _____ School _____

Grade _____ Teacher _____

Date referred for FBA _____ Referred by _____

Operational Definition of Target Behavior(s)

1 _____

2 _____

Operational Definition of Replacement Behavior(s)

1 _____

2 _____

Date FBA Initiated _____

Date FBA Procedures Completed

Record Review _____ Parent Interview _____

Teacher Interview _____ Student Interview _____

Functional Behavioral Assessment

     Screening Form _____ Behavioral Stream Interview _____

Antecedent Variables Assessment Form _____ Individual Variables Assessment Form _____

Consequence Variables Assessment Form _____ A-B-C Observation _____

Task Difficulty Antecedent Analysis Form _____ Conditional Probability Record _____

Functional Behavioral Assessment

     Observation Form _____ Interval Recording Procedure _____

Other _____

Date FBA Completed _____

Hypothesized Function(s) of Behavior(s) _____

_____

_____

Date Team Meeting Held to Discuss FBA Results _____

Date FBA Report Written _____

Date Positive Behavior Intervention Plan Written _____

Date Behavior Plan Implemented _____ **Follow-Up Dates** _____

Final Disposition of Referral (Describe) _____

_____

FIGURE 12.1. Functional Behavioral Assessment Form.

hood that a legal proceeding will arise out of the case. In the brief version of an FBA report, the main thrust is on giving overviews of information rather than in-depth findings of each procedure. The following reports are only examples of FBA and psychological reports. They are not meant to be the "gold standard" for FBA reports. Rather, they are designed to assist the reader with developing his or her own report format by either using the formats we have provided here, combining the formats, or developing his or her own. In this first example, we have double-columned the report to provide supporting rationale for the information included in the report as well as the implications for the FBA.

Example 1: Brief Functional Behavioral Assessment Report for Ward Cleaver

Identifying Information

Student: Ward Cleaver
Date of Report: 10-05-07
Date of Birth: 06-14-99
Age: 8 years, 3 months
School: Beecher Elementary
Grade: 3
Teacher: Teresa King

This part of the report is very straightforward and may include as much demographic and descriptive information as is required by the district and/or state department.

Reason for Referral

Ward was referred to the building-level teacher support team for an FBA by his classroom teacher because of his repeated verbal outbursts in class. Verbal outbursts were subsequently defined as "screaming and yelling at the teacher that may or may not include inappropriate language and physical threats."

Because this is a brief report, there is no need to provide extremely detailed information regarding the initial referral. An operational definition of "verbal outbursts" should also be included at this point.

Assessment Procedures

Record review
Teacher interview using the FAIR-T
Parent interview using the FAIR-P
Direct behavioral observations in classroom
Task difficulty analysis
Curriculum-based assessments

Although you may choose to list the assessment procedures in alphabetical order, we prefer to list them in the order they were completed. Doing so allows the reader to see the flow of the FBA process. Under "direct behavioral observations," you may also list the actual forms that were completed during the observation (e.g., Conditional Probability Record, Interval Recording Procedure) and the specific settings in which the observations were conducted.

Assessment Results

Ward's *record review* indicated a history of low grades across multiple academic areas and low standardized test scores in reading, math,

Beginning with the record review, the school psychologist should begin constructing hypotheses about the possible function of and language arts. In addition, his disciplinary reports indicate that he has been sent to the principal on numerous occasions for disrupting class. Both the *teacher* and *parent interviews* indicated that Ward was defiant and verbally abusive when tasks were assigned to him, particularly tasks that were difficult. Ms. King also indicated that if she reminded him to "get to work" or to "get busy," he often yelled at her and used inappropriate language. Ms. King reported that her typical response to Ward's verbal outbursts were to either ignore him, send him to stand in the hall, or send him to the principal's office. She has also contacted his parents on several occasions to pick him up from school for being particularly disruptive.

Direct behavioral observations confirmed the interview data in that, when academic tasks were presented to Ward, he screamed loudly at Ms. King, called her names, and threatened to hit her. A conditional probability analysis indicated that his verbal outbursts occurred 88% of the time when he was presented with an academic assignment and never when given a behavioral request (e.g., clean up around your desk, put the art materials back in the drawer).

Curriculum-based probes were administered for reading, math, and spelling. Ward was found to be lacking skills in each of these areas. For instance, his instructional reading level was first grade and he was able to add only 1-digit-by-1-digit problems. His spelling was also at a first-grade level.

the behavior as well as identifying potential antecedent stimuli. In this example, the record review indicated that Ward's academic skills might be suspect given his low grades and poor standardized test performance (a possible antecedent condition). The disciplinary data also indicated that he was frequently removed from his classroom or school contingent upon the verbal outbursts (a possible negatively reinforcing consequence). An important piece of information obtained from the interviews is that both the parents and teachers believed that he was defiant when difficult tasks were presented. This information, along with the data from the record review, has profound implications for planning the remainder of the FBA.

The information gleaned from the observation further strengthened the potential relationship between academic tasks and verbal outbursts. A very strong relationship was observed and documented with the conditional probability analysis between academic demands and verbal outbursts.

Given that his verbal outbursts were observed to occur only when Ward was presented with an academic task and it was his teacher's impression that only difficult academic tasks preceded verbal outbursts, a task difficulty analysis needed to be conducted. This type of analysis may be described as a *structural analysis* because the emphasis is on identifying antecedent stimuli that reliably evoke the problematic behavior. Before the structural analysis could be conducted, however, a curriculum-based assessment needed to be done to identify the academic materials to be used in the analysis. The analysis was then conducted by having the teacher systematically provide Ward with either difficult assignments or easy assignments and the school psychologist recording his behavior. Based on the results from the curriculum-based assessment, those tasks were selected that Ward demonstrated he could complete (easy tasks) and he could not (difficult tasks). These were then used in the task difficulty analysis. The data from the structural analysis are very consistent with the data obtained from the other methods in that a reliable antecedent for Ward's verbal outbursts is difficult academic material. Although a consequence analysis has not been conducted, it appears from the existing data that the function of Ward's verbal outbursts is escape/avoidance. That is, contingent upon his outbursts, Ward's teacher engages in behavior that allows him to either escape or avoid having to do the academic task. At this point, the school psychologist has two options: (1) conduct a brief experimental analysis to confirm the hypothesis that escape/avoidance is indeed the function of his outbursts, or (2) stop here and design a treatment plan based on the data collected thus far.

Hypothesized Function of Behavior

Based on information gathered during this FBA, it appears that Ward's verbal outbursts are triggered by being presented with academic tasks that exceed his skills and are maintained by negative reinforcement (i.e., *escape/ avoidance* of these tasks).

The title of this subsection begins with "Hypothesized" because a functional analysis was not done to demonstrate a causal relationship and to acknowledge that the function might not be stable over time and/ or circumstances. Note that the trigger or antecedent variables were mentioned as well because of their strong relationship to treatment planning.

Positive Behavior Support Plans

1. Remedial instruction will need to be provided in the areas of reading, math, and spelling to improve Ward's skill in each of these areas.

   The first two recommendations acknowledge Ward's lack of basic skills in each of these areas and the results of the functional behavioral assessment that indicated difficult tasks as an antecedent for the target behaviors. Further assessment may need to be completed in these areas including error analysis of the previously administered CBM probes and an academic functional behavioral assessment (see Witt & Beck, 1999).

2. Academic tasks that are consistent with Ward's instructional level should be provided by Ms. King instead of academic tasks that are too difficult for Ward at this time.

3. Ward should not be sent to the principal's office or be sent home when he exhibits a verbal outburst. Instead, Ms. King should wait until his verbal outburst is finished and then calmly re-present the academic task. If he exhibits another verbal outburst, then he may be removed, along with his task, to a quiet room to complete the task. The major point to remember here is to not allow him to escape the task when he exhibits verbal outbursts.

4. When Ward completes academic tasks, he should be allowed to take a short break (i.e., 5 minutes) to engage in a more preferred task that is acceptable to his teacher and does not cause disruption in the class.

5. The difficulty of academic assignments should be gradually increased as Ward becomes more skilled in each of the subjects. The indicator of moving too rapidly will probably be an escalation in Ward's inappropriate behaviors.

6. Data should continue to be collected on each of Ward's inappropriate behaviors to determine if the support plan is effective or if modifications are needed.

Recommendation 3 is derived from the results of the FBA that indicate *escape/avoidance* to be the primary function of Ward's target behaviors. The recommended procedures are called *escape extinction* (not allowing him to escape the academic task; recommendation 3) and *differential reinforcement of incompatible behavior* (allowing him to take a brief break when he finishes his work without incident; recommendation 4).

Teachers and parents often express concern when someone recommends that easier academic assignment be given, even if only for a short while. Thus, this recommendation is offered to show that our goal is not only to reduce Ward's inappropriate behaviors but to increase his academic proficiency as well. This recommendation satisfies part of the IDEA that says a positive behavior support plan must have documentation to show that a plan has been implemented and that modifications have been made if the plan was not effective.

Example 2: Functional Behavioral Assessment Report for Larry White

Identifying Information

Name: Larry White
Parents' Names: Carter and Emily White
Age: 6.5
Date of Birth: 03/17/01
Grade: 1
School: Percy Park Elementary School, Percy, MS
Date of Report: October 14, 2007

Referral Information

Larry was referred by Dr. Letsmakea Deal of the Percy School District because of concerns regarding his physically aggressive and verbal threatening behaviors that are currently occurring at school. Dr. Deal requested assistance with behavioral programming and with determining if his behaviors are related to any of his diagnosed disabilities.

Methods of Functional Behavioral Assessment

Child interview
Parent interview
Teacher interview

Record review
Direct behavioral observation
Review of behavior logs/discipline reports

Results of Functional Behavioral Assessment

Although a large amount of information was obtained during each of the procedures listed above, only information that is pertinent for either the FBA or behavioral programming is provided.

PARENT INTERVIEW

Larry's parents were interviewed at the Counseling and School Psychology Lab on the campus of Mississippi State University on September 20, 2005, for 2.5 hours. They both acknowledged that they are well aware of Larry's propensity for both verbal and physical aggression. The aggressive behavior started around age 4 and was directed toward other children and Larry's teacher. Because of his aggressive behavior, Larry was dismissed from five preschools. He began kindergarten in Harrison County, MS, at age 5, and continued to evidence "aggressive outbursts" and threatened to shoot the principal. Despite these behaviors, Mr. and Mrs. White indicated that the school worked closely with Larry and provided a "nurturing environment" which led them to view his initial school experience as positive. They reported that when he became upset, he was allowed to leave the classroom and go talk to the principal. According to the Whites, this resulted in a gradual decrease in Larry's outbursts.

During December 1998, Larry and his family moved to Percy, MS. Upon entering Percy Park Elementary School to finish his kindergarten year, his parents noted that his aggressive outbursts increased once again. They also noted that the school had difficulty in dealing with his behavior. He is currently in a first-grade class and is evidencing frequent and intense verbally and physically aggressive behaviors. He has been suspended several times thus far this year for his behavior. Sometimes, contingent upon verbal or physical aggression, he is removed to a "quiet room" where he is allowed to calm down before returning to class. The Whites indicated that he is more likely to aggress when someone either interrupts his work or provides correction while he is working. They also indicated that being physically touched when he is angry only exacerbates his aggression.

His parents noted that Larry has a hypersensitivity to textures including certain types of clothes, hard surfaces, and hard or crusty foods. At age 4 they began to notice both vocal and motor tics, which led to him being diagnosed as having Gilles de la Tourette syndrome. He is also diagnosed with attention-deficit/hyperactivity disorder (ADHD) and obsessive–compulsive disorder (OCD). Larry is currently on Luvox (25 mg/day) and Depakote (375 mg/day).

Larry's parents indicated that he continues having difficulty with sleeping, which may impact his school behavior. They noted that he did not begin sleeping completely through the night until 30–36 months of age and that he still does not sleep restfully. He grinds his teeth while asleep and is groggy upon awakening.

RECORD REVIEW

Leonard Spock, PhD, indicated in a report dated February 2, 2005, that Larry required a 504 plan to address his behavioral and emotional issues. He attributed Larry's sensitivity to criticism and difficulty in adapting to doing things in different ways to his OCD. He recommended adapting the environment to meet some of Larry's sensitivities (e.g., time-outs on a carpeted step versus a wooden chair), offering choices, assigning responsibilities, and avoiding direct criticism. When Larry becomes agitated, Dr. Spock recommended that he be given some method to release his "pent-up anxiety." He also recommended some type of reward system for work.

In a report dated May 6, 2005, Lester Pyle, MD, noted that Larry displayed the following symptoms: aggressive outbursts, hyperactivity, poor school performance, repetitive object counting, biting, fighting, motor tics, throwing objects, yelling, fits of rage, and hitting teachers and other students. He further indicated that Larry posed a long-term risk to himself and others and that he needed a highly structured, closely supervised educational environment that has few students and a high teacher–student ratio. At that time, Larry was taking Prozac, Depakote, and Risperdal.

Glenn Closely, MD, indicated in a report dated August 15, 2005, that, due to his having Gilles de la Tourette syndrome, Larry will sometimes blurt out words over which he has no control. She also attributed his desire for perfection, aversion to being touched when angry, and aversion to certain textures as being related to his OCD. She recommended that adults back off when he is angry, allow him a chance to verbalize his observation of the conflict, and then perhaps draw a picture of his feelings and write out how he feels.

REVIEW OF BEHAVIOR LOGS/DISCIPLINE REPORTS

In examining the behavior logs provided by the school, it is apparent that Larry has had a number of problems since beginning first grade. Instead of recounting these incidents in this report, the information will be reframed using an A-B-C format that is consistent with a descriptive FBA.

Date	Antecedent	Behavior	Consequence
8/16/05	Head-down time	Larry talked about breaking desk: "I can break this desk, you know."	Teacher talked to him to try to get him to lay his head down.
		"I am going to bring my shotgun and kill you. I can, you know." "I'm going to beat your butt."	Teacher told him he would have to put his name on the pad.
		Larry growled.	Teacher told him he had a check beside his name.
		Larry continued making threats.	Teacher told him they were going to the office.
	Teacher took him by the hand to go to the office.	Larry kicked the teacher.	Teacher took him to the office and Mrs. Smith was called.
8/18/05	Music/PE	Larry refused to participate.	Teacher asked him if he wanted to talk about it.
		Larry growled.	Teacher took him outside to talk and gave him a hug.

Date	Antecedent	Behavior	Consequence
8/20/05	In line at the water fountain	Larry threatened students from another class.	Teacher asked him if he needed to talk about it.
		Larry held his breath.	Teacher blew into his face.
		Larry almost started crying.	Mrs. Nyberg hugged him.
8/23/05	Handwriting worksheet Repeatedly writing Larry on his paper	Teacher reminded him to write his complete name before going to the next line.	Larry told her that he was going to write all of his "Larrys" before writing his last name.
	Teacher told him to write his complete name in a row.	He said he knew how to write his name.	Teacher said that was wonderful.
	Teacher restated the request for him to write his whole name.	Larry raised his pencil like a shotgun.	Teacher knelt beside him and asked if he needed to go to the hall to talk and calm down.
		Larry moved the pencil closer to the teacher.	Teacher told him to go to the hall.
		Larry got up and walked toward the door.	Teacher told him to give her the pencil.
		Larry threw down the pencil and left the room.	Teacher talked to him for a couple of minutes.
		Larry verbally threatened the teacher.	Teacher carried him to the principal's office.
8/25/05	Writing numbers 1–10	Larry stated that he did not have to do it that way.	Teacher asked him if he needed to go to the hall to talk.
	Teacher reminded the class to write numbers consecutively.	Larry began to crumple his paper.	Teacher went to get Mrs. Smith.
8/26/05	Writing station	Larry started drawing instead of writing.	Teacher reminded him not to draw.
	Teacher helped him form a sentence and prompted him to write it.	Larry said that he did not want to write.	Teacher gave a prompt to write.
		Larry growled.	Teacher asked him if he needed to go to the hall and talk and calm down.
		He growled again and broke his pencil in the teacher's face.	Teacher called Mrs. Maxwell to come to the room.
	Mrs. Maxwell told him that he needed to come with her.	Larry would not get up.	She warned him that if he did not get up, she would carry him to the office.

Date	Antecedent	Behavior	Consequence
	Mrs. Maxwell took him by the hands.	Larry kicked her.	Mrs. Maxwell removed him from class.
	Mrs. Maxwell let go of his hands and attempted to talk to Larry.	Larry began swinging at her and hitting her.	Mrs. Maxwell took him to the office.
8/31/05	Larry was playing on the tower in the playground; another child tried to get on.	Larry told her "No" and blocked her.	The child moved Larry's hand.
		Larry punched her in the nose.	Teacher told him to come down and talk about what happened.
9/1/05	Larry was in the cafeteria; teacher on duty gave a sticker to a child sitting beside Larry.	Larry swung at the teacher and said he could knock her butt off.	Larry was removed from the cafeteria to the office; teacher told him that could go back to the classroom if he apologized.
9/13/05	From behavior log checklist	Larry said the worksheet was boring and not fun.	Larry was removed from class for 15 minutes.
9/14/05	From behavior log checklist	Larry hit the teacher and attempted to harm himself with scissors.	He was removed to the quiet room for the remainder of the day.

TEACHER INTERVIEW

Mrs. Kotter, Larry's classroom teacher, was interviewed by phone on September 30, 2005. She noted that his behavior problems seem to occur more frequently when he is working on or has been assigned a task that involves paper and pencil. The following sequence, as related by Mrs. Kotter, is one that is typical of Larry's behavior and is used here as only one example to illustrate a behavioral chain:

Antecedent	Behavior	Consequence
Teacher tells Larry, "I need you to write this sentence," or when he has to copy from the board or color, or he has to generate an idea and write it, or he has to finish a sheet to do an activity	Larry lays head down on desk, throws paper on the floor.	Teacher allows him to lay his head down or verbally encourages him to do his work.
	Larry slides desk around, bounces desk, yells out, verbally threatens.	Teacher tells him he can either do his work or his name will be written on the pad.
	Verbal threats increase.	He is removed from the classroom.

DIRECT BEHAVIORAL OBSERVATION

Larry was observed in his classroom by two separate observers, Wanda Hemp and Dr. Mike Richards, on October 5, 2005. During one part of the observation in which the class was transitioning to reading at their desk, Larry was observed to be out of his seat during 75% of the intervals. (*Note:* a 15-second partial-interval recording procedure was used.) During those intervals in which he was out of his seat, 50% of those resulted in either teacher or aide verbal attention. Thus, the probability that Larry received attention for engaging in out-of-seat behavior was .50. At the end of this observation, he began scooting his desk around the back of the room. This evoked a good deal of verbal attention from both the teacher and the aide.

The next observation began during a snack period in which Larry sat quietly and was out of his seat only 16% of the intervals. He did not call out or disturb anyone during snack time. The remainder of this observation occurred during a math worksheet assignment. Larry was off-task during 45% of the intervals. Thus, he was on-task for 55% of the intervals. Most of his off-task behavior involved looking around the room or laying his head down on his desk. When Larry was off-task, the teacher/aide attended to him during 30% of those intervals. Conversely, when he was on-task, they attended to him during 6% of the intervals.

An A-B-C log was also completed during the classroom observations. These are summarized below:

Antecedent	Behavior	Consequence
Teacher told him to throw his trash in the trash can.	Larry threw his trash in the trash can.	
Aide gave him a direction.	Larry looked down.	Aide walked away.
Aide gave him a direction.	Larry looked away.	Aide returned to her desk.
Teacher said, "I am going to count to 2 and then I am going to write your name on the pad if you are not facing forward."	Larry sat with his back to the teacher.	Teacher continued with the lesson.
Teacher told Larry to return his desk to the proper place.	Larry put his head on his desk.	Larry got his snack and a piece of art paper from the teacher.
Larry was doing written work at his seat.	Larry made several negative comments.	Teacher told him that he could do the work.
A classmate walked by his desk.	Larry growled.	Teacher told him not to growl.

An interesting behavioral sequence occurred in which Larry was leaning out of his desk; the teacher told him to get in his seat; he then said, "I have an idea"; the teacher said, "I don't want to know what it is"; to which Larry replied, "I'm going to kill you," and the teacher responded by saying, "That's enough." Apart from the formal observations in which data were recorded for specific behaviors, other interactions were also noted. For instance, Larry was extremely quiet and compliant while drawing and coloring during snack time. In the afternoon, the teacher was reading to the class. Larry was extremely still and quiet during this time, even more so than most of his classmates. Larry was also attentive and behaved appropriately during a large-group instructional period where the teacher was doing a lesson on patterns at the board and calling on various children to come to the board and point to the correct answer.

CHILD INTERVIEW

Larry was interviewed on October 5, 2005, for the purpose of conducting a reinforcer preference assessment. A preference assessment is considered to be essential when designing a school-based intervention where reinforcement strategies will be used to increase appropriate behaviors. Eighteen items/events to be used in the preference assessment were gleaned from interviews with Larry's teacher, teacher aide, principal, and parents. Each of the 18 items were paired with each other and presented to Larry in a forced-choice format. The results of the assessment are as follows, with higher numbers indicating stronger preference:

1.	Popsicle	15
2.	Play a game for 5 minutes with Mrs. Maxwell	15
3.	Play a game for 5 minutes with Mrs. Kotter	13
4.	5 minutes of outside play	13
5.	Being read to for 5 minutes by Mrs. Meadows	11
6.	Play a game for 5 minutes with Mrs. Meadows	10
7.	Be the classroom helper	10
8.	Listen to music for 5 minutes	10
9.	Two stickers	9
10.	1 piece of candy	9
11.	Being read to for 5 minutes by Mrs. Smith	7
12.	5 minutes of computer time	7
13.	Being read to for 5 minutes by Mrs. Wiggins	6
14.	Break from work for 5 minutes	5
15.	Talk with Mrs. Maxwell for 5 minutes	5
16.	Being read to for 5 minutes by Mrs. Kotter	4
17.	5 minutes of drawing/coloring	4

Determination of Function

Based on the information presented here, including historical data (from behavior logs/discipline reports), anecdotal data (from interviews), and direct observation data, it appears that the primary function(s) of Larry's aggressive behaviors are *attention* and *escape*. Further, it appears that the primary function of his verbally aggressive/inappropriate behavior is attention, while escape seems to be the primary variable maintaining physically aggressive behavior. However, it is likely that both attention and escape are functional for verbal and physical aggression. In other words, Larry uses inappropriate language primarily because adults in his environment respond quickly and reliably when he does so. He physically aggresses primarily because doing so results in the cessation of an unpleasant task (e.g., a paper–pencil task) or removal from an aversive situation (e.g., the classroom). In addition there is a definite pattern, or behavioral chain, that starts with a command or direction that Larry does not follow, which results in an adult either reprimanding him or talking to him in some manner, which then results in even more refusal and inappropriate language. Occasionally these sequences end in physical aggression.

Manifest Determination

It seems unlikely that Larry's inappropriate verbalizations are due to his having Gilles de la Tourette syndrome, primarily because they occur in response to specific environmental stimuli and are not stereotypic, rapid, or nonrhythmic. As for the other conditions being related to either his verbal or nonverbal behaviors, it is extremely difficult to say with certainty that they are or aren't. Based on the diagnostic criteria for ADHD and OCD, one could make a valid argument that his behaviors are indeed related to these disorders. On the other hand, one could make an equally valid argument that stimuli in the environment are evoking and maintaining these behaviors and are thus unrelated to either ADHD or OCD. For purposes of school-based *treatment*, it does not matter whether or not these behaviors are determined to be related to a particular diagnostic category. What is known is that if certain changes are made in Larry's environment, behavior changes will soon follow.

General Recommendations

1. Despite the intensity of Larry's inappropriate verbal behavior, it appears that he can be maintained within the regular classroom environment if appropriate behavioral support is given to his teacher.

2. Based on the observation and interview data, it is likely that if his verbal behavior and noncompliance can be successfully addressed, his physical aggression will diminish as well.

3. The focus of intervention should be on:

   a. Reinforcing compliance with commands/directions.
   b. Not reinforcing noncompliance.
   c. Reinforcing appropriate verbal behavior.
   d. Not attending to inappropriate verbal behavior.
   e. Using the results from the preference assessment to guide selection of reinforcers.
   f. Disallowing escape from unpleasant activities contingent upon inappropriate verbal and/or physical behavior.
   g. Allowing escape from unpleasant activities contingent upon appropriate verbal and/or physical behavior.

4. Continue with the 10-minute morning transition time with Mrs. Maxwell. This seems to be helping to transition Larry from home to school.

5. Make certain that instructions and directions are followed up to increase compliance. Do not give a direction and then walk away. Give the direction, wait for compliance, assist as necessary, and reinforce compliance. For example, if it is snack time and Larry has moved his desk from its appropriate location, he should not get his snack until he returns the desk. This is only one example, and the basic principle should be followed throughout the day.

6. On a daily basis, monitor Larry's target behaviors and provide him feedback on successful performance. It is best, from an intervention perspective, not to point out difficulties but rather to focus on the positives.

7. Also on a daily basis, monitor to what degree the intervention is actually implemented.

Comments Regarding Current Behavioral Programming

The comments made in this section are relative to the behavior intervention plan (BIP) that was to have started on September 13, 2005. The purpose of this section is not to criticize the existing plan but rather to use the data from the current assessment, which obviously was not available when the BIP was written, to highlight effective and ineffective strategies.

1. It is fine to offer Larry choices, but do not offer him the opportunity to escape as one of those choices. For example, do not say you can either do your work or you can go to the office with Mrs. Smith. Instead, say something like "You can either do your work now and then you may _____, or you can choose not to do your work and not get _____." It is still a choice for Larry but one that does not run the risk of reinforcing inappropriate behavior. Be forewarned, however, that Larry's inappropriate behavior will escalate for a brief period of time because he is no longer receiving reinforcement for previously reinforced responses.

2. If adults are going to talk with Larry about his feelings and the like, then this should be done contingent upon *appropriate* behavior and not inappropriate behavior. That is, Larry should not get access to one-on-one adult attention for using inappropriate language or by being physically aggressive.

3. Do not give Larry hugs contingent upon inappropriate behavior. Hugs are fine, but make certain that hugs are given for appropriate behaviors.

4. To the greatest extent possible, do not remove Larry from the classroom contingent upon inappropriate behavior. Doing so reinforces his behavior by allowing him to escape the classroom. If he absolutely must be removed from the classroom, do so without talking to him, counseling him, or correcting his behavior. As soon as he has calmed down, return him immediately to the classroom and reissue the command or direction or have him finish the assignment on which he was working.

It is hoped that the information contained in this report is helpful in understanding Larry's behavior as well as in designing interventions that take into account the resources available at the school and district and the needs of the teacher. If I can be of further assistance, please do not hesitate to call.

_____   _____
Mike Richards, PhD   Date

Example 3: Psychological Evaluation Report (Extended Report Version) for Eric Trout

The following example illustrates a case in which a student, Eric Trout (see also Chapter 13), was referred for a 3-year reevaluation and demonstrates the assessment–intervention continuum. For many years, the Salmon Elementary School student assistance team (SAT) viewed the role of the school psychologist as one of an "evaluator" whose job was to conduct diagnostic assessments to determine a student's eligibility for special education placement. In the case of 3-year reevaluations of students with developmental disabilities, psychological evaluations typically included norm-referenced assessments (e.g., cognitive and adaptive behavior assessments), anecdotal observations and narrations, and record review.

In this case example, the school psychologist decided to offer a more comprehensive evaluation of Eric Trout. In addition to addressing the issue of continued eligibility for special education services, the school psychologist met with team members prior to conducting the evaluation to identify concerns and questions team members had regarding (1) behaviors that interfered with Eric's acquisition of skills and (2) strategies for addressing these behaviors. During the preevaluation team meeting, it was determined that team members were particularly concerned about Eric's stereotypic, self-injurious, and tantrum behaviors.

Identifying Information

Student: Eric Trout
Date of Birth: 06/23/2000
Age: 7-6
Grade: 2
School District: Sebago Lake, ME
School: Salmon Elementary School
Evaluation Dates: October 15, 22, 24, and 26, 2007
Report Date: 11/12/07

Reason for Referral

Eric was referred for psychological evaluation by the Salmon Elementary School student assistance team (SAT). The psychological evaluation was conducted to (1) determine if Eric continues to qualify for special education services, (2) evaluate behaviors that were interfering with Eric's educational progress, and (3) offer recommendations for the design of PBS interventions.

Assessment Procedures

Record Review
Scales of Independent Behavior—Revised
Social Skills Rating System
Indirect FBA:

- Interviews with Ms. Jones (special education teacher)
- Interviews with Mr. and Mrs. Trout
- Functional Behavioral Assessment Screening Form (FBASF)
- Antecedent Variables Assessment Form (AVAF)
- Individual Variables Assessment Form (IVAF)
- Consequence Variables Assessment Form (CVAF)
- Behavioral Stream Interviews (BSIs)

Direct descriptive FBA:

- Anecdotal observations
- Interval Recording Procedure (IRP)
- Structural assessment

Background Information

Eric lives with his parents, Stuart and Sandy Trout, and one elder brother, in Sebago Lake, Maine. Review of records provided by the Department of Behavioral Services indicated that Eric's history is significant for developmental delays, long-standing problem behaviors (e.g., aggression, self-injury, tantrum, stereotypy, refusal to eat solid foods), and the diagnosis of autistic disorder. Prior to entering kindergarten, Eric received home-based developmental therapy services for 20 hours per week over the course of 18 months. He also received biweekly speech/language services.

The most recent psychological evaluation was conducted in May 2006 by Dr. George Curious (school psychologist). The results of intellectual and adaptive behavior assessments indicated that compared to other children of the same age, Eric evidenced significant delays. Dr. Curious indicated that Eric's history was significant for severe impairments in language and social skills. He also indicated that Eric displayed the following problem behaviors: self-injury, tantrum, and stereotypic behaviors. Dr. Curious recommended that Eric receive comprehensive special education support services. In June 1999 the Salmon Elementary School multidisciplinary team determined that Eric was eligible for special education services under the handicapping condition of autism. He was placed in a self-contained program for students with developmental disabilities. Special education supports included speech/language and occupational therapy services.

Presently, Eric attends the Salmon Elementary School on a full-time basis and is enrolled in a self-contained classroom for students with developmental disabilities. He is mainstreamed into recess, lunch, and music. Since the first day of the 2006–2007 school year, Salmon Elementary School staff have expressed concerns regarding Eric's display of stereotypic, self-injurious, and tantrum behaviors. During a preevaluation team meeting, it was determined that the psychological evaluation would focus on the following: (1) assessment of Eric's current levels of adaptive behavior skills and (2) FBA of behaviors that interfere with Eric's educational progress. Behavioral consultation in the design and implementation of positive behavioral support interventions was also requested.

Assessment Results

The Scales of Independent Behavior—Revised (SIB-R) was completed with Ms. Jones and Mrs. Trout serving as informants. The SIB-R is an adaptive behavior assessment that compared Eric's performance to that of same-age peers. Domains assessed include gross and fine motor skills, social interactions, language, self-care skills, domestic skills, money, time, and community participation.

Results are reported as standard scores and percentile ranks. An average standard score is 100, with scores from 85 to 115 constituting the broad average range. A score of 50 is considered to be an average percentile rank and would mean that a student's score was higher than or equal to 50% that of similar-age peers in the norm group. Results are as shown in the accompanying table.

Domain	Standard score	Percentile rank
Motor skills	75	1
Social interaction and communication skills	48	1
Personal living skills	68	1
Community living skills	62	1
Broad independence	57	0.2

These results indicated that, compared to other children of the same age, Eric evidenced delays across all domains. Eric's areas of strength within the adaptive behavior domain included visual discrimination skills, visual matching skills, specific personal living skills (e.g., independent toileting), fine motor skills, willingness to try new tasks, recently acquired ability to transition between tasks and settings, and developing expressive verbal language skills. Areas of relative weakness included reciprocal social interactions, cooperative play with peers, independent leisure/play, community living skills, and specific self-help skills (toothbrushing, bathing, and bed making, among others).

To further assess social skills delays that were identified through adaptive behavior assessment, the Social Skills Rating System (SSRS) was administered, with Ms. Jones serving as the informant. The SSRS utilizes rating scales to provide a broad assessment of a student's social behaviors. The SSRS is a norm-referenced assessment in which the results of Eric's performance were compared to that of male peers of the same age to yield Standard Scores and Percentile Ranks. Results indicated that Eric received a Standard Score of 60 and a Percentile Rank of 1, and he is described as having significantly below-average skills when compared to those of same-age peers.

The results of social skills assessment suggested that Eric evidences relative social skills strengths with regard to his social interest and desire to interact with others. Assessment results indicated that the following skills are particular areas of weakness for Eric: group participation with peers, imitation of appropriate behavior of peers, ignoring peer distractions, using free time in an acceptable way, initiating conversations with peers, inviting peers to join activities, and cooperating with peers without prompting. During interviews regarding Eric's social behaviors, Ms. Jones and Mrs. Trout reported that Eric typically avoids eye contact with others, rarely responds to social interactions that have been initiated by peers/classmates/siblings, rarely initiates social interactions with others, and prefers to manipulate and be occupied with inanimate objects. They reported that Eric has marked weaknesses in independent leisure and cooperative play skills.

Indirect FBA included administration of structured interviews to assess current areas of behavioral concern, relevant antecedents (or "triggers") to problem behavior, relevant internal/individual variables, and relevant consequence variables. This involved the use of the following assessment forms:

- The Functional Behavioral Assessment Screening Form (FBASF)
- The Antecedent Variables Assessment Form (AVAF)
- The Individual Variables Assessment Form (IVAF)
- The Consequence Variables Assessment Form (VAF)
- Behavioral Stream Interviews (BSIs)

The interviews were conducted with Ms. Jones and Mrs. Trout serving as informants.

Identification and Description of Interfering Behaviors

The following behaviors interfere with Eric's acquisition of academic, social, and adaptive living skills:

1. *Stereotypic behaviors*—defined as hand flapping, scratching, rubbing, pounding, or tapping of objects/surfaces.
2. *Self-injurious behaviors*—defined as harm to self including hitting of head/face with open hand or closed fist, separated by 10 seconds of no-hitting behaviors.
3. *Tantrum behaviors*—defined as a response set including two or more of the following: screaming, crying, flopping to the floor, or throwing materials, separated by 30 seconds of no-tantrum behaviors.

Identification of Antecedent, Individual, and Consequence Variables

The following *antecedent* variables were identified as "triggers" (i.e., variables that occurred prior to the onset of interfering behaviors):

1. Unstructured time appears to contribute to the occurrence of stereotypic behavior.
2. Language-based instructional activities contribute to the occurrence of stereotypic behaviors.
3. Physically prompting Eric to stop stereotypic behaviors contributes to the occurrence of self-injurious behaviors and tantrum behaviors.

The following *individual* variables were identified as factors that appear to contribute to the occurrence of interfering behaviors:

1. Social skills deficits.
2. Expressive and receptive communication skill delays.
3. Delays in independent and cooperative leisure skills.

The following variables were identified as *consequences* of interfering behaviors (i.e., variables that follow the occurrence of interfering behaviors):

1. Sensory consequences (arousal induction) appear to be a result of stereotypic behaviors.
2. Withdrawal of staff physical prompting typically occurs following self-injurious and tantrum behaviors.

Direct descriptive FBA included (1) anecdotal observations and behavior-recording procedures, (2) the interval recording procedure (IRP), and (3) structural assessments. The results of anecdotal observation and recording indicated that stereotypic behaviors occurred at high rates across multiple classroom settings, activities, and staff. Self-injury was observed to occur less frequently, but it also occurred across settings, activities, and staff. To document the occurrence and to identify antecedent conditions associated with these behaviors, the IRP was implemented for several school days. The IRP is an ongoing functional behavioral assessment and monitoring system where Eric's behavior was monitored and recorded every 15 minutes throughout his school day. Prior to implementing the IRP, each interfering behavior was described and a corresponding data recording was identified for each behavior. Training sessions with Ms. Jones and one educational technician involved both role play and coaching in how to complete the IRP. The results of documentation of interfering behaviors using the IRP are as shown in the accompanying table:

Behavior	Description	Data recording	Current levels of occurrence
Stereotypy	Hand flapping; scratching rubbing/ pounding/tapping objects or surfaces	Performance-based (0, 1, 2, 3, 4, 5)	61% daily average
Self-injury	Occurrences of harm to self including hitting head/face with open hand or closed fist	Frequency (recording of each discrete event)	7.85 occurrences/ hour
Tantrum	A response set including two or more of the following: screaming, crying, flopping to the floor, throwing materials	Duration (recording the length of each occurrence of tantrum behaviors)	8.75 minutes/ hour

Note. Current level of occurrence (CLO) was determined by averaging behavioral data from April 16, 2002 through April 26, 2002.

Review of the completed IRP data indicated that stereotypic behaviors occurred across a wide range of conditions. Stereotypic, self-injurious, and tantrum behaviors occurred at the highest levels during unstructured and language-based instructional situations and at lower levels during structured situations and when Eric was engaged in functional tasks that involved experiential learning activities. To further evaluate these behaviors, functional behavioral analysis procedures were implemented.

Structural Assessment

To further evaluate interfering behaviors, a structural assessment was conducted. The structural assessment involved observing Eric within *naturally occurring classroom situations* and recording occurrences of appropriate and interfering behaviors using a 6-second partial-interval recording procedure. Eric was observed within the following situations: free play (no instructional expectations were placed on Eric and no social interactions were provided), individual visual–motor (VM) instructional tasks, and individual language-based (LB) instructional tasks. Within each situation, active participation was defined as Eric's visual, verbal, and/or motor on-task behavior. The previous definitions of self-injurious, stereotypic, and tantrum behaviors were used during these observations. The results of the structural assessment are shown in the following table (data are presented as percentage of occurrence).

Setting	Active participation	Self-injury	Stereotypy	Tantrum
Free play	12%	0%	74%	0%
Individual VM instructional tasks	68%	2%	12%	0%
Individual LB instructional tasks	22%	24%	66%	12%

During the structural assessment it was observed that Eric exhibited higher levels of stereotypic behavior when prompted to participate in language-based instructional tasks (e.g., expressive labeling) and free-play situations. Conversely, he exhibited lower levels of stereotypic behavior during visual–motor tasks (e.g., putting together a puzzle, performing a visual discrimination task). Also self-injurious and tantrum behaviors occurred at much higher levels during the language-based instruction but at very low (2%) to no occurrences during the visually based and free-play situations.

An additional structural analysis was conducted to further evaluate these findings. This additional assessment involved observing and recording Eric's behavior across naturally occurring classroom situations using a 6-second partial-interval recording procedure. Results are shown in the following table.

Setting	Active participation	Self-injury	Stereotypy	Tantrum
Language-based tasks	18%	84%	16%	21%
Visually based tasks	89%	14%	0%	0%
Language-based tasks	12%	78%	0%	16%
Visually based tasks	94%	12%	2%	0%

These results confirmed the hypothesis that high levels of stereotypic behavior were associated with language-based instructional tasks/activities. Conversely, active participation was much higher during visually based instructional tasks/activities. These data also revealed another finding, namely, that self-injury occurred at higher levels during language-based tasks as compared to visually based instructional situations.

Note: During these observations it was found that self-injury occurred only when the educational technician physically prompted Eric to disengage from stereotypic behaviors. Also tantrum behaviors occurred following physical prompts (i.e., response interruption) to block occurrences of self-injury. Based on the results of FBA procedures, the following hypotheses are offered:

HYPOTHESIZED FUNCTIONS OF INTERFERING BEHAVIORS

Stereotypy. Stereotypic behaviors appear to be motivated by automatic positive reinforcement (i.e., sensory consequences, arousal induction).

Example. When "alone" and not engaged in functional tasks/activities, Eric exhibited hand flapping and tapping of objects/surfaces. It is highly likely that stereotypic behaviors are also motivated by negative reinforcement (i.e., escape/avoidance of nonpreferred tasks/activities).

Example. When prompted to participate in language-based instruction, Eric exhibited high levels of stereotypic behavior and low levels of active participation.

Self-Injury. Self-injurious behaviors appear to be motivated by negative reinforcement (i.e., escape/avoidance of nonpreferred social interactions, such as prompting by staff to disengage from stereotypic behaviors) *and* positive reinforcement (i.e., continued opportunity to engage in stereotypic behaviors).

Example. The educational technician was attempting to implement a language-based instructional activity. Eric exhibited high levels of stereotypic behavior. The educational technician physically prompted Eric from stereotypic tapping of objects and cued him to the task. Eric immediately exhibited self-injury (i.e., hit his face with a closed fist). The educational technician withdrew the physical prompt. Eric immediately stopped self-injury and began to exhibit stereotypic behavior.

Tantrum. Tantrum behaviors appear to be motivated by negative reinforcement (i.e., escape/avoidance of nonpreferred social interactions, such as physical intervention from staff to interrupt or block self-injurious behaviors) *and* positive reinforcement (i.e., continued opportunity to engage in stereotypic behaviors).

Example. During a free-play situation, Eric exhibited stereotypic behaviors. The educational technician provided physical prompts to redirect Eric from tapping objects. Eric exhibited self-injury (i.e., he hit himself on the side of his head with a closed fist several times). The educational technician blocked the self-injury with her hand and attempted to stop Eric from hitting himself. He flopped to the floor, screamed, and threw objects. Eric was physically directed to a time-out area where he exhibited high levels of stereotypic behaviors.

The results of assessments indicated a response chain involving stereotypic, self-injurious, and tantrum behaviors. It was hypothesized that interventions that focused on decreasing stereotypic behaviors would also result in reductions in self-injurious and tantrum behaviors.

IMPLEMENTATION AND PRELIMINARY EVALUATION OF INTERVENTION

Based on the results of the assessment it was determined that Eric demonstrated strengths in visual discrimination and visual matching skills. It was also noted that Eric was in the early stages of learning to use visual communication strategies under the direction of Ms. Peabody (a speech–language pathologist). In collaboration with Ms. Peabody, an intervention involving dialogue displays (DDs) was implemented. The DDs included picture symbols (with the paired written word) depicting the content of the language-based instructional tasks/activities, rules regarding appropriate behaviors, and a symbol that indicated a direction to stop engaging in stereotypic behaviors. The team agreed to implement the DD procedures on a trial basis. To evaluate the efficacy of this intervention, an alternating treatments design was used in which the DD procedures were used within the context of three language-based instructional sessions but were not used in three comparable language-based instructional sessions. Active participation, stereotypy, self-injury, and tantrum behaviors were recorded using a 6-second partial-interval recording procedure.

Note: Because self-injury typically occurred during attempts to physically redirect Eric from stereotypic and tantrum behaviors occurred when staff attempted to block self-injury, staff were instructed not to provide contingent physical redirection or response interruption procedures when Eric displayed stereotypical behaviors.

The results are shown in the accompanying table. These results demonstrated that the implementation of the DD procedure within the context of language-based instructional tasks/activities resulted in much lower levels of stereotypic behavior and higher levels of active participation compared to comparable instructional sessions in which the DD procedures were not implemented. Also by not providing physical redirection contingent on self-injury, the levels of self-injury were very low to nonexistent. In fact, there were no occurrences of self-injury during those situations in which the DD procedures were used. Moreover, by not blocking self-injury, tantrum behavior was eliminated.

Situation	Active participation	Self-injury	Stereotypy	Tantrum
Language-based (no DD)	16%	0%	80%	0%
Language-based (with DD)	59%	0%	27%	0%
Language-based (no DD)	14%	0%	69%	0%
Language-based (with DD)	72%	0%	20%	0%
Language-based (no DD)	21%	2%	74%	0%
Language-based (with DD)	83%	0%	10%	0%

Psychological Impressions and Considerations for the Team

The results of adaptive behavior and behavioral checklists indicate that compared to other children of the same age, Eric evidences delays across all domains. He exhibits stereotypic, self-injurious, and tantrum behaviors that significantly interfere with his acquisition of academic, social, personal living, community living, and social skills. While over the past year he has gained numerous skills, he continues to display many of the characteristics within the autism spectrum. The diagnosis of autistic disorder is offered. Eric appears to continue to meet the criteria for special education services under the handicapping condition of autism.

The results of adaptive behavior and social skills assessments indicate that Eric is in need of comprehensive social skills training programs. Social skills instruction that focuses on increasing reciprocal social interactions with teachers and classmates and cooperative play skills are supported. Social skills instruction will need to incorporate individualized and group instruction as well as role-play and live practice of a variety of identified social skills. The following types of instructional procedures are suggested:

- Discrete trial teaching methods to teach specific social skills.
- Incidental teaching procedures within naturally occurring situations as methods of teaching and generalizing social skills.
- Social skills instruction to focus on the acquisition and generalization of socially meaningful skills within self-contained, community, home, and mainstream settings.
- The use of behavioral coaching models of instruction to teach and generalize social skills within mainstream classroom settings.
- The utilization of a team composed of the special education teacher, special education consultant, school psychologist, and speech/language pathologist to work collaboratively following a problem-solving process so as to develop, implement, and evaluate social skills interventions.

The results of FBA of interfering behaviors indicate that these behaviors appear to have multiple functions. Accordingly, interventions addressing these behaviors need to take into consideration the respective triggers, internal/individual variables, and consequences for each target behavior.

It is expected that increasing Eric's repertoire of prosocial behaviors within the context of an educational setting that is relevant, effective, and efficient will result in marked decreases in stereotypic, self-injurious, and tantrum behaviors.

The use of the time-out from reinforcement contingent on the occurrence of interfering behaviors, especially those behaviors motivated by negative reinforcement, is *not supported*.

In general, interventions incorporating the following strategies are supported:

- Planned ignoring of interfering behaviors.
- Differential reinforcement of appropriate behavior (DRA).
- Differential reinforcement of incompatible behavior (DRI).
- Embedded instruction procedures using both high-probability response sequence and Premack principle procedures are recommended to establish "behavioral momentum" and to reinforce active participation.

Continued development of the application of DD procedures is suggested as a method for decreasing stereotypic behavior that interferes with Eric's active participation within instructional settings. Further evaluation of the effectiveness of this intervention needs to be conducted across a variety of instructional situations.

Systematic instruction focusing on teaching Eric independent play, cooperative play, and reciprocal social interactions is suggested as the primary means to decease stereotypy during free-play situations. Physical redirection and/or physical response interruption procedures when Eric is exhibiting stereotypic and tantrum behaviors should only be used in those situations in which Eric is in danger of harming himself. Use of a picture schedule/picture rules procedure will provide Eric with visual cues of expected behaviors. Redirection involving gesturing to the picture schedule or picture rules is suggested as an alternative to physical prompts during most situations.

Ongoing data recording using the interval recording procedure (IRP) is suggested as a method of documenting current levels of occurrence of behaviors. It is recommended that the IRP be expanded from its present use of documenting only interfering behaviors to include the documentation of appropriate behaviors (e.g., active participation, initiation of social interactions with peers).

Ongoing behavioral consultation to include (1) ongoing FBA of interfering behaviors and (2) design, implementation, and evaluation of positive behavioral support interventions is suggested.

Ima Angler, EdS, NCSP
School Psychologist

Example 4: Functional Behavioral Assessment Report for Hal Alou-Ya

Identifying Information

Student: Hal Alou-Ya
Date of Report: November 14, 2008
Date of Birth: 9/24/97
Age: 11-1
Home Community: Skinner Island, ME
School: Burris Elementary
Grade: 4
Evaluation Dates: September 29; October 10, 15, 20, and 24; November 3, 6, and 10, 2008
A copy of this report was reviewed with and provided to parent/guardian on November 17, 2008.

Reason for Referral

Hal was referred for a functional behavioral assessment (FBA) by the IEP team on September 22, 2008. The FBA was conducted to:

- Identify behaviors that are interfering with Hal's acquisition and performance of academic, social, and personal living skills.
- Describe those interfering behaviors in objective, observable terms.
- Document the level of occurrence of interfering behaviors.
- Identify variables (i.e., antecedent, individual, and consequence) that are associated with the occurrence of interfering behaviors.
- Develop hypotheses regarding the function(s) of interfering behaviors.
- Identify evidence-based and function-based interventions.

Relevant Background Information

Hal lives with his parents (Fred and Wilma Alou-Ya) and two younger siblings on Skinner Island. Hal is identified as a student with autism and is enrolled in the self-contained with supported inclusion special education classroom at Burris Elementary School in Blueberry Cove, Maine. He receives the following related services: (1) psychology (i.e., behavioral consultation and social skills training), (2) speech and language (i.e., direct and consulting), and (3) occupational therapy (i.e., consulting). A review of school records indicated that Hal has received special education services since the fall of 2001.

The most recent psychological evaluation was conducted in March 2008 by Mr. Norm Referenced. Based on the results of the BASC-2, Social Skills Rating System, Vineland II Adaptive Behavior Scale, and Autism Rating Scale, Mr. Referenced reported that "compared to other children of the same age Hal evidences clinically significant externalizing behaviors, significant social skills deficits, significant delays across all adaptive domains, and characteristics of autistic disorder (e.g., language delays, fine and gross motor delays, stereotypy, poor eye contact, impaired social relationships, inattention, hyperactivity, and impulsivity)."

During an IEP team meeting on September 20, 2008, team members expressed concerns about Hal's multiyear history of inappropriate behaviors that significantly interfere with his educational performance. The following interfering behaviors were identified: stereotypy, property destruction, aggression, and self-injury.

Description of Evaluation Procedures

INDIRECT FBA PROCEDURES

- Record review
- Interviews with school staff
- Interviews with Mrs. Alou-Ya
- Antecedent Variables Assessment Form (AVAF)
- Individual Variables Assessment Form (IVAF)
- Consequence Variables Assessment Form (CVAF)
- Behavioral Stream Interviews

The AVAF, IVAF, and CVAF are semistructured interviews that are used to identify the events that occur prior to the occurrence of interfering behavior, individual variables (e.g., skill deficits or personal issues) that contribute to interfering behavior, and the reinforcing events that follow interfering behavior. Behavioral stream interviews involve identifying the antecedent–behavior–consequence chains that unfold when interfering behaviors occur.

DIRECT DESCRIPTIVE FBA PROCEDURES

- Anecdotal and systematic observations
- Interval Recording Procedure (IRP)
- Brief functional analyses
- Assessment of reinforcer preferences

Anecdotal and systematic observations were conducted within multiple school settings (i.e., special education class, mainstream class, lunchroom, and gym) and during a variety of activities (i.e., 1:1 instruction, small-group instruction, and large-group instruction).

The IRP involves direct observation and recording of interfering behaviors and associated contextual variables within 15-minute intervals during the school day. The IRP is useful in:

- Identifying specific settings/activities/tasks in which interfering behavior occurs.
- Recording the magnitude of appropriate behaviors.
- Recording the magnitude of interfering behaviors.
- Identifying corelationships among appropriate and interfering behaviors.
- Identifying corelationships among different interfering behaviors.
- Identifying relationships between specific staff and both appropriate and interfering behaviors.

The Interval Recording Procedure (IRP) was designed in collaboration with Skinner Elementary School staff. A 3 hour in-service with role play and performance feedback was provided to all staff working with Hal prior to the implementation of the IRP. Staff have been using the IRP to record interfering behaviors since October 1, 2008. Table 12.1 includes the identification and definition of interfering behaviors, the behavior recording procedure used to measure each behavior, and the levels of occurrence of interfering behavior from October 1 through November 7, 2008.

A brief functional analysis was conducted to test hypotheses derived from interviews and anecdotal observations about variables controlling interfering behaviors. This included direct observations and 6-second partial-interval recording of both interfering behavior and on-task (OT) behavior within five 10-minute assessment conditions (see Figure 12.2 for description of assessment conditions and results).

Based on the results of anecdotal observations and the results of the initial functional analysis, a second brief functional analysis was conducted to assess the specific antecedent variations that occasioned/evoked interfering behavior. This involved using a 6-second partial-interval recording procedure to measure occurrences of disruptive behavior (i.e., any occurrence of property destruction, aggression, or self-injury) and on-task (OT) behavior during two types of instructional sessions: (1) instruction using verbal prompts and (2) instruction using gesture and symbol prompts and *no* verbal prompts (see Figure 12.3 for results).

Assessment of reinforcer preferences was conducted in three ways: (1) interviewing Skinner Island School staff and Mrs. Alou-Ya, (2) placing items identified through interviews as being preferred within the classroom environment and recording which items Hal selected, and (3) a stimulus preference assessment that involved a set of trials in which Hal was presented two items and recording his choice (i.e., reach for and engage with the item).

TABLE 12.1. Identification/Definition of Target Behaviors, Recording Procedures, and Levels of Occurrence

Target behavior	Definition of behavior	Recording procedure	Levels of occurrence (10/1–11/7), 25 school days
Property destruction (PD)	Throwing items, swiping materials, and/or ripping work materials	Duration	Daily average: 44.4 minutes/day Range: 10–175 minutes (0% of days with no PD)
Aggression (AGG)	Occurrences of hitting, kicking, scratching, and/or biting others	A. Frequency	Daily average: 32.5 occurrences/day Range 0–84 (16% of days with no AGG)
Self-injurious behavior (SIB)	Occurrences of biting, hitting, and/or scratching self	B. Frequency	Daily average: 17.3 occurrences/day C. Range: 0–128 (24% of days with no SIB)
Stereotypy (ST)	Flapping loose items of clothing (e.g., jacket sleeve, shirt sleeve), pieces of thread, or string in front of face	Performance-based scale: 0 (no ST) to 5 (high ST)	Daily average: 2.7 Range: 0.75–3.25 (0% of days with no PS)

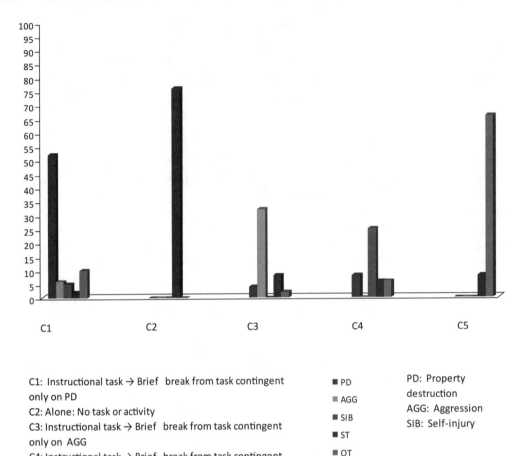

FIGURE 12.2. First Brief Functional Analysis conditions and results.

FORMING HYPOTHESES

The Behavior Analytic Problem Solving (BAPS) model was used following the completion of the indirect, direct descriptive and functional analysis procedures to organize and summarize assessment results. The BAPS addresses the dynamic relationships among the various variables that maintain interfering behaviors. This information was used as the foundation for designing function-based interventions.

Results of Evaluation Procedures

The results of indirect and direct descriptive FBA procedures are summarized in the following tables and figure:

- Table 12.1: identification/definition of interfering behaviors, recording procedures, and level of occurrence of interfering behaviors
- Figure 12.2: description of the first brief functional analysis conditions and results
- Figure 12.3: description of the second brief functional analysis conditions and results
- Tables 12.2 and 12.3: summary of the variables that contribute to interfering behaviors

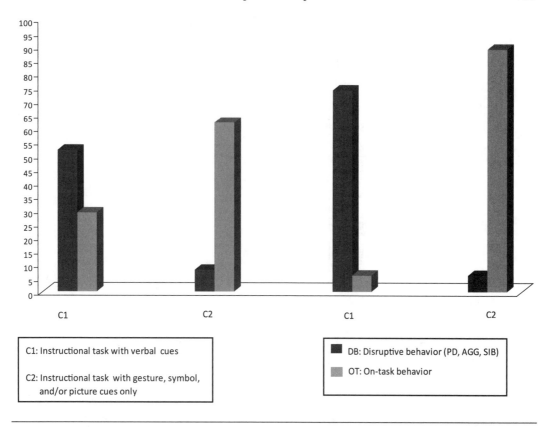

FIGURE 12.3. Second Brief Functional Analysis conditions and results.

Interpretation of the Results of Assessments

STEREOTYPY

The results of assessment indicated that stereotypy typically occurs when Hal is not engaged in instruction or preferred activities. Stereotypy often occurs in unstructured situations (e.g., transitions from one task to another, during a brief break). When Hal is participating in preferred activities, stereotypy occurs at very low levels (see Table 12.2).

- Hypothesis: Stereotypy is reinforced by automatic positive reinforcement (i.e., sensory consequences that induce stimulation).

SELF-INJURY

The results of assessment indicated that self-injurious behavior (SIB) occurred in unstructured situations in which Hal was *not* actively participating in tasks or activities and was exhibiting stereotypy. When staff used specific and repeated verbal cues to redirect Hal from stereotypy, he often exhibited self-injury. When self-injury occurred, staff usually stopped delivering verbal cues. When staff walked away, self-injury abruptly stopped. At that point, Hal often engaged in stereotypy (see Table 12.2).

TABLE 12.2. Behavior-Analytic Problem-Solving (BAPS) Model: Physical Stereotypy and Self-Injury

Contextual variables: Probable contexts in which interfering behavior occurs	Individual mediating variables: Individual sensitivities, preferences, internal states, etc., that contribute to interfering behavior	Individual behavior deficits: Behavior deficits (e.g., communication, academic, and/or social) that contribute to the interfering behavior	Antecedent—unconditioned motivating operation (UMO): Unlearned stimulus condition that increase the *value* of a reinforcing consequence	Antecedent—conditioned motivating operation (CMO): Learned stimulus condition that increases the *value* of a reinforcing consequence	Antecedent—discriminative stimuli (SD): Stimuli or events that signal the *availability* of a reinforcing consequence	Behavior: Interfering behavior	Reinforcing consequence: Specify the events that follow and strengthen interfering behavior	Parameters of reinforcement: Specify: • Schedule of reinforcement • Quality of reinforcement • Magnitude of reinforcement • Timing of reinforcement
Unstructured situations when Hal is not provided access to appropriate leisure items	Mild visual impairment	Independent play skills Functional communication skills	Deprivation of sensory stimulation increases motivation to engage in stereotypy	Deprived access to preferred leisure items (e.g., videos, toys) increases motivation to engage in stereotypy	Personal clothing, pieces of paper, loose strings/thread trigger stereotypy	Stereotypy	Automatic positive reinforcement (sensory input/arousal induction)	Continuous schedule Highly preferred High amount/duration Immediate
Unstructured situations when Hal is exhibiting stereotypy	Sensitive to repeated verbal cues Hal requires a latency of 5–10 seconds between delivery of verbal cues and response	Independent play skills Functional communication skills	Presentation of repeated verbal cues is aversive and increases motivation to engage in self-injury	Repeated verbal cues to stop stereotypy signal a worsening condition (i.e., the interruption of stereotypy) and increases motivation to engage in self-injury	Specific verbal cues to stop stereotypy (e.g., "Hal, stop doing that") trigger occurrences of self-injury	Self-injury	Negative reinforcement (cessation of verbal cues) Negative reinforcement (cessation of interactions with staff)	Intermittent schedule Highly preferred High amount/duration Immediate

TABLE 12.3. Behavior-Analytic Problem-Solving (BAPS) Model: Property Destruction, Aggression, and Self-Injury

Contextual variables: Probable contexts in which interfering behavior occurs	Individual mediating variables: Individual sensitivities, preferences, internal states, etc., that contribute to interfering behavior	Individual behavior deficits: Behavior deficits (e.g., communication, academic, and/or social) that contribute to the interfering behavior	Antecedent—unconditioned motivating operation (UMO): Unlearned stimulus condition that increase the value of a reinforcing consequence	Antecedent—conditioned motivating operation (CMO): Learned stimulus condition that increases the value of a reinforcing consequence	Antecedent—discriminative stimuli (SD): Stimuli or events that signal the availability of a reinforcing consequence	Behavior: Interfering behavior	Reinforcing consequence: Specify the events that follow and strengthen interfering behavior	Parameters of reinforcement: Specify: • Schedule of reinforcement • Quality of reinforcement • Magnitude of reinforcement • Timing of reinforcement
Instructional sessions	Seizure disorder	Functional communication skills	Sleep deprivation following seizures and presentation of repeated verbal cues are aversive and increase motivation to engage in interfering behaviors	Presentation of instructional tasks signal a worsening condition (i.e., high response effort, repeated verbal cues) and increase motivation to engage in interfering behaviors	Specific verbal cues to begin instruction (e.g., "Hal, it's time to work") triggers interfering behavior	Property destruction	Negative reinforcement (avoidance of or escape from instruction)	Intermittent schedule
Academic tasks		Academic skills				Aggression		Highly preferred
Functional life skills tasks		Functional life skills				Self-injury		High amount/duration
								Immediate

- Hypothesis: Self-injury is reinforced by negative reinforcement (i.e., escape from staff cues and social interactions with staff).

  Response Chain: The following response chain was observed:

  Unstructured → ST → staff verbal redirection → SIB → staff stop verbal cues and walk away → ST

PROPERTY DESTRUCTION, AGGRESSION, AND SELF-INJURY

The results of assessment indicated that these behaviors typically occur when Hal is participating in systematic instructional sessions. The results of the brief functional analysis (Figure 12.1) showed that PD, AGG, and SIB increased when instruction was briefly halted (see Table 12.3).

- Hypothesis: Property destruction, aggression, and self-injury are reinforced by negative reinforcement (i.e., the avoidance of or escape from instructional tasks/activities).

Additionally, these behaviors appear to members of the same response class. This means that these behaviors are directly related to the same antecedents ("triggers") and reinforcing consequences. Within the context of instructional sessions, these behaviors often occur as part of a predictable response chain (i.e., response class hierarchy) that begins with property destruction (PD). Then, when PD does not result in the cessation of instruction, Hal typically displays aggression (AGG), and when that does not result in the stopping of instruction he typically displays self-injury (SIB).

The following diagrams depict the chain of events that contribute to occurrences of PD, AGG, and SIB

(Instructional Task) → PD → (Task Discontinued) → PD stops
(Instructional Task) → PD → (Redirect to Task) → AGG →
(Task Discontinued) → PD and AGG stop
(Instructional Task) → PD → (Redirect to Task) → AGG → (Redirect to Task) →
SIB (Task Discontinued) → PD, AGG, and SIB stop

The results of assessment of the second brief functional analysis (see Figure 12.2) indicated that Hal exhibited higher levels of interfering behavior and lower levels of on-task behavior when verbal cues were used during instructional sessions. In contrast, Hal exhibited markedly lower levels of disruptive behaviors and higher levels of on-task behavior when nonverbal (e.g., gesture, picture, symbol) instructional cues were used during instructional sessions.

Assessment of Reinforcer Preferences: the results of assessments of reinforcer preferences identified that the following items/activities are reinforcing to Hal:

- Food: pieces of sausage, chocolate chips, frozen blueberries, cheese pizza, strawberry ice cream
- Drink: chocolate milk, apple juice
- Activity: videos (e.g., "Thomas the Train"), battery-operated toys

Specific Educational Recommendations

On November 10, 2008, Skinner Elementary team members used a behavior analytic collaborative problem-solving approach to identify evidence-based and function-based interventions to (1) minimize interfering behaviors, (2) maximize Hal's participation in educational programming, and

(3) increase Hal's acquisition of appropriate behaviors (see Tables 12.4 and 12.5 for a summary of intervention strategies). Following is a brief description of the recommended interventions:

RECOMMENDATIONS ADDRESSING ANTECEDENTS (MODIFY THE ENVIRONMENT TO REDUCE OR ELIMINATE THE VARIABLES THAT "TRIGGER" INTERFERING BEHAVIORS)

- Reduce unstructured situations to reduce ST and SIB.
- Minimize access to loose clothing, strings, and thread to decrease opportunities for ST.
- Minimize or eliminate repeated verbal prompts; use gesture/symbol/picture instructional cues to reduce PD/AGG/SIB and to increase on-task behavior during instructional sessions.
- Minimize or eliminate specific verbal prompts; use gesture/symbol/picture instructional cues to reduce PD/AGG/SIB.
- To minimize occurrences of PD/AGG/SIB, modify instructional contexts by rearranging the instructional environment, providing instruction in varied settings, and scheduling two or more teachers to provide instruction.
- Once behavioral stability is maintained and Hal has consistently responded to nonverbal prompts, begin to fade in naturally occurring verbal prompts during instructional programming.
- Neutralize the motivation for ST through the use of noncontingent reinforcement (e.g., provide access to functional activities that provide visual stimulation; access to preferred activities) on a fixed interval schedule throughout the school day.
- Neutralize the motivation for PD/AGG/SIB through the use of noncontingent reinforcement (e.g., brief breaks) on a fixed-interval schedule throughout the school day.
- Reduce the motivation for PD/AGG/SIB during instructional sessions by using errorless teaching strategies to minimize errors and the use of repeated verbal instructional prompts.
- Program stimuli that are discriminative for compliance (e.g., use gesture/symbol prompts to cue the start of instructional sessions).
- Reduce the motivation for PD/AGG/SIB during instructional sessions by using incidental teaching procedures within naturally occurring situations.
- Reduce the motivation for PD/AGG/SIB during instructional sessions by modifying response effort (i.e., number of trials prior to a break, length of assignment, instructional level).
- Reduce the motivation for PD/AGG/SIB by providing rest then low-interest, low-demand, and dense reinforcement following occurrences of seizures.
- Reduce the motivation for PD/AGG/SIB during instructional sessions by using a high-probability response sequence method (i.e., schedule a series of preferred and/or low effort and/or high-fluency activities prior to the start of challenging/difficult/novel instructional sessions) to increase the probability of on-task behavior during instructional sessions and to reduce interfering behaviors.
- Use a visual activity schedule to illustrate the schedule of tasks and reinforcing activities.

RECOMMENDATIONS ADDRESSING REPLACEMENT BEHAVIOR (STRATEGIES FOR TEACHING AND INCREASING BEHAVIORS TO REPLACE INTERFERING BEHAVIORS)

- In general, to compete with interfering behaviors, it is important to teach replacement behaviors that are relevant (e.g., functional, appropriate to the setting, useful, meaningful), efficient (i.e., low response effort with minimal errors), and effective (i.e., result in reinforcement).
- Functional communication training (FCT): Teach appropriate communication behavior as

TABLE 12.4. Evidence-Based and Function-Based Behavior Supports: Stereotypy and Self-Injury

Interfering behavior: Specify the interfering behavior and the reinforcing consequence	Contextual modifications: Alter the setting characteristics that trigger interfering behavior	Unconditioned motivating operations (UMO) manipulations: Neutralize the deprivation or presentation of unlearned stimuli that motivate interfering behavior	Conditioned motivating operations (CMO) manipulations: Manipulate the learned events that motivate interfering behavior	Discriminative stimulus (SD) modifications: Alter the specific stimuli that occasion interfering behavior	Replacement behavior: Identify behaviors that replace interfering behaviors	Reinforcement procedures: Determine the specific strategies to be used to reinforce replacement behaviors	Parameters of reinforcement: Determine the schedule, type, amount, and timing of reinforcement procedures	Extinction procedure: Alter the functional relationship between behavior and reinforcement	Reactive procedures: Specify the strategies to use in the event that interfering behavior occurs
Stereotypy — Positive automatic reinforcement (arousal induction)	Reduce the number and duration of unstructured situations; Increase planned activities (see activity schedule)	Noncontingent access to a functional activity that provides visual stimulation	Noncontingent reinforcement (e.g., access to preferred reinforcing activities during the school day)	Reduce access to loose clothing, strings/thread	Increase independent play/leisure skills; Increase functional communication skills (requesting substitutable toys and activities)	Differential reinforcement of appropriate (DRA) behavior	Fixed and continuous; Highly preferred toys/activities; High amount/duration; Immediate	NA	Gesture and visual redirection to appropriate behavior
Self-injury — Negative reinforcement (avoidance/escape)	Reduce the number and duration of unstructured situations; Increase planned activities (see activity schedule)	Minimize verbal cues when stereotypy occurs	FCT procedures at the onset of unstructured situations to teach Hal to request reinforcing activities (an improving condition); Increase delivery of neutral verbal comments throughout the school day	Eliminate specific verbal cues that trigger self-injury	Increase independent play/leisure skills; Increase functional communication skills (requesting substitutable toys and activities)	Differential reinforcement of appropriate and incompatible behaviors (DRA and DRI)	Continuous then fading to intermittent; Highly preferred; High amount/duration; Immediate	Staff maintain presence (do not walk away)	Nonverbal response interruption; Gesture and visual redirection to functional communication procedure

TABLE 12.5. Evidence-Based and Function-Based Behavior Supports: Property Destruction, Aggression, and Self-Injury

Interfering behavior: Specify the interfering behavior and the reinforcing consequence	Contextual modifications: Alter the setting characteristics that trigger interfering behavior	Unconditioned motivating operations (UMO) manipulations: Neutralize the deprivation or presentation of unlearned stimuli that motivate interfering behavior	Conditioned motivating operations (CMO) manipulations: Manipulate the learned events that motivate interfering behavior	Discriminative stimulus (SD) modifications: Alter the specific stimuli that occasion interfering behavior	Replacement behavior: Identify behaviors that replace interfering behaviors	Reinforcement procedures: Determine the specific strategies to be used to reinforce replacement behaviors	Parameters of reinforcement: Determine the schedule, type, amount, and timing of reinforcement procedures	Extinction procedure: Alter the functional relationship between behavior and reinforcement	Reactive procedures: Specify the strategies to use in the event that interfering behavior occurs
Property destruction Negative reinforcement (avoidance/escape)	Visual activity schedule Rearrange instructional environment	Modify daily schedule following seizures: allow rest, low demand, high interest, dense reinforcement	Modify response effort (i.e., number of trials prior to a break, length of assignment, instructional level)	Eliminate specific verbal cues that trigger PD, AGG, SIB	Increase academic and functional life skills	Premack principle DRA	Continuous then fading to intermittent	Staff maintain presence (do not walk away)	Response interruption Redirection
Aggression Negative reinforcement (avoidance/escape)	Provide instruction in varied settings Two or more teachers provide instruction	Minimize verbal cues during instruction	Noncontingent reinforcement (e.g., access to preferred reinforcing activities during the school day)	Program stimuli that are discriminative for compliance (e.g., use gesture/symbol prompts to cue the start of instructional sessions).	Increase functional communication skills	Food, drink and activity reinforcers contingent on appropriate behaviors	Highly preferred (vary reinforcers to avoid satiation)	Do not stop instruction when interfering behavior occurs	DRA
Self-injury Negative reinforcement (avoidance/escape)	Minimize repeated verbal cues	Minimize repeated verbal cues: allow 5–10 seconds between verbal cues and additional prompts	Errorless teaching strategies High-probability response sequence				High amount/duration Immediate		Crisis intervention procedures

245

a replacement for interfering behavior. Use a visual communication strategy (e.g., picture/symbol) to teach Hal to access "break" and "play."
- Increase independent play skills as a replacement for stereotypy.
- Increase academic and functional life skills as a replacement for property destruction, aggression, and self-injury during instructional sessions.
- Incidental teaching procedures to program for generalization of skills learned during instructional sessions.
- Provide reinforcement (e.g., food, drink, activity) following replacement behaviors.
- Premack principle (i.e., provide activity reinforcement following replacement behaviors).
- Differential reinforcement of alternative (DRA) behavior by providing reinforcement contingent on Hal displaying alternative/appropriate behavior (e.g., on-task, appropriate social behaviors).

RECOMMENDATIONS OUTLINING REACTIVE PROCEDURES (PROCEDURES TO USE WHEN INTERFERING BEHAVIORS OCCUR)

- Extinction: avoid providing reinforcement following interfering behaviors
  - Avoid providing breaks immediately following PD, AGG, SIB
  - Response Interruption/Redirection: gesture to the visual activity schedule; point to the use of the visual communication strategy.
- Differential reinforcement: Following redirection, provide DRA behavior by providing reinforcement contingent on Hal displaying alternative/appropriate behavior (e.g., OT, communication response).
- Crisis intervention: In the event that PD, AGG, or SIB persist or intensify to a level where Hal is in danger of hurting self or others, use school-approved crisis intervention procedures.

PROGRESS MONITORING AND BEHAVIORAL CONSULTATION

- Implementation of the Task Analysis Recording Procedure (TARP) during instruction of functional life skills (e.g., toileting, tooth brushing, washing hands, preparing snack) to measure levels of independence, effective and ineffective instructional prompts, and corresponding interfering behaviors is recommended.
- Continued use of the Interval Recording Procedure to measure occurrences of interfering behavior throughout the school day is recommended.
- Ongoing progress monitoring with weekly analysis of graphed data to evaluate the effectiveness of interventions is recommended.
- Ongoing behavioral consultation in collaboration with Skinner Elementary School staff in the design, implementation, and evaluation of evidence-based and function-based behavior supports plans could be given consideration by the IEP team.
- Direct behavioral consultation methods in which the consultant uses modeling and performance-feedback procedures to coach staff in the implementation of interventions is recommended.

Erin Hooligan, PsyD
School Psychologist
Nationally Certified School Psychologist
Board Certified Behavior Analyst

SUMMARY

This has been a lengthy chapter—for us as well as you. How's that for stating the obvious? We have attempted to illustrate how the results of a FBA are documented and communicated in written format and how those results are linked to the intervention process. We have also provided some basic supporting documentation forms and examples of FBA reports. Please remember, there is no best FBA report format. You must use the one that is best suited for the teams with which you work and the types of interfering behaviors that are being addressed.

13

Direct Behavioral Consultation

Or, "How Do We Get People to Implement Interventions Accurately and Consistently?"

Many readers will no doubt be alerted by the term "behavioral consultation" in the title of this chapter. After all, behavioral consultation (BC) has consistently been endorsed by school psychologists as the preferred method of consultation in schools. Without writing an entire book on consultation (which we plan to do as soon as this one is finished), we have written this chapter to provide a brief overview of what consultation is (and, of course, what it is not), why it is important to know how to do correctly, the advantages and disadvantages of other approaches, and finally, a description of how we think consultation should conducted in schools. The term *direct* in our model of consultation should be a huge clue as to how we think, and data show, consultation is most effective, particularly in difficult cases.

Stated very simply, consultation is one means by which intervention services are delivered in schools. Consultation, itself, is not an intervention. Rather, it is a model by which interventions are provided to teachers. Within the FBA framework, after all of the assessment data have been collected and the components of the positive behavioral intervention have been detailed, the next step is to implement the BIP in the classroom. And therein lies the rub. Just because an IEP team has designed an intervention, even one that is function-based, there is no guarantee that the classroom teacher will have the knowledge and skills to implement the treatment with any reasonable degree of integrity. That is where consultation comes in! After the BIP is designed, someone must assist the teacher with implementing the plan. Sometimes this assistance is only minimal as it merely requires fine-tuning existing classroom practices. In other cases, the teacher may have to significantly alter his or her instructional practices or other environmental variables to make meaningful behavior change occur. In the latter case, the role of the consultant is paramount in the sense that he or she has to be able help the teacher to accurately and consistently implement the intervention in the classroom. The big question, for many school-based practitioners is "How do I help teachers implement interventions with integrity so that meaningful change occurs?" This is indeed a critical question and one that we are going to answer in this chapter. Before we do, however, let's take a look at what typically happens in such situations.

PLAN, HOPE, AND CHECK-IN

Many readers are familiar with this scenario: A teacher is given a well-thought-out positive behavior *plan*, with the *hope* that he or she will be able to implement the recommendations and steps, and a promise by the plan-giver to *check-in* after a few days—or a couple of weeks—to see how things are going. In some instances, this might actually be ok:

- The teacher is experienced in implementing the strategies suggested by the IEP team.
- The teacher is essentially already doing the plan, but he or she just needs to alter the consistency or the timing of when he or she does it.
- The plan is one that the teacher has implemented before.

In each of these situations, the teacher has experience and/or knowledge in implementing the BIP and may only need verbal guidance on how to integrate the procedures with a specific student. In most cases, at least in our collective experiences, the plan is *not* one that teachers have a wealth of knowledge and/or experience implementing and will find it extremely difficult integrating the plan into their daily classroom routine.

SELECT FROM THE MENU, PLEASE

This represents one of the worst situations that a teacher can face. She has made a referral to the student assistance team and the team, in their infinite wisdom, provides her with a list of possible strategies that she can choose from on any given day. In fact, the implicit message of such a list is threefold: (1) we (i.e., the team) don't really expect *any* of these strategies to be effective, so it doesn't matter which one you select; (2) we have no idea what to do, so here ya go; and (3) try a strategy two or three times and if it doesn't seem to be working, move on to something else. In any case, the teacher is left hanging and has no real basis on which to select an intervention strategy, much less to determine which one gives her the best shot.

CONSULTATION

The term "behavioral consultation" was coined by John Bergan in 1977 and referred to a four stage problem-solving model. Bergan conceptualized consultation as an *indirect* model whereby a teacher was assisted in the four stages:

- Problem identification (really the first step in an FBA—operationalizing the interfering behavior).
- Problem analysis (what FBA is all about).
- Plan implementation (the BIP part).
- Plan evaluation (sort of the second part of a BIP, determining if the BIP was implemented with integrity and if it was effective).

As we just said, Bergan conceptualized the interaction between a consultant (usually a school psychologist) and a consultee (the teacher) as indirect. That is, identifying the problem, analyzing the problem, designing an intervention, and evaluating that intervention resulted from a verbal interaction between the consultant and the consultee.

The indirect model was hailed as something of a godsend because it was believed that more teachers and students could be assisted if the consultant did not have to spend time gathering data, observing the student, and so on, and it kind of let the consultant "off the hook" because he or she was not directly responsible for the accuracy of data, correctly identifying the problem, or the success of the intervention. Although the indirect model is seductive for these reasons, and a couple of others, there are a number of problems associated with the indirect nature of providing this assistance, namely:

- There are no data indicating that services delivered through an indirect model are more cost efficient than those delivered more directly.
- There are no data indicating that services delivered through an indirect model are more effective than those delivered more directly.
- There are no data indicating that what is *said* during consultation is important for student/teacher behavior change.
- There is no focus on teacher skill development in the indirect model.
- There is no immediate performance or corrective feedback available to the teacher.
- There is no demonstration of the intervention with the target student prior to the teacher attempting to implement the intervention.

DIRECT BEHAVIORAL CONSULTATION

In response to these criticisms and limitations, Watson and Robinson (1996) described direct behavioral consultation (DBC) in which the focus is on teacher skill acquisition through interactions with the target student, measuring treatment integrity, measuring student behavior change, and promoting generalization of teacher skills. Figure 13.1 illustrates the process of direct behavioral consultation.

Within the FBA/BIP framework, the teacher is still the consultee and someone from the IEP or student assistance team can act as the consultant. The overriding theme in DBC is that someone with expertise acts as collaborator/coach with the teacher to teach him or her the skills he or she needs, encourage him or her, and problem-solve difficulties with the intervention.

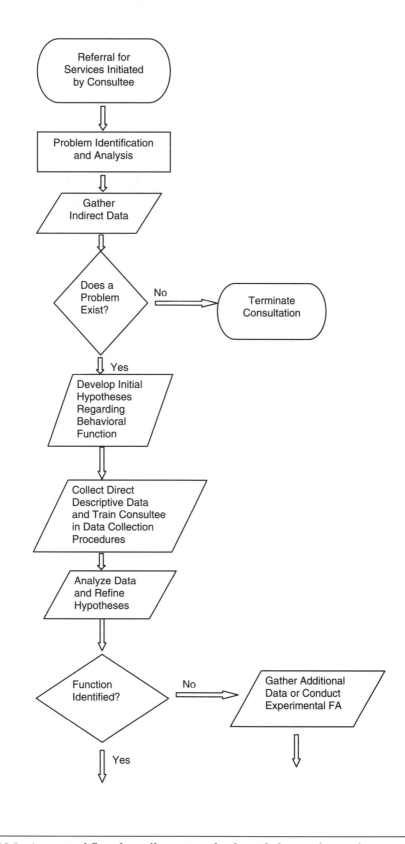

(continued)

FIGURE 13.1. A practical flowchart illustrating the direct behavioral consultation process.

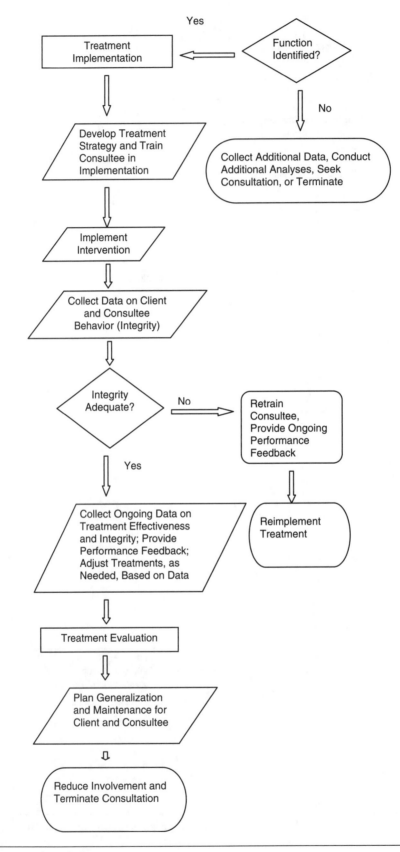

FIGURE 13.1. *(continued)*

Problem Identification

During problem identification, the consultant (or team) can use the indirect procedures described in this book to help the consultee accurately *identify* the problem. To operationally define the problem, both indirect and direct descriptive procedures can be used. The primary difference between most models of consultation and DBC is that in DBC the consultant takes an active role in data collection, student observation, and data analysis instead of relying on verbal reports of student behavior.

Problem Analysis

Data collected from all the FBA procedures are used to develop and confirm hypotheses about behavioral function. In some instances, the consultant may have to conduct some brief functional *analysis* to accurately ascertain function or at the very least coach the teacher in conducting the analyses.

Plan Implementation

This stage of problem solving is where the consultant should be of considerable value. Instead of merely pointing the teacher in one direction or another, giving him or her a list of possible interventions, or giving him or her a detailed BIP and telling him or her to "have at it," the consultant can help design an individualized BIP based on the data from the FBA *and* then train the teacher on implementing the intervention. In many cases, this will require the consultant to actually go into the classroom and demonstrate for the teacher how and when the intervention should be implemented. Additionally, the consultant must observe the teacher, not only to collect some initial integrity data, but also to provide feedback on aspects performed well and those that can be strengthened.

Plan Evaluation

The final stage of DBC consists of evaluating the efficacy of the intervention *plus* determining if the treatment has been implemented with accuracy and consistency (Watson, 2004). One simply can not make statements or draw conclusions about treatment effectiveness without some kind of data showing that the treatment has actually been implemented the way it was intended. This is not only a "best practices, data-based approach," it is also a requirement under IDEIA (see Chapter 3). By collecting integrity data, the consultant can decide whether treatments need to be redesigned or whether additional teacher training is necessary.

Research on Direct Behavioral Consultation

The research on using the DBC model to assist teachers is very strong. Early studies showed that using DBC either resulted in high treatment integrity or integrity greater than that obtained from indirect methods (Sterling-Turner & Watson, 2002; Sterling-Turner, Watson,

& Moore, 2002; Sterling-Turner, Watson, Wildmon, Watkins, & Little, 2001; Watson & Kramer, 1995) and teacher skill in functional methodology (Moore et al., 2002; Watson, Ray, Sterling-Turner, & Logan, 1999). Two additional studies demonstrated that teachers trained using DBC were able to generalize their skills across students and classrooms (Freeland, 2003; Watkins-Emonet, 2001).

Consultation Summary Report

Many of you using a consultation model to deliver services, whether team-based or not, will utilize some type of summary report to detail your activities as well as to document your findings. The following is an example of a consultation summary report that is consistent with the DBC model that we have found particularly useful. (See also Chapter 12.)

Example of a Consultation Summary Report for Eric Trout

Student: Eric Trout
Age: 8-4
Date of Birth: 06/23/2000
Grade: 3
School District: Sebago Lake, ME
School: Salmon Elementary School
Report Date: 10/23/08

CONSULTATION SERVICES PROVIDED

Direct behavioral consultation services were provided within the context of a collaborative problem-solving process. Consultation services were provided throughout the following stages:

1. Functional behavioral assessment of behaviors (see previous reports).
2. Design of positive behavioral support interventions (see the foregoing PBS plan).
3. Implementation of PBS interventions.
   - Staff training in intervention strategies.
   - Staff training in data collection.
   - Observation of staff implementation of the strategies and data collection procedures (treatment integrity).
   - Weekly team meetings to discuss intervention strategies, review data, and to make modifications as needed.
4. Evaluation of the effectiveness of the interventions.
   - Weekly analysis of data.
   - Graphing of data.

STAFF TRAINING AND SUPPORTS

Staff training was conducted prior to implementing the intervention procedures. Staff training included reviews of the FBA report and the PBS plan, discussions of the PBS interventions, role play of PBS interventions and data-recording procedures, and guided practice in implementation of the procedures.

Performance feedback was provided to staff during implementation of intervention procedures to improve treatment integrity. Through observations of staff and weekly consultation meetings it was determined that staff implemented the intervention strategies consistently and accurately (evidence of treatment integrity).

IMPLEMENTATION

During the baseline and intervention phases, data were recorded for each of the target behaviors according to the procedures outlined in the PBS plan. Following a 3-week baseline, the interventions strategies outlined in the PBS plan were implemented. To date, these interventions have been implemented for 21 weeks.

OUTCOMES

Included here are graphs that depict the effectiveness of the PBS plan for Eric. Figure 13.2 shows both his active participation and his stereotypic behaviors. Figures 13.3 and 13.4 show his tantrum and self-injurious behaviors, respectively.

In general, these data support the overall effectiveness of the PBS plan. Each of the behaviors showed marked improvement compared to baseline levels. Although stereotypic behaviors continue to occur daily (approximately 30%), these behaviors occurred at much higher levels prior to the implementation of the PBS plan (65%). Both self-injury and tantrum behaviors currently occur at much lower rates compared to baseline levels.

We view active participation (AP) as a critical component of any student's educational program. AP is directly related to on-task behavior (i.e., engagement in the educational process). Eric's AP has increased from a baseline level of 45% to current levels of 80–85%. This is a marked increase in AP.

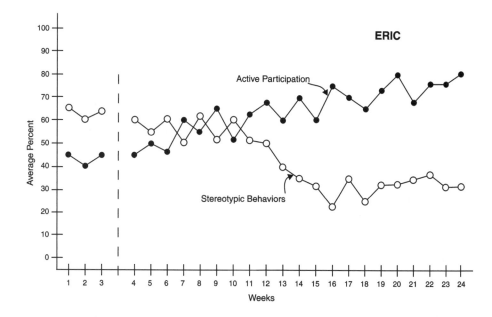

FIGURE 13.2. Effectiveness of the PBS plan. Note the decline of Eric's stereotypic behaviors and increase in his active participation after the intervention strategy was implemented. (Baseline behaviors are shown at the left.)

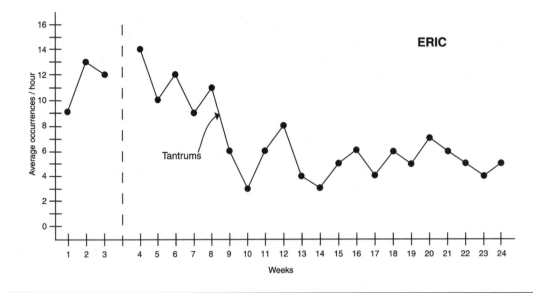

FIGURE 13.3. Decline in Eric's tantrum behaviors after implementation of the PBS plan. (His baseline behavior is shown at the left.)

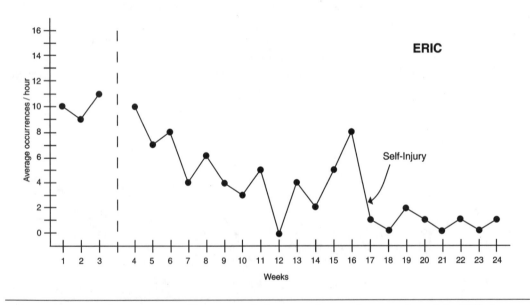

FIGURE 13.4. Decline in Eric's self-injurious behaviors after implementation of the PBS plan. (His baseline behavior is shown at the left.)

REPORT SUMMARY

These data document the effectiveness of the PBS plan in both increasing appropriate behaviors and in reducing interfering behaviors. The current support team has done an excellent job of implementing the PBS plan with Eric. Continued implementation of the PBS plan is suggested.

Review of the effectiveness of the PBS plan needs to be conducted on an ongoing basis. It is important to keep in mind that strategies that have been effective with Eric in the past may not be effective in the future. Also, behaviors that were motivated by a specific function at one point in his life (e.g., behaviors motivated by negative reinforcement) may be motivated by a different function (e.g., positive reinforcement) in the future. Consequently, ongoing FBA of interfering behaviors and ongoing evaluation of the effectiveness of interventions is recommended.

Ima Angler, EdS, NCSP
School Psychologist

PARTING SHOTS

Well, this is it! We have said (written) probably far more than we needed to. In some cases we may have provided too much information, at other times not enough, perhaps at times the information has been confusing, and maybe, just maybe, we have provided the right amount of useful information. Please bear with us and read the following two situations. They are ones that we encounter frequently and that still bother us greatly. We hope that, with your careful consideration, we can remedy these and help even more children!

The Quiet Crisis

Consider the case of Lucy, a student with mild developmental disabilities who was fully included with minimal instructional supports within a fifth-grade class. Lucy has a history of exhibiting both physical and verbal aggression. The results of previous assessments showed that these behaviors were reinforced by negative reinforcement (i.e., escape from academic demands) and that her academic skills were in the first- to second-grade range. At the end of fourth-grade, the IEP team decided to give Lucy a "fresh start and place her in the full inclusion program within the middle school." After 4 months of placement a meeting was held. Team members reported: "Lucy's doing great. She fits right in and she's not a problem at all." Lucy's parents requested observations of Lucy within the mainstream setting to document her progress. Anecdotal observations revealed that Lucy displayed very low rates of on-task behavior and extremely low rates of interfering behavior. Moreover, in spite of the fact that a primary purpose of the placement was " . . . for purposes of socialization and to foster social relationships with typically developing classmates," Lucy rarely interacted with her peers. The results of systematic observations over two full school days (i.e., 12 hours) using a 6-second partial-interval recording procedure to measure academic engagement documented that Lucy displayed "on-task" behavior during only 11% of the intervals. In addition, during the same observation period, Lucy initiated three (3) social interactions with classmates and eight (8) social interactions with teachers. Finally, using the student's IEP as a reference, only four (4) instructional objectives were addressed during the 2-day period. Consistent with anecdotal observations, Lucy displayed no occurrences of interfering behaviors. During interviews with team members, it became apparent that "doing great" meant no interfering behaviors. With Lucy, and countless of other cases like this, teams define the success of placement by the lack of interfering behaviors. These are the cases we refer to as the "Quiet Crisis." These are the cases that rarely lead to a referral for an FBA. From our perspective, Lucy *should* be referred for a comprehensive FBA. She has a history of severe interfering behaviors that appear to be addressed by simply reducing academic demands and educational opportunities. A comprehensive FBA will examine the variables that trigger and maintain interfering behaviors and inform the design of interventions that will result in both the acquisition of skills and the reduction/elimination of interfering behavior (see the case of Jerry in Chapter 11).

American Idle

Throughout this book, we have discussed the importance of teaching and reinforcing appropriate behaviors as replacements for interfering behaviors. An extension of this model is to make sure that students are actively engaged in a dense schedule of a wide range of socially significant, meaningful, and functional educational opportunities throughout the school day. We have seen way too many cases in which interfering behavior is directly related to students not having much, if anything, to do. We have also conducted too many observations within group homes over the years where the staff complete nearly all of the household chores (e.g., shopping, cooking, cleaning, laundry, yard work) while the clients are basically idle . . . and this is not ideal . . . well, you get the idea. Within these programs the clients are just basically "hanging out." Remember the old adage "Idle hands . . . idle minds. . . ." Left to their own devices and to create an interesting environment, children (and adults too) will often engage in mischievous, annoying, loud, and sometimes dangerous behaviors. Focusing on improving academic engagement is one easy way to *prevent* a wide range of interfering behaviors. The lack of engagement in academic programming as well as chronic delays in academic, social, personal living, community living, communication, vocational, and recreation-leisure skills *is a crisis*. IEP teams should be just as alarmed about the lack of progress and low levels of engagement as they are about severe interfering behaviors.

This is the next frontier, but certainly not uncharted territory. We assert that the next logical step in supporting persons with disabilities is to aggressively address these "Quiet Crises." We have the knowledge. We have the technology. We need to conduct comprehensive assessments and design person-centered habilitative and educational interventions that result in socially meaningful and durable behavior change. It is then, when we have both reduced interfering behaviors and have increased a wide range of functional skills, that we will be able to say that we have adequately addressed the needs of our most vulnerable citizens.

NOW WE HAVE SAID IT ALL!!!

References

Alex R. by Beth R. v. Forrestville Valley Community Unit School District #221, 375F3d 603 (7th Cir. July 2004).

Asmus, J. M., Ringdahl, J. E., Sellers, J. A., Call, N. A., Andleman, M. S., & Wacker, D. P. (2004). Use of a short-term inpatient model to evaluate aberrant behavior: Outcome data summaries from 1996 to 2001. *Journal of Applied Behavior Analysis, 37*, 283–304.

Ayllon, T. (1960). The application of reinforcement theory toward behavior problems: The psychiatric nurse as a behavioral engineer. *Dissertation Abstracts, 20*, 3372.

Ayllon, T., & Azrin, N. H. (1965). The measurement and reinforcement of behavior of psychotics. *Journal of the Experimental Analysis of Behavior, 7*, 327–331.

Ayllon, T., & Azrin, N. H. (1968). Reinforcer sampling: A technique for increasing the behavior of mental patients. *Journal of Applied Behavior Analysis, 1*, 13–20.

Azrin, N. H. (1960). Use of rests as reinforcers. *Psychological Reports, 7*, 240.

Azrin, N. H. (1961). Time-out from positive reinforcement. *Science, 133*, 382–383.

Azrin, N. H., & Lindsley, O. R. (1956). The reinforcement of cooperation between children. *Journal of Abnormal and Social Psychology, 52*, 100–102.

Azrin, N. H., & Powell, J. (1968). Behavioral engineering: The reduction of smoking behavior by a conditioning apparatus and procedure. *Journal of Applied Behavior Analysis, 1*, 193–200.

Baer, D. M., Peterson, R. F., & Sherman, J. A. (1967). The development of imitation by reinforcing behavioral similarity to a model. *Journal of Experimental Analysis of Behavior, 10*, 405–416.

Baer, D. M., & Sherman, J. A. (1964). Reinforcement control of generalized imitation in young children. *Journal of Experimental Child Psychology, 1*, 37–49.

Berg, W. K., Wacker, D. P., Cigrand, K., Merkle, S., Wade, J., Henry, K., et al. (2007). Comparing functional behavioral analysis and paired-choice assessment results in classroom settings. *Journal of Applied Behavior Analysis, 40*, 545–552.

Bergan, J. R. (1977). *Behavioral consultation.* Columbus, OH: Merrill.

Bijou, S. W., Peterson, R. F., & Ault, M. H. (1968). A method to integrate descriptive and experimental field studies at the level of data and empirical concepts. *Journal of Applied Behavior Analysis, 1*, 175–191.

Billington, E. J., & DiTommaso, N. M. (2003). Demonstrations and applications of the matching law in education. *Journal of Behavioral Education, 12*, 91–104.

259

Borgmeier, C., & Homer, R. H. (2006). An evaluation of the predictive validity of confidence ratings in identifying functional behavioral assessment hypothesis statements. *Journal of Positive Behavior Interventions, 8,* 100–105.

Braden, J. P., & Kratochwill, T. R. (1997). Treatment utility of assessment: Myths and realities. *School Psychology Review, 26,* 475–485.

Carbone, V. J., Morgenstern, B., Zecchin-Tirri, G., & Kolberg, L. (2007). The role of the reflexive conditioned motivating operation during discrete trial instruction of children with autism. *Journal of Early and Intensive Behavior Intervention, 4,* 658–673.

Carr, E. G. (1977). The motivation of self-injurious behavior: A review of some hypotheses. *Psychological Bulletin, 84,* 800–816.

Carr, E. G., & Durand, V. M. (1985). Reducing behavior problems through functional communication training. *Journal of Applied Behavior Analysis, 18,* 111–126.

Charlop-Christy, M. H., & Haymes, L. K. (1996). Using obsessions as reinforcers with and without mild reductive procedures to decrease inappropriate behaviors of children with autism. *Journal of Autism and Developmental Disorders, 26,* 527–546.

Charlop, M. H., Kurtz, P. F., & Casey, F. G. (1990). Using aberrant behaviors as reinforcers for autistic children. *Journal of Applied Behavior Analysis, 23,* 163–181.

Cihak, D. A., Alberto, P. A., & Frederick, L. D. (2007). Use of brief functional analysis and intervention evaluation in public settings. *Journal of Positive Behavior Interventions, 9,* 80–93.

Cooper, J. O., Heron, T. E., & Heward, W. L. (2007). *Applied behavior analysis* (2nd ed.). Upper Saddle River, NJ: Pearson.

Crone, D. A., & Horner, R. H. (2003). *Building positive behavior support systems in schools: Functional behavioral assessment.* New York: Guilford Press.

Derby, K. M., Wacker, D. P., Sasso, G., & Steege, M. (1992). Brief functional assessment techniques to evaluate aberrant behavior in an outpatient setting: A summary of 79 cases. *Journal of Applied Behavior Analysis, 25,* 713–721.

District No. 211 v. Michael R., 44 IDELR 36 (N. D. Ill. 2005).

Dittmer-McMahon, K. I. (2001). *An evaluation of functional behavior assessments as implemented by teacher support teams after training.* Unpublished doctoral dissertation, Mississippi State University.

Dufrene, B. A. (2005). Functional behavior assessment: A preliminary investigation of convergent, treatment, and social validity. *Dissertation Abstracts International, Section A, 66*(4-A), 1272.

Dufrene, B. A., Doggett, R. A., Henington, C., & Watson, T. S. (2007). Functional assessment and intervention for disruptive classroom behaviors in preschool and Head Start classrooms. *Journal of Behavioral Education, 16,* 368–388.

Edwards, R. P. (2002). A tutorial for using the Functional Assessment Informant Record—Teachers (FAIR-T). *Proven Practice: Prevention and Remediation Solutions for Schools, 4,* 31–38.

English, C. L., & Anderson, C. M. (2006). Evaluation of the treatment utility of the analog functional analysis and the structured descriptive assessment. *Journal of Positive Behavior Interventions, 8,* 212–229.

Erbas, D., Tekin-Iftar, E., & Yucesoy, S. (2006). Teaching special education teachers how to conduct functional analysis in natural settings. *Education and Training in Developmental Disabilities, 41,* 28–36.

Ervin, R. A., & Ehrhardt, K. E. (2000). Behavior analysis in school psychology. In J. Austin & J. E. Carr (Eds.), *Handbook of applied behavior analysis* (pp. 113–135). Reno, NV: Context Press.

Ervin, R. A., Ehrhardt, K. E., & Poling, A. (2001). Functional assessment: Old wine in a new bottle. *School Psychology Review, 30,* 173–179.

Flanagan, B., Goldiamond, I., & Azrin, N. H. (1959). Instatement of stuttering in normally fluent individuals through operant procedures. *Science, 130,* 979–981.

Freeland, J. T. (2003). Analyzing the effects of direct behavioral consultation on teachers: Generalization of skills across settings. *Dissertation Abstracts International Section A: Humanities and Social Sciences, 63*(10-A), 3471.

Goldfried, M., & Sprafkin, J. (1976). *Behavioral personality assessment.* Morristown, NJ: General Learning Press

Grayslake CCSD #46 37 IDELR 239 (2002).

Gresham, F., Watson, T. S., & Skinner, C. H. (2001). Functional behavioral assessment: Principles, procedures, and future directions. *School Psychology Review, 30,* 156–172.

Hacienda La Puente Unified School District v Honig, 976 F. 2d 487, 491 (9th Cir. 1992).

Hager, K. D., Slocum, T. A., & Detrich, R. (2007). No Child Left Behind, contingencies, and Utah's alternate assessment model. *Journal of Evidence-Based Practices for Schools, 8,* 63–83.

Hagopian, L. P., Fisher, W. W., Thompson, R. H., Owen-DeSchryver, J., Iwata, B. A., & Wacker, J. P. (1997). Toward the development of structured criteria for interpretation of functional analysis data. *Journal of Applied Behavior Analysis, 30,* 313–326.

Hanley, G. P., Iwata, B. A., & McCord, B. E. (2003). Functional analysis of problem behavior: A review. *Journal of Applied Behavior, 36,* 147–185.

Herrnstein, R. J. (1961). Relative and absolute strength of a response as a function of frequency of reinforcement. *Journal of the Experimental Analysis of Behavior, 4,* 267–272.

Herrnstein, R. J. (1970). On the law of effect. *Journal of the Experimental Analysis of Behavior, 13,* 243–266.

Hoch, H., McComas, J. J., Johnson, L. A., Faranda, N., & Guenther, S. L. (2002). The effects of magnitude and quality of reinforcement on choice responding during play activities. *Journal of Applied Behavior Analysis, 35,* 171–181.

Hoff, K. E., Ervin, R. A., & Friman, P. C. (2005). Refining functional behavioral assessment: Analyzing the separate and combined effects of hypothesized controlling variables during ongoing classroom routines. *School Psychology Review, 34,* 45–57.

Holz, W. C., Azrin, N. H., & Ayllon, T. (1963). Elimination of behavior of mental patients by response-produced extinction. *Journal of the Experimental Analysis of Behavior, 6,* 449–456.

Horner, R. H. (1994). Functional assessment: Contributions and future directions. *Journal of Applied Behavior Analysis, 27,* 401–404.

Individuals with Disabilities Education Act, 20 U.S.C. § 1400 *et seq.* (1997).

Iwata, B., Dorsey, M. F., Slifer, K. J., Bauman, K. E., & Richman, G. S. (1982). Toward a functional analysis of self-injury . *Analysis and Intervention in Developmental Disabilities, 2,* 3–20. [Reprinted in *Journal of Applied Behavior Analysis, 27,* 197–209 (1994).]

Iwata, B., Pace, G., Kissel, R., Nau, P., & Farber, J. (1990). The Self-Injury Trauma (SIT) Scale: A method for quantifying surface tissue damage caused by self-injurious behavior. *Journal of Applied Behavior Analysis, 23,* 99–110.

Iwata, B. A., Smith, R. G., & Michael, J. (2000). Current research on the influence of establishing operations on behavior in applied settings. *Journal of Applied Behavior Analysis, 33,* 411–418.

Jones, K. M., & Lugaro, C. J. (2000). Teacher acceptability of functional assessment-derived treatments. *Journal of Educational and Psychological Consultation, 11*(3–4), 323–332.

Jones, V., & Jones, S. (1998). *Comprehensive classroom management: Creating communities of support and solving problems* (5th ed.). Boston: Allyn & Bacon.

Kahng, S. W., & Iwata, B. A. (1998). Computerized systems for collecting real-time observational data. *Journal of Applied Behavior Analysis, 31,* 253–261.

Kamps, D., Wendland, M., & Culpepper, M. (2006). Active teacher participation in functional behavior assessment for students with emotional and behavioral disorders: Risks in general education classrooms. *Behavioral Disorders, 31,* 128–146.

Kantor, J. R. (1959). Evolution and the science of psychology. *Psychological Record, 9,* 131–142.

Kazdin, A. E. (2001). *Behavior modification in applied settings* (6th ed.). Belmont, CA: Wadsworth/Thomson Learning.

Kennedy, C. H., Meyer, K., Knowles, T., & Shukla, S. (2000). Analyzing the multiple functions of ste-reotypical behavior for students with autism: Implications for assessment and treatment. *Journal of Applied Behavior Analysis, 33,* 559–571.

Kern, L., Bailin, D., & Mauk, J. E. (2003). Effects of a topical anesthetic on non-socially maintained self-injurious behavior. *Developmental Medicine & Child Neurology, 45,* 769–771.

Knoff, H. M. (2002). Best practices in facilitating school reform, organizational change and strategic planning. In A. Thomas & J. Grimes (Eds.), *Best practices in school psychology IV.* Bethesda, MD: National Association of School Psychologists.

Koegel, L. K., Koegel, R. L., & Dunlap, G. (Eds.). (1996). *Positive behavioral support: Including people with difficult behavior in the community.* Baltimore: Brookes.

Kwak, M. M., Ervin, R. A., Anderson, M. Z., & Austin, J. (2004). Agreement of function across methods used in school-based functional assessment with preadolescent and adolescent students. *Behavior Modification, 28,* 375–401.

Lalli, J. S., Browder, D. M., Mace, C. F., & Brown, K. D. (1993). Teacher use of descriptive analysis data to implement interventions to decrease students' problem behaviors. *Journal of Applied Behavior Analysis, 26,* 227–238.

Lalli, J. S., Vollmer, T. R., Progar, P. R., Wright, C., Borrero, J., Daniel, D., et al. (1999). Competition between positive and negative reinforcement in the treatment of escape behavior. *Journal of Applied Behavior Analysis, 32,* 285–296.

Langthorne, P., McGill, P., & O'Reilly, M. (2007). Incorporating "motivation" into the functional analysis of challenging behavior: On the interactive and integrative potential of the motivating operation. *Behavior Modification, 31,* 466–487.

Laraway, S., Snycerski, S., Michael, J., & Poling, A. (2003). Motivating operations and terms to describe them: Some further refinements. *Journal of Applied Behavior Analysis, 36,* 407–414.

LaRue, R. H., & Handleman, J. (2006). A primer on school-based functional assessment. *The Behavior Therapist, 29,* 48–52.

Lewis-Palmer, T., & Barrett, S. (2007). Establishing and sustaining statewide positive behavior supports implementation: A description of Maryland's model. *Journal of Evidence-Based Practices for Schools, 8,* 45–62.

LIH v New York City Board of Education, 103 F. Supp. 658 2d (E.D.N.Y. 2000).

Lockley, J. R. (2001). Teacher acceptance of and utilization of functional assessment techniques. *Dissertation Abstracts International, Section A: Humanities and Sciences, 61*(9-A), 3439.

Mace, C. F., Gritter, A. K., Johnson, P. E., Malley, J. L., & Steege, M. W. (2007). Contingent reinforcement in context. *European Journal of Behavior Analysis, 7,* 115–120

Mace, C. F., & Lalli, J. S. (1991). Linking descriptive and experimental analyses in the treatment of bizarre speech. *Journal of Applied Behavior Analysis, 24,* 553–562.

Mace, C. F., & Roberts, M. L. (1993). Developing effective interventions: Empirical and conceptual considerations. In J. Reichle & D. P. Wacker (Eds.), *Communicative alternatives to challenging behavior: Integrating functional assessment and intervention strategies* (pp. 113–133). Baltimore: Brookes.

Martens, B. K., Halperin, S., Rummel, J. E., & Kilpatrick, D. (1990). Matching theory applied to contingent teacher attention. *Behavioral Assessment, 12,* 139–155.

Martens, B. K., & Houk, J. L. (1989). The application of Hernstein's law of effect to disruptive and on-task behavior of a retarded adolescent girl. *Journal of the Experimental Analysis of Behavior, 51,* 17–27.

Mason City Community School District, 32 IDELR 216(2001).

McAfee, J. K. (1987). Classroom density and the aggressive behavior of handicapped children. *Education and Treatment of Children, 10,* 134–145.

McComas, J. J., & Mace, C. F. (2000). Theory and practice in conducting functional analysis. In E. S. Shapiro & T. R. Kratochwill (Eds.), *Behavioral assessment in schools: Theory, research, and clinical foundations* (2nd ed., pp. 78–103). New York: Guilford Press.

McGill, P. (1999). Establishing operations: Implications for the assessment, treatment, and prevention of problem behavior. *Journal of Applied Behavior Analysis, 32,* 393–418.

Michael, J. (1982). Distinguishing between discriminative and motivational functions of stimuli. *Journal of Experimental Analysis of Behavior, 37,* 149–155.

Michael, J. (1993). Establishing operations. *The Behavior Analyst, 16,* 191–206.

Michael, J. (2000). Implications and refinements of the establishing operation concept. *Journal of Applied Behavior Analysis, 33,* 403–410.

Miltenberger, R. G. (1997). *Behavior modification: Principles and procedures.* Pacific Grove, CA: Brooks/ Cole.

Miltenberger, R. G. (2001). *Behavior modification: Principles and procedures* (2nd ed). Belmont, CA: Wadsworth/Thomas Learning.

Monastra, V. J. (2008). *Unlocking the potential of patients with ADHD: A model for clinical practice.* Washington, DC: American Psychological Association.

Moore, J. W., Edwards, R. P., Sterling-Turner, H. E., Riley, J., DuBard, M., & McGeorge, A. (2002). Teacher acquisition of functional analysis methodology: Didactic versus direct training. *Journal of Applied Behavior Analysis, 35,* 73–77.

Nelson, R. O., & Hayes, S. C. (1981). Theoretical explanations for reactivity in self-monitoring. *Behavior Modification, 51,* 314.

Newcomer, L. L., & Lewis, T. J. (2004). Functional behavioral assessment: An investigation of assessment reliability and effectiveness of function-based interventions. *Journal of Emotional and Behavioral Disorders, 12,* 168–181.

Oak Park and River Forest H. S. District #200, 34 IDELR 161 (2001).

Office of Special Education Programs. (2007). *Letter to Christianses,* 48, IDELR 161.

O'Neill, R. E., Horner, R. H., Albin, R. W., Sprague, J. R., Storey, K., & Newton, J. S. (1997). *Functional assessment and program development for problem behavior: A practical handbook* (2nd ed.). Pacific Grove, CA: Brooks/Cole.

Powell, J., & Azrin, N. H. (1968). The effects of shock as a punisher for cigarette smoking. *Journal of Applied Behavior Analysis, 1,* 63–71.

Radford, P. M., Aldrich, J. L., & Ervin, R. A. (2000). An annotated bibliography of 102 school-based functional assessment studies. *Proven Practice: Prevention and Remediation Solutions for Schools, 3,* 24–43.

Ray, K. P., & Watson, T. S. (2001). Analysis of the effects of temporally distant events on school behavior. *School Psychology Quarterly, 16,* 324–342.

Rodiriecus L. v Waukegan School District, No. 60, 90 F. 3d 249 (7th Cir. 1996).

Sandwich Community Unit School District No. 430, 35 IDELR 173 (2001).

Sattler, J. M. (2001). *Assessment of children: Behavioral and clinical applications* (4th ed). La Mesa, CA: Author.

Shapiro, E. S., & Kratochwill, T. R. (Eds.). (2000). *Behavioral assessment in schools: Theory, research, and clinical foundations* (2nd ed.). New York: Guilford Press.

Shriver, M. D., Anderson, C. M., & Proctor, B. (2001). Evaluating the validity of functional behavior assessment. *School Psychology Review, 30,* 180–192.

Shriver, M. D., & Kramer, J. J. (1997). Application of the generalized matching law for description of student behavior in the classroom. *Journal of Behavioral Education, 7,* 131–149.

Shriver, M. D., & Watson, T. S. (2001). A survey of behavior analysis and behavioral consultation courses in school psychology: Implications for training school psychologists. *Journal of Behavioral Education, 9,* 211–221.

Skinner, B. F. (1938). *The behavior of organisms: An experimental analysis.* New York: Appleton-Century.

Skinner, B. F. (1953). *Science and human behavior.* New York: Macmillan.

Skinner, C. H., Dittmer, K. I., & Howell, L. A. (2000). Direct observation in school settings: Theoretical issues. In E. S. Shapiro & T. R. Kratochwill (Eds.), *Behavioral assessment in schools: Theory, research, and clinical foundations* (2nd ed., pp. 19–45). New York: Guilford Press.

Skinner, C. H., Rhymer, K. H., & McDaniel, C. E. (2000). Naturalistic direct observation in educational settings. In E. S. Shapiro (Ed.), *Conducting school-based assessments of child and adolescent behavior* (pp. 21–54). New York: Guilford Press.

Steege, M. W., Brown-Chidsey, R. B., & Mace, C. F. (2002). Best practices in evaluating interventions. In A. Thomas & J. Grimes (Eds.), *Best practices in school psychology—IV* (pp. 517–534). Washington, DC: National Association of School Psychologists.

Steege, M. W., Davin, T., & Hathaway, M. (2001). Reliability and accuracy of a performance-based behavioral recording procedure. *School Psychology Review, 30,* 252–261.

Steege, M. W., Mace, F. C., & Brown-Chidsey, R. B. (2007). Functional behavioral assessment of classroom behavior. In S. Goldstein & R. Brooks (Eds.), *Understanding and managing children's classroom behavior: Creating sustainable, resilient classrooms* (2nd ed., pp. 43–63). Hoboken, NJ: Wiley.

Steege, M. W., Mace, F. C., Perry, L., & Longenecker, H. (2007). Applied behavior analysis: Beyond discrete trial teaching. *Psychology in the Schools, 44,* 91–99.

Steege, M. W., & Northup, J. (1998). Brief functional analysis of problem behavior: A practical approach for school psychologists. *Proven Practice: Prevention and Remediation Solutions for Schools, 1,* 4–11, 37–38.

Steege, M. W., Wacker, D. P., Berg, W. K., Cigrand, K. C., & Cooper, L. J. (1989). The use of behavioral assessment to prescribe and evaluate treatments for severely handicapped children. *Journal of Applied Behavior Analysis, 22,* 23–33.

Steege, M. W., Wacker, D. P., Cigrand, K. C., Berg, W. K., Novak, C. G., Reimers, T. M., et al. (1990). Use of negative reinforcement in the treatment of self-injurious behavior. *Journal of Applied Behavior Analysis, 23,* 459–467.

Steege, M. W., Wacker, D. P., & McMahon, C. M. (1987). Evaluation of the effectiveness and efficiency of two stimulus prompt strategies with severely handicapped students. *Journal of Applied Behavior Analysis, 20,* 293–299.

Steege, M. W., & Watson, T. S. (2008). Best practices in functional behavioral assessment. In A. Thomas & J. Grimes (Eds.), *Best practices in school psychology V.* Bethesda, MD: National Association of School Psychologists.

Sterling-Turner, H. E., & Watson, T. S. (2002). An analog investigation of the relationship between treatment acceptability and treatment integrity. *Journal of Behavioral Education, 11,* 39–50.

Sterling-Turner, H. E., Watson, T. S., & Moore, J. W. (2002). The effects of direct training and treatment integrity on treatment outcomes in school consultation. *School Psychology Quarterly, 17,* 47–77.

Sterling-Turner, H. E., Watson, T. S., Wildmon, M., Watkins, C., & Little, E. (2001). Investigating the empirical relationship between training type and treatment integrity. *School Psychology Quarterly, 16,* 56–67.

Tapp, J. T., & Walden, T. A. (2000). A system for collecting and analysis of observational data from videotape. In T. Thompson, D. Felce, & F. J. Symons (Eds.), *Behavioral observation: Technology and applications in developmental disabilities* (pp. 61–70). Baltimore: Brookes.

Tapp, J. T., & Wehby, J. H. (2000). Observational software for laptop computers and optical bar code readers. In T. Thompson, D. Felce, & F. J. Symons (Eds.), *Behavioral observation: Technology and applications in developmental disabilities* (pp. 71–81). Baltimore: Brookes.

Thompson, R. H., & Iwata, B. A. (2005). A review of reinforcement control procedures. *Journal of Applied Behavior Analysis, 38,* 257–278.

Thorndike, E. L. (1898). Animal intelligence: An experimental study of the associative processes in animals. *Psychological Monographs, 2,* 1–109.

Touchette, P. E., MacDonald, R. F., & Langer, S. N. (1985). A scatter plot for identifying stimulus control for problem behavior. *Journal of Applied Behavior Analysis, 18,* 343–351.

Valdovinos, M. G., Ellringer, N. P., & Alexander, M. L. (2007). Changes in the rate of problem behavior associated with the discontinuation of the antipsychotic medication quetiapine. *Mental Health Aspects of Developmental Disabilities, 10,* 64–67.

Valleley, R. J. (2004). Treatment acceptability. In T. S. Watson & C. H. Skinner (Eds.), *Encyclopedia of school psychology* (pp. 355–356). New York: Kluwer Academic/Plenum.

VanAcker, R., & Borenson, L. A. (2008). Blueprints for success: Instructional strategies to promote appropriate student behavior. Retrieved May 24, 2008, from *http://dpi.wi.gov/sped/edbluepri. html*

Volkert, V. M., Lerman, D. C., & Vorndran, D. M. (2005). The effects of reinforcement magnitude on the outcomes of functional analysis. *Journal of Applied Behavior Analysis, 38,* 147–162.

Wacker, D. P., Steege, M., Northup, J., Reimers, T., Berg, W. K., & Sasso, G. (1990). Use of functional analysis and acceptability measures to assess and treat severe behavior problems: An outpatient clinic model. In A. C. Repp, C. Allen, & N. N. Singh (Eds.), *Perspectives on the use of nonaversive and aversive interventions for persons with developmental disabilities* (pp. 349–359). Sycamore, IL: Sycamore.

Walker, H. M., Block-Pedego, A. E., Todis, B. J., Severson, H. H., & Pedego, A. (1991). *School archival records search.* Longmont, CA: Sopris West.

Watkins-Emonet, C. E. (2001). Evaluating the teaching components of direct behavioral consultation on skill acquisition and generalization in Head Start classrooms. *Dissertation Abstracts International: Section B: The Sciences and Engineering, 61*(10-B), 5547.

Watson, J. B., & Rayner, R. (1920). Conditioned emotional reactions. *Journal of Experimental Psychology, 3,* 1–14.

Watson, T. S. (2004). Treatment integrity. In T. S. Watson & C. H. Skinner (Eds.), *Encyclopedia of school psychology* (pp. 356–358). New York: Kluwer.

Watson, T. S., & Kramer, J. J. (1995). Teaching problem solving skills to teachers-in-training: An experimental analysis of three methods. *Journal of Behavioral Education, 5,* 281–293.

Watson, T. S., Ray, K. P., Sterling, H. E., & Logan, P. (1999). Teacher implemented functional analysis and treatment: A method for linking assessment to intervention. *School Psychology Review, 28,* 292–302.

Watson, T. S., & Robinson, S. L. (1996). Direct behavioral consultation: An alternative to traditional behavioral consultation. *School Psychology Quarterly, 11,* 267–278.

Watson, T. S., & Steege, M. W. (2003). *Conducting school-based functional behavioral assessments: A practitioner's guide.* New York: Guilford Press.

Weigle, K. L., & Scotti, J. R. (2000). Effects of functional analysis information on ratings of intervention effectiveness and acceptability. *Journal of the Association for Persons with Severe Handicaps, 25,* 217–228.

Wilder, D. A., Chen, L., Atwell, J., Pritchard, J., & Weinstein, P. (2006). Brief functional analysis and treatment of tantrums associated with transitions in preschool children. *Journal of Applied Behavior Analysis, 39,* 103–107.

Wilder, D. A., Harris, C., Reagan, R., & Rasey, A. (2007). Functional analysis and treatment of noncompliance by preschool children. *Journal of Applied Behavior Analysis, 40,* 173–177.

Witt, J. C., & Beck, R. (1999). *One minute academic functional assessment and interventions.* Longmont, CO: Sopris West.

Wright-Gallo, G. L., Higbee, T. S., Reagon, K. A., & Davey, B. J. (2006). Classroom-based functional analysis and intervention for students with emotional/behavioral disorders. *Education and Treatment of Children, 29,* 421–436.

Yell, M. L. (2006). *The law and special education* (2nd ed.). Upper Saddle River, NJ: Pearson.

Zarcone, J. R., Lindauer, S. E., Morse, P. S., Crosland, K. A., Valdovinos, M. G., McKerchar, T. L., et al. (2004). Effects of risperidone on destructive behavior of persons with developmental disabilities: III. Functional analysis. *American Journal on Mental Retardation, 109,* 310–321.

WEBSITES ON FBA AND PBS

The following websites are offered as resources for practitioners seeking additional information about the FBA-PBS process.

cecp.air.org/fba/default.htm
www.pbis.org/english
www.childpsychologist.com/fba_bip/
nasponline.org/publications/cq263funcassessbibl.html
www.nasponline.org/publications/cq277fba.html

Author Index

Subject Index

A-B-C assessment, 23, 58–60, 74, 75, 106–110, 223
Academic assessments, 71–72
Adaptive behavior scales, 70, 72
Alex R. by Beth R. v. Forrestville Valley Community Unit School District #221, 40
Altered states, 53
Anecdotal record keeping, 74
Antecedents, 43–44, 46–54, 58–59
   using during intervention, 198–200
Antecedent Variables Assessment Form (AVAF), 101, 110–115
Automatic reinforcement, 23, 55, 57, 71, 182. *see also* Sensory reinforcement

Behavior
   defining, 83–84
   operant, 20 -23, 56
   recording, 23, 71, 73, 83, 87–93
   respondent, 19–21
   Behavior-Analytic Problem-Solving model, 176–195, 238, 240–241
Behavior Intervention Plans, 28–30, 32–34, 40–42, 248–250
Behavior modification, 22, 173–174
Behavior rating scales, 15, 70, 72
Behavioral consultation, 248–254
Behavioral Stream Interview (BSI), 101, 106–110
Behavioral stream observation, 158–159

Case-based intervention, 4
Conditional Probability Record (CPR), 131–134

Consequences, 27, 43–44, 54–59
   using during intervention, 203–205
Consequence Variable Assessment Form (CVAF), 110–111, 118–121
Consultation summary report, 254
Conceptual models, 58–62
Conditional Probability Record, 131–134
Contextual variables, 177
Coping skills, teaching of, 181, 202

Descriptive assessments, 74–75
Diagnosis 2–3, 34, 36
Direct descriptive FBA, 15–17, 70–71, 73–77, 128–129, 158–160, 163
Direct observation, 16, 86–87
Discriminated operant, 47
Discriminative stimuli, 26–27, 46–50, 52–53, 60–61, 177–178
District No. 211 v. Michael R., 42
Duration recording, 87–89

Embedded instructions, 234
Errors during FBA
   of association, 8
   of exaggeration, 11
   of generalization, 11–12
   of inaccurate FBA, 9–11
   of misplaced precision, 9–10
Establishing operations, 47, 102
Extinction, 185–186, 203–204

FBA brief report, 215–218
FBA errors, 6–12, 29–30. *see also* Errors during FBA
Frequency recording, 87–88

Functional analysis, 15–17, 76, 162–165, 173–174
Functional Assessment Informant Record for Teachers (FAIR-T), 73, 122–126
Functional behavioral analysis
   brief model, 16–17, 24, 162–175
   consequence analysis, 168
   extended model, 16, 26, 57, 173
   structural analysis, 165–168
Functional Behavioral Assessment Observation Form (FBAOF), 78, 134–138, 142, 145, 159–161
Functions of behavior
   automatic reinforcement, 23, 55, 57, 71, 182
   negative reinforcement, 48–51, 55–57, 204–205
   social attention, 55–57, 63
   tangible reinforcement, 161, 164, 204
Functional behavioral assessment (FBA)
   behavioral triggers for, 32–33
   brief report, 215–218
   bus behavior, 38–39
   criteria for student disability, 31–32, 36
   decision tree, 67–69, 99
   definition, 7
   direct descriptive, 15–17, 73–76, 128–129, 163, 230, 236
   documentation form, 213–215
   errors, 6–12, 29–30
   extended day programs, 39
   free and appropriate public education (FAPE), 41

269